The
CHARLESTON,
SAVANNAH &
COASTAL ISLANDS
Book

A Complete Guide

Wade Spees

THE CHARLESTON, SAVANNAH & COASTAL ISLANDS BOOK

A Complete Guide

FOURTH EDITION

CECILY McMILLAN

Berkshire House Publishers
Lee, Massachusetts

The Charleston, Savannah & Coastal Islands Book: A Complete Guide
© 1993, 1997, 1998, 2001 by Berkshire House Publishers
Cover and interior photographs ©1993, 1997, 1998, 2001 by Wade Spees and other credited sources

Library of Congress Cataloging-in-Publication Data

McMillan, Cecily.

     The Charleston, Savannah & coastal islands book : a complete guide /
Cecily McMillan. — 4th ed.
          p.   cm. — (Great destinations series, ISSN 1056-7968)
     Includes bibliographical references (p.) and index.
     ISBN 1-58157-024-4
     1. Charleston (S.C.)—Guidebooks. 2. Savannah (Ga.)—Guidebooks. 3. Sea Islands—
Guidebooks. 4. Charleston Region (S.C.)—Guidebooks. 5. Savannah Region (Ga.)—
Guidebooks. I. Title: Charleston, Savannah, and Coastal Islands book. II. Title. III Series.
     F279.C43 M38   2001
     917.57'9150444—dc21   2001025000

ISBN 1-58157-024-4
ISSN: 1056-7968 (series)

Editor: Susan Minnich. Managing Editor: Philip Rich. Design and composition: Dianne Pinkowitz. Cover design and composition: Jane McWhorter. Index: Diane Brenner.

No complimentary meals or lodgings were accepted by the author and reviewers in gathering information for this work.

Berkshire House Publishers'
Great Destinations™ travel guidebook series

Recommended by NATIONAL GEOGRAPHIC TRAVELER and TRAVEL & LEISURE magazines.

. . . a crisp and critical approach, for travelers who want to live like locals.
USA TODAY

Great Destinations™ guidebooks are known for their comprehensive, critical coverage of regions of extraordinary cultural interest and natural beauty. The authors in this series are professional travel writers who have lived for many years in the regions they describe. Each title in this series is continuously updated with each printing, in order to insure accurate and timely information. All of the books contain over 100 photographs and maps.

Neither the publisher, the authors, the reviewers, nor other contributors accept complimentary lodgings, meals, or any other consideration (such as advertising) while gathering information for any book in this series.

Current titles available:
The Adirondack Book
The Berkshire Book
The Charleston, Savannah & Coastal Islands Book
The Chesapeake Bay Book
The Coast of Maine Book
The Finger Lakes Book
The Hamptons Book
The Monterey Bay, Big Sur & Gold Coast Wine Country Book
The Nantucket Book
The Newport & Narragansett Bay Book
The Napa & Sonoma Book
The Santa Fe & Taos Book
The Sarasota, Sanibel Island & Naples Book
The Texas Hill Country Book
Wineries of the Eastern States

If you are traveling to, moving to, residing in, or just interested in any (or all!) of these enchanting regions, a **Great Destinations**™ guidebook is a superior companion. Honest and painstakingly critical, full of information only a local can provide, **Great Destinations**™ guidebooks provide you with all the practical knowledge you need to enjoy the best of each region. Why not own them all?

To the memory of George McMillan, who first brought me to the Lowcountry and turned my eyes to its subtleties, and to our son, Tom, with whom I continue to love it.

Contents

CHAPTER ONE
"No Fayrer or Fytter Place"
HISTORY
1

CHAPTER TWO
Getting Here, Getting Around
TRANSPORTATION
27

CHAPTER THREE
A City of Stories
CHARLESTON
48

CHAPTER FOUR
An Old City, A Modern City
SAVANNAH
119

CHAPTER FIVE
Sea Island Gems
BEAUFORT, EDISTO, AND BLUFFTON
163

CHAPTER SIX
Courts, Courses, Sails, and Sand
HILTON HEAD
204

CHAPTER SEVEN
Practical Matters & Seasonal Events
INFORMATION
244

Acknowledgments

This book gathers together for readers both a sense of Lowcountry history and all the details that make for a successful visit. Such a project required the efforts of friends and assistants.

In Charleston, Langhorne Howard and Nina McCully gave me valuable insights into their native city. Wade Spees, although not a native of that city or this region, has in his photographs for this book and other articles of mine, portrayed the Lowcountry as a place of serene beauty, humanity, and vitality.

In Beaufort and on St. Helena Island, my home, I was helped by Dale Friedman, Susan Graber, Cheryl and Roger Steele, Molly McDonald and Jonathan Gelber, Mary Mack, and Gracie Reddicks.

Beth Scott deepened my knowledge of Savannah and Hilton Head. Steve Wise, author, museum curator, and military historian, kindly critiqued my History chapter.

Jenny Stacy at the Savannah Area Convention and Visitors Bureau and her counterparts in Charleston remain great sources. The staff of the Chambers of Commerce in Beaufort, Hilton Head Island, and Charleston were thorough and prompt in answering my questions. Special thanks goes to the Charleston Museum for the use of archival photos.

Thanks to Philip Rich at Berkshire House and Susan Minnich, to my Lowcountry friends, and especially to Priscilla Johnson McMillan who continues to nurture my Lowcountry life.

Introduction

There are some places about which we have such strong impressions that when we finally go there they seem familiar, as if we had known them forever. For many people the Lowcountry is such a place. It seems to have lodged itself so securely in so many imaginations that I often find, when I am asked about it, that what I have to say matters less than the opportunity I may be giving someone to fine-tune the picture they already have.

Where these clustered impressions come from, whether learned in a history lesson on the Civil War, gathered from a friend, understood in a novel, or viewed on a movie screen, seems less important than the fact that they feel fully conceived. This isn't surprising: the Lowcountry has earned our permanent attention. It is a compelling world. Like other places that have witnessed tremendous historic upheavals and whose residents have had to adjust to changed circumstances, it evokes a natural sympathy in us for its stories.

I first stepped foot in the Lowcountry late in the summer of 1979, and ever since I have been listening in on its history. I return again and again to places where I feel the presence of the past and its rituals: to the shores of St. Helena Sound, where I catch crabs on a string or dig for oysters much as Native Americans might have done; to Drayton Hall where beds of lilies bloom as they did in Jefferson's Monticello garden; to Penn Center, where descendants of slaves honor their heritage and the strength of their forebears in song; to the squares of Savannah, laid out more than 250 years ago and still possessing a power of geometry that untangles nature and orders the pace of urban life.

The region's physical beauty is just as evocative. The landscape is soft, uninterrupted by hills on land, carpeted with marsh grass and flowing waters at its edges. The air itself seems to press down, weighted by all the humidity, wrapping the Lowcountry like a package. There are distinctive seasons here which bring their own changes in color and light, in bird migrations and blossoms. Every day the shoreline is redefined by the tides.

This book is intended to both introduce you to some of the long-standing pleasures and pastimes found in the Lowcountry and point you in directions where you might discover ones of your own. In individual chapter openings, and in Chapter One, *History*, it lays out a broad context into which you may place yourself, as a traveler looking to plan a day or as a reader adjusting the imaginary pictures you arrived with to those you observed first hand.

Sometimes, your efforts may be studious — admiring architecture, exploring sites of historic and cultural significance. At other times, you will be content to satisfy your senses: to feel the beach between your toes, smell the salt marsh, watch a pelican dive, taste fresh shrimp. Don't neglect to listen for old stories, either.

It may turn out that, having come to the Lowcountry for a vacation, you end up joining the ranks of those who return for good. The glossy residential resorts on the developed islands like Kiawah, Dataw, and Hilton Head have drawn national attention to the area; Beaufort has appeared on so many "Best Small Town" lists and attracted so many new visitors that it is possible, as it was not even fifteen years ago, to walk down its main street and see only unfamiliar faces. The Spoleto Festival has put Charleston on an international map.

Yet the inexorable need in many of us for community, for a sense of continuity that comes from bringing the past forward, keeps the Lowcountry alive, keeps it from resting solely on the life of its past for vitality. Today, restaurants, bookstores, jazz and blues clubs, clothing shops, galleries, and B&Bs are embedding themselves in the old Lowcountry places. They are enlarging the remnant world, just as spats fasten on oyster banks and make them grow.

Cecily McMillan
St. Helena Island, South Carolina

THE WAY THIS BOOK WORKS

This book is divided into seven chapters. Several of them cover specific regions of the Lowcountry. But, like a shelf of individual volumes, it encourages browsing: you may want to thumb through the opening sections of individual chapters, for example, to get an overview of the subject. Or you may want to start with the History chapter and pick and choose among the others as your visit unfolds and your needs become apparent.

If you're interested in finding a place to eat or sleep — and during the high season in spring you're encouraged to consider advance planning — look over the restaurant and lodging charts in the *Index* (organized by area and price); then turn to the pages in the general index and read the specific entries for the places that most interest you.

Some entries, most notably those in the **Lodging** and **Dining** sections of chapters, include specific information (telephone, address, hours, etc.) organized for easy reference in blocks in the left-hand column. All such information has been checked for accuracy as close to the time of publication as possible, but details change so it's best to call ahead.

PRICES

Prices change, too, and for that reason we've avoided listing specific prices in favor of noting their range. Lodging price codes are based on a per-room rate, double-occupancy in the high season months. Low season rates, which generally apply in December and January, are usually about 20 percent less. In the high season many places, small and large, require a minimum two-night stay and may also have specific rules regarding adequate notice and refunds in the event of cancellation. Check ahead.

You might also confirm information that we've provided about policies in effect concerning such things as handicapped access and smoking.

Restaurant prices indicate the cost of a meal including appetizer, entree, and dessert, but not bar beverages, tax, or tip. Prix-fixe menus are noted. Here again, the season of your visit may bring on special conditions: when there are crowds, most restaurants extend their hours of operation, serving meals both earlier and later. In the winter, they may shut down for a day or two.

Price Codes

	Lodging	*Dining*
Inexpensive	Up to $60	Up to $10
Moderate	$60 to $120	$10 to $20
Expensive	$120 to $200	$20 to $30
Very Expensive	Over $200	Over $30

Credit cards are abbreviated as follows:

AE — American Express	DC — Diner's Card
CB — Carte Blanche	MC — MasterCard
D — Discover Card	V — Visa

For year-round tourist information see the sources listed on the last page of the Information chapter.

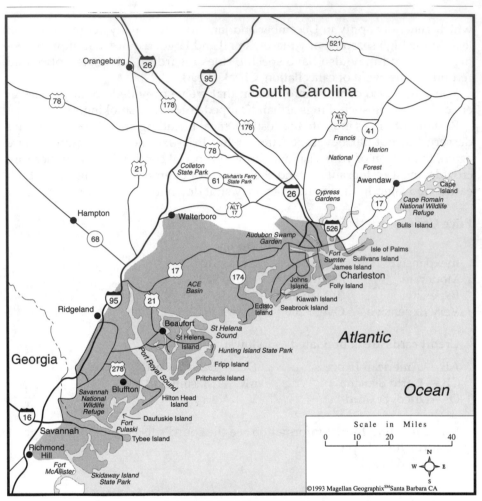

THE LOWCOUNTRY

The
CHARLESTON, SAVANNAH & COASTAL ISLANDS
Book

A Complete Guide

CHAPTER ONE
"No Fayrer or Fytter Place"
HISTORY

Toward the middle of the 16th century, European adventurers were spreading across the Atlantic Ocean in a wild burst of exploring, hoping to claim for their sovereigns and sponsors vast territories of land and the riches they believed to flourish there. Aboard what now seem to be preposterously small ships and guided by hopeless maps (few of these expeditions ever landed where they intended), they arrived, established forts, and set to their business. One of the places they landed — Spanish, French, and English in succession — was the region we now know as the Lowcountry of South Carolina and Georgia.

Wade Spees

The vastly rich, tidal world the explorer Ribaut praised: "No fayrer or fytter place."

The next 150 years was a period of settling and retreating, of establishing colonies and defending them — from one another, from the Native Americans who lived there, and from the twin scourges of disease and deprivation. Motivated by religious zeal and political unrest at home, as well as by the drive to acquire real estate, slaves, or converts to Christianity, the Europeans kept returning to build, to trade, to map, to start life over in new places on which they imposed an Old World order. In the end, it was the English who dominated the Lowcountry.

While the accounts of these years outdo one another in their use of superlatives to describe God and king, they contain even richer praise for the new country. Captain Jean Ribaut, a Frenchman who led a group of 150 Huguenot colonists to the Lowcountry in 1562, claimed in a report (translated into English the following year) that there was "no fayrer or fytter place" than the area of Port Royal Sound, near present-day Beaufort, one of the "goodlyest, best and frutfullest countres that ever was sene"; where egrets were so plentiful the bushes "be all white covered with them"; where there were "so many sortes of fishes that ye may take them without net or angle."

On a site which is now at the edge of a golf course at the Marine Corps Recruit Depot on Parris Island, Ribaut and his settlers built Charlesfort. It was a basic defensive structure measuring 96 feet by 78 feet, barricaded with palisades, and surrounded by a moat. There were gun platforms at its corners and, inside, a rude house with a straw roof. Modest though it may have been, Charlesfort represented the first attempt by the French to establish a colony in what is now the United States. The effort took place three years before the founding of St. Augustine by the Spanish, and 45 years before the English settled Jamestown.

Impressed with the Lowcountry and confident of its potential, Ribaut quickly returned to France, intending to return with supplies and recruits. He never made it back; the colony itself collapsed soon afterwards. The well-situated site did not lie fallow for long, however. In 1566 the Spanish expanded their reach north from St. Augustine and constructed Fort San Felipe on the ruins of Charlesfort. It seemed inevitable that a place so plentifully endowed would not go begging.

A typical Lowcountry walk: mild day, sandy road, under the oaks, in the afternoon light.

Wade Spees

To a modern traveler who chances upon a rookery in Hunting Island State Park, or to the youngster throwing a cast net and needing the strength of two to draw it in, perhaps nothing has changed. Today, as centuries ago, the natural resources of the Lowcountry are breathtakingly impressive wherever you go. There will be schools of dolphin by your boat off Hilton Head, dozens of crabs in the basket you hauled to Kiawah Island, hundreds of eggs in the log-gerhead turtle's nest on Pritchard's Island, and thousands of terns, which — when they rise all at once off Egg Bank in St. Helena Sound — appear as a cloud of smoke on the horizon. There will be late-afternoon light so intense and golden it makes the dun bark of the grayest sycamore shimmer.

And remember: when Ribaut called the Lowcountry a place "where nothing lacketh," Charleston, Beaufort, and Savannah had not even been invented.

By 1740, each of these towns had developed the intense self-consciousness — the spirit of place — that is apparent there today. You can find it in the water-colors of a native artist, in the concert of an African-American chorus, in the words of a docent, in the tales of a fisherman. Before the first roads were laid, the wharves constructed, or the means of governance fully conceived, the conti-nuity of culture that characterizes all the Lowcountry was begun. It is the rare American place to have evolved intact, with its monuments and houses and symbols of achievement still pointing to a documented and recognized past.

So overwhelming is the sense of place in the Lowcountry that I have often felt of people I know that, if they ever left the city limits of Charleston — or Beaufort or Savannah — they would vaporize.

There's no doubt, to read from their accounts, that visitors from the earliest days of settlement have shared the feeling that the Lowcountry is a special place, a dramatic place apart. Looking backwards, it is hard to pinpoint pre-cisely when the term "Lowcountry" — or even, as it is sometimes spelled, "Low Country" — became widely used. It is certainly an apt geographical description for an area that is hill-less and hardly above sea level. But to accurately define the Lowcountry, to comprehend it at its broadest, you must consider that it is many things: a place of dozens of distinctive, interconnected natural communities and ecosystems; a site where historical forces have been converging, sometimes with disastrous consequences, for 400 years; a region whose tiny society influenced national culture; a self-conscious political subdi-vision of the United States.

Technically, the Lowcountry is divided from what is known as the South Carolina Upcountry by the fall line, that feature of geography which bisects the state from the Georgia border at Augusta, approximately 90 miles from the coast, to North Carolina. Upland of the fall line the soil is red clay, and it is hilly; downward the land flattens and spreads, creating broad alluvial plains which meet the sea.

As to its other defining attributes, the Lowcountry that stretches from Charleston to Savannah and encompasses the Sea Islands in between seems to be characterized by a sense of pride that will never leave it. Old families, old houses, old customs, old loyalties remain, if not guiding principles, then ones whose legacy is passed on, as one might give a quilt to the next generation. As the writers of the classic WPA Guide, *South Carolina, A Guide to the Palmetto State*, wrote in 1941, the Lowcountry inhabitant "may live in Charleston, a city that competes with the New Jerusalem in his dreams; or he may live in a drafty

Georgian country house" but he "recalls his past glory with a pride that surpasses his ability to appreciate thoroughly the good things of the present."

Of course, the protection of this vital spirit has come at a price. Lowcountry residents were willing to pay it once, to take the drastic measure of firing on Fort Sumter, and they are continuing that commitment. Maintaining Historic Districts, scenic vistas, two-lane island roads, Gullah communities, marine sanctuaries comprising tens of thousands of acres — these are among the accomplishments of present-day preservationists who seek to insure the presence of the past in everyday life. Their victories are for you to savor, too.

NATURAL HISTORY

The coastline that defines the Lowcountry was, until about 245 million years ago, still more or less attached to the eastern rim of what became present-day Europe and Africa. The shifting of geologic plates that caused the movement of the landmass and created the southern Appalachians, among other mountain ranges, led to the formation of the Atlantic Ocean and the Lowcountry coastal plain.

Sand Hills

I continued through this forest nearly in a direct line towards the sea coast, five or six miles, when the land became uneven, with ridges of sand hills, mixed with sea shells, and covered by almost impenetrable thickets, consisting of Live Oaks, Sweetbay, Myrica, Ilex, . . . The dark labyrinth is succeeded by a great extent of salt plains, beyond which the boundless ocean is seen. Betwixt the dark forest and the salt plains, I crossed a rivulet of fresh water, where I sat down a while to rest myself, under the shadow of sweet Bays and Oaks; the lively breezes were perfumed by the fragrant breath of the superb Crinum, called by the inhabitants, White Lily. This admirable beauty of the sea-coast islands dwells in the humid shady groves, where the soil is made fertile and mellow by the admixture of sea shells . . . and the texture and whiteness of its flowers at once charmed me.

—From *Travels of William Bartram*
(First published in 1791)

In the geologic history of the southeast region, the coastal plain is a rather new development. Long before the present-day coastline obtained its shape, toward the end of the Miocene — third epoch of the Cenozoic Era — the upcountry regions already were well established. They were formed in an earlier era, the Mesozoic (220–70 million years ago, the time when the dinosaurs came and went), and their ancient mineral formations contrast sharply with those of the coast.

Over time, a cycle was begun. Eroded material from these highland ridges was carried by streams draining the Blue Ridge and Piedmont uplands and deposited, again and again, to the south and east. This Cretaceous material extended the landmass. Periodic inundation by the sea followed, thus covering the sediment and creating distinctive geologic layers of clay, sand, and gravel. At least seven such terraces have been identified, ranging in elevation from 25 feet to 270 feet. Mining activity near Charleston has unearthed fossils of sharks' teeth and mammoth vertebrae.

In short, millions of years ago much of the present-day Lowcountry was under water, while as recently as thousands of years ago, the Native Americans who lived here probably collected oysters and shellfish from beds that, were we to locate them today, would lie some 95 miles out to sea.

Today, well beneath the sandy soil, ranging in thickness from 1000 to 3000 feet, lie the sandstone, silt stones, shale, and limestone that were dumped there. They undergird the land and stretch well beyond it into the ocean to form the continental shelf and the upper slope. The oldest rocks of the coastal plain lie in scattered sections under these layers and it is activity in their faults that can, and has, caused earthquakes, such as the one that damaged Charleston in 1886.

The geologic history of the Lowcountry has given its farmers, residents, and for a time its phosphate-mining industry, some unique advantages. Unlike northern coastal areas such as New England, the area is free of surface rocks. Preparing a field never required the building of a stone wall beside it. The nature of subterranean rock formations has provided some especially good soils for timber cultivation. More important, the deeper layers of rocks serve as aquifers to provide potable water for agriculture, industry, and homes — not an idle resource given the near sea-level elevation of the Lowcountry.

Finally, if the Lowcountry were without the plentiful deposits of easily eroded rock that tumbled from the highlands over the years, the region would have no beaches. The sand you traverse, across miles of coastal and barrier beach, is their legacy.

The phenomenon of rocks-into-sand is one piece of the Lowcountry's geologic history. Another is the transformation of one massive ocean into a landscape of sculptured sounds, estuaries, and marshes. Their evolution has defined the Lowcountry as the site of one of the nation's most productive fisheries, a home to dozens of species of native and migratory birds, and a habitat for mammals small and large. Even the trees and plants of the coast flourish in direct response to these various bodies of water.

THE MARINE ENVIRONMENT

The Lowcountry marine environment includes several distinctive parts: swamps, estuaries, marshes, maritime forests, dunes and interdune meadows, tidal creeks and sounds, alluvial and blackwater rivers. Their functions

Great blue heron are commonly seen in the Lowcountry, and so are endangered species like the bald eagle.

Wade Spees

are interdependent; to all, tidal action — about six to eight feet throughout the region — is significant. Evidence of the complexity of the marine ecosystem is best seen at any number of points where the land meets the sea, for it is here that some of the most dynamic and subtle dramas of nature are played out. To witness them, a traveler need do no more than lean over a bridge at low tide, step out of the car by a rural creek, or walk the beach.

Perhaps the most common sight of the Lowcountry is the field of smooth cordgrass *(Spartina alterniflora)* that makes up the salt marsh, and the muddy banks and flats that cut through it. Rimmed by wax myrtle and Carolina cherry laurel on its banks, overshadowed by huge live oaks whose limbs are draped with Spanish moss (an air plant, member of the pineapple family) and dotted with resurrection fern, the salt marsh is probably nature's most productive nursery.

What you will see here is this: filter-feeders such as snails, crabs, oysters, shrimp, and mullet ingesting the detritus — a potent mixture of decomposed marsh grass, animal matter, algae, and fungi. Or something larger, a heron, say, or a bottle-nose dolphin (locally called porpoise), or a raccoon eating its smaller prey. The fiddler crabs with their lopsided claws will gather and disperse by the hundreds, a muddy cavalry. Look up and there are the shrimp boats, nets dragging at their sides. Behind them flock the gulls scavenging for cast-off fish. As the tide recedes, you will hear the marsh pop like 100 pricked balloons. The earthy smell of "pluff mud" will fill the air.

A Pleasing Music

A beautiful green frog inhabits the grassy, marshy shores of these large rivers. They are very numerous, and their noise exactly resembles the barking of little dogs, or the yelping of puppies: these likewise make a great clamour, but as their notes are fine, and uttered in chorus, by separate bands or communities, far and near, rising and falling with the gentle breezes, affords a pleasing kind of music.

—From *Travels of William Bartram*, 1791

In brackish marshes slightly farther inland, along the tidal rivers, there will be more sediment, flushed from the upland, and greater plant diversity. In the shelter of the vegetation lie the nests of waterfowl; in the highest trees is, perhaps, the nest of a bald eagle. Three of the rivers, the Ashepoo, Combahee, and Edisto, form one of the largest estuarine systems on the East Coast— the ACE Basin, located in and around U.S. Highway 17 south of Charleston. Protection and expansion of the basin is assured by a consortium of federal, state, and private interests. Farther south, the Savannah Wildlife Refuge offers another opportunity to see these natural forces at work.

THE WORLDS OF ISLANDS AND CITIES

The barrier islands offer another view of the marine ecosystem. Developed or not, they maintain a sense of isolation and fragility at "the edge of the world." Even as they appear solid, they are in fact changing shape all the time, their dunes migrating, growing, eroding, their forests shaped by the unforgiving winds and salt spray. The lives of the birds and mammals that make their homes here are impacted daily by the elements. If the beach has suffered from erosion, oak-tree roots and upended palmettos will obstruct your path. As if to mock this

---

Voluptuous Charm

Picket life was of course the place to feel the charm of the natural beauty on the Sea Islands. We had a world of profuse and tangled vegetation around us, such as would have been a dream of delight to me, but for the constant sense of responsibility and care which came between. Amid this preoccupation, Nature seemed but a mirage, and not the close and intimate associate I had before known. I pressed no flowers, collected no insects or birds' eggs, made no notes on natural objects, reversing in these respects all previous habits. Yet now, in the retrospect, there seems to have been infused into me through every pore the voluptuous charm of the season and the place; and the slightest corresponding sound or odor now calls back the memory of those delicious days.

—From *Army Life in a Black Regiment*
by Thomas Wentworth Higginson (First published in 1869)

---

rough beauty, dozens of sanderlings play at the water's edge, while overhead, the big brown pelicans impose an order of their own as they fly in unerring formation.

You may be lucky enough to participate in a late-night "turtle watch" when groups of residents observe the 300-pound loggerhead sea turtles drag themselves up the beach, dig holes, and lay eggs. On several barrier islands, teams of people are charged with marking the nests and moving the eggs to a secure hatchery, away from predators, poachers, and high tides. At the time of release, the hatchlings make their way to the ocean in groups of two and three, and then somehow, miraculously, paddle with their tiny fins to the open sea.

Precisely where these turtles go is not known. From Lowcountry marinas, it takes a big fishing boat several hours to reach the Gulf Stream, where, as every fisherman knows, the big, fighting fish swim — creatures that might eat a turtle in a second. And there are other giants in this marine wildness — the right whales and the manatees.

Coastal refuges show life in abundance; but even in the cities, away from the water's edge, you will be surrounded by natural beauty. In downtown Savannah, the parkways are filled to bursting with azaleas and flowering dogwood in the spring. Honeysuckle, jessamine, wisteria, and trumpet vine tumble wildly over garden walls or race up the trunks of trees. And then there are the birds: the tiny Carolina wren, practically domesticated as it makes its nest in a flower box; mourning doves cooing on telephone wires, and the ever-present mockingbird.

The Mock-Bird

This ancient sublime forest, frequently intersected with extensive avenues, vistas and green lawns, opening to extensive savannas and far distant Rice plantations, agreeably employs the imagination, and captivates the senses by scenes of magnificence and grandeur. The gay mock-bird, vocal and joyous, mounts aloft on silvered wings, rolls over and over, then gently descends, and presides in the choir of the tuneful tribes.

—From *Travels of William Bartram*, 1791

Mark Catesby, the naturalist who "discovered" the mockingbird in this region over 250 years ago, noted its fantastic ability to mimic. Today it is said that the bird can imitate 39 songs and 50 call notes, not to mention the cackling of hens, the creak of old gates, and the croaking of frogs. Given the diversity and abundance of Lowcountry life, the mockingbird has songs enough for a lifetime.

SOCIAL HISTORY

This sculpture, "Landing Brave" by Peter Toth, stands at Charles Towne Landing. It honors the Native Americans who lived off the area's natural bounty and taught the early settlers of Charles Town to do so.

Wade Spees

EARLY HUMAN INHABITANTS

The Native Americans who ranged along the coast from the earliest days — as far back as 10,000 B.C. — have left the merest impression of their lives in patterned pottery shards, woven reed baskets, huge shell middens and shell rings, cypress-log canoes, and the remains of burial or religious sites scattered throughout the region. They also left their names, now anglicized in common usage, to confirm their presence in a dozen Lowcountry places. Some of the most prominent archaeological remains have been found on coastal islands — Hilton Head, Callawassie — suggesting that these early inhabitants possessed both geographic agility and a sense of territorial significance. Their population is thought to have numbered 50,000 at its peak.

The Native Americans of the Lowcountry were divided into loose tribal confederations, each of which may have communicated in its own tongue. They spent the summers along the coast and on the coastal islands, farming and harvesting fish and shellfish; in winter they retreated inland, where they hunted deer and small game. An apparently abundant food supply and an absence of harshness in the climate or geography seem to have helped insure the stability of these native societies. Communal farming produced several crops a year of corn and bounteous harvests of beans, peas, pumpkin, and watermelon. The forests yielded wild fruits, nuts, berries, and plants for food; roots and bark for medicinal drinks. Well-fortified towns, rimmed with circular stockades and enclosing an ever-burning ceremonial fire, established their home base.

The Native Americans' houses had the appearance of Quonset huts, long and domed. They were constructed of wooden frames over which mats, woven from palmetto fronds, could be draped, or, during hot weather, removed. Inside, the walls were lined with benches for sleeping. Some houses were grander than others, featuring rooms and pillared platforms usually reserved for a chief or tribe member believed to have unusual wisdom or healing powers.

A larger structure, perhaps 200 feet in diameter, served as a community center for religious and social activities. Early European observers noted devout attention to ritual celebrations in praise of the harvest, accompanied by singing, dancing, and playing of instruments — cane flutes, drums, and rattles made from shells and seed pods. Some Native American games included forms of bowling and lacrosse. They laid their dead to rest, wrapped like swaddled babies, atop high scaffoldings.

ENCOUNTERS WITH EUROPEANS

B y the time of their first encounters with white men, the coastal Native Americans had sorted themselves into various confederacies. From Charleston to the Savannah River lived a group of tribes known collectively as the Cusabo, including the Combahee, Ashepoo, Edisto, Stono, Wando, Kiawah, and Etiwan.

Their responses to the incursion of Europeans were mixed: some were generous and open to trade, teaching the newcomers how to fish and make secure shelter, and in so doing probably saved their lives. Some Native Americans also shared farming techniques. One white settler told of his success in cultivating with one tribe such crops as grape vines, pomegranates, orange and fig trees, barley, onions, and garlic. Some Native Americans and their chiefs, known as *caciques*, helped the Frenchmen of Charlesfort build a ship, caulked with moss, for a return voyage to Europe. Some delivered to English explorers the prime high-bluff settings on which the newcomers laid the cities of Charles Town and Savannah. Some boarded ships and went abroad, or to Barbados.

Other accounts, however, report canoe flotillas fleeing in shock, the villagers hiding for days in the woods. Fighting and massacres were not unknown. Among the Europeans, the toll was largely on French and Spanish settlers, who were the first to land.

If the settlers faced an uneasy alliance with the Cusabo, the Cusabo themselves knew an even stronger enemy in the Westo, a vigorous inland tribe. Over time, the Westo dominated until they in turn were swept out by stronger tribes and the English settlers of early Charles Town.

By the time of persistent English colonization, toward the end of the 17th century, another tribe, the Yemassee, had gained prominence in the region. Once friendly with the Spanish explorers to the south and educated in their ways of civilization, this group shifted its allegiance to the English as its members migrated north. They proved to be loyal supporters of Colonel "Tuscarora Jack" Barnwell, a flamboyant Irishman who had recently come to the Low-country, in a campaign to subdue hostile North Carolina tribes. Barnwell, who is buried in St. Helena's Episcopal Churchyard in Beaufort, proved to be a diplomat, as well: in 1719, he was called on by the settlers of Charles Town to represent their grievances to the Lords Proprietors, an action that resulted in the formal establishment of a royal colony.

The Yemassee carried on a healthy deerskin trade with the new Europeans, and there developed over time a far-ranging network of agents, outposts, and agreements. Yet, finally, the very success of the enterprise and the pressure of increased migration onto native lands proved to be the colonists' undoing. Long-simmering resentment of unscrupulous traders, unfair taking of land, and abuse of their people led to a gathering of fifteen Native American nations, who directed an assault from the Yemassee town at Pocotaligo. They attacked on Easter Sunday, 1715, killing as many traders as they could and sending the residents of Beaufort to their ships. The bloody Yemassee War lasted two years. At times, hundreds of warriors were dangerously close to Charles Town, reminding its residents of their isolation and pitiful protection under the crown. Eventually, the Yemassee forces disbanded and moved out of the region for good. By the middle of the 18th century, the last remnant tribes near Savannah had left the area.

THE SETTLING OF CHARLES TOWN

Carolina was originally known to Europeans as "Carolana," and it was the dream of the kings of Spain and France to have it. Their struggle for domination, played out on lands far distant from their own, and among native inhabitants who had been there for centuries, marked the earliest days of settlement.

The Spanish arrived first, in 1521, under the leadership of Francisco Gordillo: he named the Sea Island area Santa Elena. Further colonization was planned for but never materialized. Five years later, another Spaniard, Vasquez de Ayllon, having heard marvelous stories of the rich, vast land of Santa Elena, gathered 500 settlers and established his party at a point farther north along the coast. Their hopes, too, were to be dashed — by illness, a revolt among the slaves they had brought, attacks by Native Americans, and unusually harsh winter weather.

In 1562, Captain Jean Ribaut established Charlesfort, the first Protestant colony in North America, in the area he named Port Royal. Charlesfort, too, soon petered out, and by 1566, the area belonged to the Spanish, who commenced to build a string of forts along the coast. In 1629, Charles I of England announced his intentions of ownership. In the end, it was the English claim that stuck, although the early residents of Charles Town faced down Spanish, French, and Native forces several times before they were secure.

Time passed, however, before the English pursued their claim by actually settling. It took a monarch pressed to return favors — and a group of men with means, entrepreneurial spirit, and a keen sense of the market — to reap the benefits imagined for so long by so many. The monarch was Charles II, king of England during the Restoration. The group of men was Carolina's Lords Proprietors: Sir John Colleton, the Duke of Albermarle (George Monk), Lord Craven, Lord Berkeley, Sir William Berkeley, Sir George Carteret, the Earl of Clarendon, and Lord Ashley (Anthony Ashley Cooper).

The familiar nursery rhyme that calls Old King Cole a "merry old soul" might aptly have applied to Charles II. By 1663, restored to the throne after the dispatch of Cromwell, Charles found himself short of cash and facing obligations to those who had helped him in the late civil war. As a token of his appreciation, he gave to his loyal friends the territory "described in the parts of America not yet cultivated or planted, and only inhabited by some barbarous people who have no knowledge of Almighty God." This was to be the Carolina Province. Its development, particularly along the lower coast, was to define a society that exists today.

Planning for colonization began immediately. Sir John Colleton, who had lived among the planters in Barbados, convinced his associates of the need for expansion of the society there (already nearly 40 years old) and of the profits to be made in overseeing its relocation. In the summer of 1663, Captain William Hilton sailed the ship *Adventure* into Port Royal Sound, and their project began in earnest.

Hilton's successful foray and contact with friendly natives led to another exploratory trip three years later under the leadership of Captain Robert Sandford. This time, the English left behind Henry Woodward, a surgeon whose interest in the culture, language, and habits of the Native Americans

Reenactments of candle–making at Charles Towne Landing show the self-sufficiency of early settlers.

Wade Spees

was to ease the way, several years hence, for the first settlement at Charles Town. That day finally came in 1670 with the arrival of the ship *Carolina*, the only one of three ships to complete the voyage from England via Barbados.

It was at first unclear precisely where to settle — whether in the vicinity of Port Royal Sound, which Hilton had explored, or farther north, along the North Edisto River, where Sandford had ventured. Finally, after further viewing of both sites under the piloting and careful guidance of the *cacique* of the Kiawah tribe, the colonists established a fort at Albermarle Point, in the lands of the Kiawah, at Old Towne Creek up the Ashley River from present-day Charleston.

The earliest years of this colony have been brought to life at Charles Towne Landing which today offers a true sense of the importance of siting —high on a bluff from which unfriendly Spanish ships might be seen — and evidence of agricultural successes and failures. Small-scale farming worked; large cash crops, upon which rested the hopes of the Barbadian planters, didn't as yet.

In 1671, another shipload of colonists arrived, including more from Barbados, accompanied by their slaves; and by the following year the colony consisted of 30 houses and 200 people.

The colonists prospered and gained confidence, such that by 1680 they had removed themselves from Albermarle Point to a site on the peninsula at the mouth of the harbor, where they laid out their city. From this time forward, the development of Charles Town — indeed of the entire Lowcountry of which it was the capital — proceeded rapidly.

EARLY GROWTH AND PROSPERITY

Between 1690 and 1720, according to the historian Carl Bridenbaugh, the population of Charles Town tripled. New immigrants included French Huguenots and Irish, who established themselves in business and government. Wharves, churches, protective sea walls, defensive bastions, and homes were built. Streets were named (Church, Broad, Meeting, Tradd, and Queen are among those you can see today) and some of them were even paved with oyster shells. Trade with the Native Americans was lively, and exports thrived: deerskins and fur were shipped to England; pork, corn, naval stores, and lumber went to Barbados and the southern islands. The vast natural networks of creeks and rivers opened up the countryside to planters who raised beef and pork, cultivated cotton, rice, and indigo, and harvested lumber. And of course the waterways were crucial to transporting all these goods to Charles Town.

In governance, the influence of the Barbados colony continued to be felt in the key areas of law and representation by parish, and in the adoption of the slave code. The settlers from Barbados also imposed their architecture — the classic design with its raised basement and upstairs piazzas —and their intent to develop plantations outside the city limits. The increasing importation of slaves followed, an absolute essential in making large-scale agriculture a success.

Thus, from the very beginning, Charles Town was a society in which profitability and expansion — not to mention ease of living, even among the less grand — were inextricably tied to slaves and their management by law and custom. The historian Peter Wood estimates that by 1715 the slave population exceeded the European population.

Prosperity did not guarantee security, though. Charles Town faced threats from outsiders: there were skirmishes with Native Americans, Spanish soldiers, even pirates such as Blackbeard (Edward Teach) and Stede Bonnet. In 1718, 49 pirates were hanged.

Success in trade and a growing, more diverse population did, however, embolden the citizens to improve their lot. Prompted by resentment toward England (which refused to help pay for the defense of the city, attempted to enact trade restrictions, and raised the colonists' quitrents, among other heavy-handed actions), the citizens challenged the very form of proprietorship under which their colony had been established. In 1721, after much to-and-fro with England, the Carolina Province became a royal colony. By the 1730s, it was referred to by its new name, Charlestown. Only after the Revolution, when it was incorporated as the new state of South Carolina's first city, would it finally adopt the now-familiar spelling as Charleston.

EXPANSION IN THE COLONIAL LOWCOUNTRY

Once people were settled, once they were safe, once they had established their markets and their means of production in slaves, the Lowcountry around colonial Charlestown started its meteoric climb to achieve what it eventually became: person for person, the wealthiest region in the colonies. It

Drayton Hall, an Ashley River Plantation considered the finest Georgian-Palladian dwelling in the country, represents early 18th century refinement.

Wade Spees

started with rice; then came indigo, and finally cotton. The fact that all these crops were suited to Lowcountry cultivation, that there was land to support them and slaves to work them, that there was desire abroad for their harvest (in some cases a bounty paid for it), and hefty profit to be made on it, left only a need for a class of men to seize the opportunity to grow rich. As was the case in other colonies, there were plenty of them, and they promptly did so.

The world they began to establish, the ways they embellished it, the physical order they imposed on it, and the choices they made to keep it alive defined Lowcountry culture right up to the Civil War. Even after that, even today, the echoes of those efforts resound in Lowcountry political, social, and economic life. In the deepest way, they form the basis of the stories people tell themselves about who they are.

As planters and their families spread out — and as new colonists continued to arrive from Barbados — they ventured across the Ashley River to Magnolia and Drayton Hall and Middleton Plantation; they went to Goose Creek and points inland, to Beaufort, across the Sea Islands of Kiawah, Seabrook, John's, Edisto, St. Helena, Lady's, and Hilton Head. In addition to their main house in the city, they might establish a "big house" on one plantation and then own several others that were far more rustic, run by overseers and a slave crew. Profits were turned to acquire new land and slaves. A merchant, having amassed a fortune in town, would follow a path similar to the one taken by this newly landed gentry. Planters were businessmen, and vice versa.

Thus emerged a small society that was at once far-flung across the Lowcountry but glued together by shared aspirations, tastes, assumptions about plantation life and the treatment of blacks, even by marriage.

The relation between city and country was intimate. Charlestown, already the throbbing commercial heart of this society, came to display all its wealth. There were theatrical performances, clubs of every variety, subscription concerts followed by elaborate balls, racetracks, even a "season" that included "Race Week" in February, which was marked by nonstop celebrations, balls, co8 of the wilderness a life of refinement." In fact, there was still a lot of wilderness. To the south, it was just being tamed. By 1742, when there were nearly 7,000 people living in Charlestown, Savannah's population numbered only in the hundreds.

THE FOUNDING OF SAVANNAH

By comparison with the settling of Charlestown, the founding of Savannah in 1733 was seen as a far less ambitious enterprise — and perhaps a morally loftier one. The colony began as the idea of a group of twenty Englishmen, who petitioned the Crown for a grant of land. They were known as the Trustees, and they had idealistic, philanthropic goals: land would be held communally, settlers would be selected from "impoverished classes"; Trustees would pay for passage of settlers; there would be no liquor, slavery,

A "single house" of the Georgian period, built of cypress and adorned, as the best houses might be, with a drawing-room mantel by Thomas Elfe. Single refers to the style of a building that is only one-room deep.

Wade Spees

or land speculation. The Trustees were given executive and legislative powers for 21 years. They could distribute land to settlers, but land was held in the Trustees' name.

The 114 or so settlers who arrived under the flag of King George were mostly of modest means, and their goal — as outlined by the Trustees — was the development of exports, including wine and silk. They were also supposed to defend the colony from the Spanish, and thus provide a buffer for prosperous Charlestown.

They were led by General James Oglethorpe, a high-minded Englishman with a caretaker's concern for his flock. Many addressed him as "Father." Such was his sense of mission that when the ship *Ann* arrived in Charlestown harbor for consultations with the royal governor, the passengers were required to remain aboard and fish for their supper, so as not to have their heads turned by the glamorous city ashore.

Continuing south, the *Ann* stopped at tiny Beaufort. Here passengers *were* allowed to fraternize with the residents, whose standard of living probably appeared to be more in line with what the newcomers, in the best of circumstances, might hope to accomplish. General Oglethorpe chose as his site for Savannah a place where "the river forms a half-moon, along the south side of which the banks are about 40 feet high, and on the top a flat, which they call a bluff." He was assisted by Colonel William Bull, a engineer from Charlestown with local surveying experience, and guided by Tomochichi, a friendly Yamacraw chief. The site was about 18 miles from the river's mouth on the

Atlantic, on water sufficiently deep for ships drawing up to 12 feet to navigate within 10 yards of the shore.

Oglethorpe and Bull immediately set themselves to the task of planning the city, and it is the legacy of their inspired effort that distinguishes Savannah today. The city was, and is, a meticulously planned urban environment stretching back from the river in a series of squares and boulevards which, then as now, are landscaped focal points. The basic form consisted of blocks of five symmetrical 60 by 90 foot lots encompassing 20 squares. Space was designated for public buildings and market areas, as well as for secure retreats, in which settlers living outside the city limits could take cover in the event of Native American uprisings. The plan has been designated a National Historic Civil Engineering Landmark.

As things turned out, relations with the Native Americans remained friendly. Tomochichi supported the colonists' work throughout his life and was instrumental in winning the trust of tribes in the area. He was also willing to support Oglethorpe in battles with the Spanish, which were to occur sporadically over the next 10 years. The existence of a trading post nearby — run by John Musgrove, from South Carolina and his wife, Mary, who was part Creek — also smoothed the way for natural contact.

Given such a propitious start, it was up to the settlers to dig in, to clear and build, hunt and farm, and establish the Trustees' Garden. This they did, on the grants of 50 acres received by heads of families (five acres in the city, 45 outside it for farming). The settlers were also the beneficiaries of hundreds of head of livestock from their South Carolina neighbors, as well as rice and horses. For quite some time, even after Savannah got on its feet, South Carolina, and the port of Charlestown in particular, was to dominate the commercial life of the southern coast.

More settlers, including Irish, Scots, Swiss, Germans, and Italians, came very quickly. Jews and Protestant Salzburgers from the German-Austrian border area sought refuge from religious persecution. By 1741, there were 142 houses, a courthouse, jail, storehouse, market building, and a 10-acre, fenced public garden. By 1742, the liquor ban was repealed due to popular demand.

Soon enough the settlers found that some of the original restrictions intended to guide development were hampering it. By 1749, the ban on slavery was repealed because settlers felt they could not compete with South Carolina's productivity and overseas trade. In 1750, the Trustees relinquished their hold on land (again, by popular demand): private property ownership ensued.

In 1752, when the original Trustee Charter was up for review, Parliament refused further aid. As a result, in 1754, the colony became a royal province with governance by a royal council appointed by the King. As such, the province was subject to all the taxes, levies, duties, etc. that the other American colonies endured.

Thus in a sense released from Oglethorpe's idealism, the colonists proceeded to develop plantations as their neighbors had. However, it took until the close of the French and Indian War in 1763 (when Florida was ceded to England) for Savannah to begin to flourish as a colonial city and primary port serving the Georgia backcountry. By the time of the Revolution, the South Carolina and Georgia colonies had settled lingering border disputes, were engaging freely in trade, and were communicating through four Lowcountry newspapers. The region had pulled together, united by shared commercial and social goals, and a culture deeply affected by slavery.

In 1775, a Provincial Congress was called because Savannah residents were as fed up with English governance and taxation as the rest of the colonies. In a show of solidarity and goodwill, the colony joined the Revolution.

THE AMERICAN REVOLUTION

Ten years before reports of the battles of Lexington and Concord reached the Lowcountry, its residents were taking independent action to defy British rule, especially its methods of colonial governance and taxation. By the time of the Stamp Act in 1765, they had become wealthy, self-confident and better-organized in their own military defense. Having built their cities from scratch, they were in no mood to be further subjugated, and their responses were violent. In Charlestown, long-festering political disagreements between the colonists and the royal governor burst to the surface. They bitterly resented his order to move the Assembly and center of government to Beaufort, a day's journey by boat. In Savannah, where relations between colonists and governor had been more cordial, groups of Liberty Boys nevertheless were openly challenging loyalists and destroying British property.

Fear of fire in homes relegated cooking to adjacent "kitchen houses" like this one behind the Heyward-Washington House. Thomas Heyward, Jr. signed the Declaration of Independence; George Washington stayed here in 1791.

Wade Spees

By 1774, many colonists had become defiant. The merchants of Charlestown refused to buy tea that had been taxed, preferring to let it mold in the Exchange Building, which you can see today at the foot of Broad Street. British products were boycotted. Five delegates were sent to the First Continental Congress. In Savannah, leaders gathered at Tondee's Tavern to sign a petition denouncing the acts Parliament had passed in response to the Boston Tea Party (the Intolerable Acts) and insisting on their independent rights.

At this point, war seemed inevitable, even though there were loyalists throughout the Lowcountry who urged negotiation and reconsideration of non-importation policies. In 1776, four South Carolinians and three Georgians signed the Declaration of Independence. Colonial rule was over, but the fighting had just begun.

In the first significant victory of the Revolution (June 28, 1776, a day that is still celebrated in Charleston), General William Moultrie, outnumbered and outgunned, defeated an invading fleet of 50 British warships from his position on Sullivan's Island, in a fort built of palmetto logs. Visitors to the site today are impressed by the degree of risk and bravery that battle entailed.

But the Lowcountry was not yet secure. In December 1778, the British captured Savannah, and in May 1780, after a one-month siege, they finally subdued Charlestown. The British wreaked vengeance on the colonists by imprisoning and executing patriots. When they finally left the Lowcountry, in 1782, they were loaded down with war booty.

The American Revolution had a profound effect on the heretofore stable Lowcountry society. It was nothing less than a civil war dividing families and generations. According to Robert Rosen in *A Short History of Charleston*, William Bull was for the king; his nephews for the revolutionaries. Daniel Heyward was a Tory, but his son Thomas signed the Declaration of Independence. Similar clashes of ideals and politics occurred in other prominent Lowcountry families such as the Draytons, Pinckneys, Manigaults, Horrys, and Hugers.

Old Sheldon Church in Beaufort County, built in the style of a Greek Temple, was a casualty of the American Revolution, as the British fought desperately to hold on to the Lowcountry.

Wade Spees

The political questions raised by the conflict sensitized new classes of people to their own self-interest. The governments that came into place afterwards reflected these diverse new motivations. No longer were mechanics and other artisans — "the little people" — satisfied with government dominated by the planter class, especially when planters' slaves soaked up most of the available work. As for the wealthy, they were forced to read the handwriting on the wall; fortunately, some of the Lowcountry's planters were themselves ardent patriots, and they adjusted to democratic government, though their influence remained out of proportion to their numbers.

The years following the Revolution saw a fantastic boom in population, in building, and in commerce. Many of the houses of the Lowcountry date from this Federal period, in which new fortunes were made and old ones even further enhanced. If the architecture of the Lowcountry can be read as a book, this is its first great chapter.

In March, a broad hillside of flowering azaleas borders the rice mill pond at Middleton Place; the formal gardens were built by slaves in the middle of the 18th century.

Wade Spees

Entrepreneurs, ship captains, military people, and merchants from New England came to the cities and the Sea Islands to build their plantations. While the bounty on indigo was a casualty of war and led to a decline in that crop, the invention in 1793 of the cotton gin, on a plantation near Savannah, meant that the process of removing seeds from cotton could occur with greater ease and speed. Slaves working in the ginhouses still plucked by hand seeds from the most highly prized strain then being grown: Sea Island cotton, whose long, silky fibers would be broken by the action of the gin. These seeds were saved, talked about, compared, and the best of them used for the following crop. Despite ups and downs in the cotton market and competition from the rest of the new American republic, for most of the next 60 years the Lowcountry flourished.

PLANTATION LIFE AND GULLAH CULTURE

The first African-American slave came to the Lowcountry to stay in 1670. Ever since then, slaves, freedmen, and their heirs have defined in the most essential way imaginable the politics, growth, lifestyle, culture, language, and habits of the Lowcountry. The complexity of relations between blacks and whites — who, in city or country, lived in close quarters and experienced daily contact but were governed by strict social codes enforced by penalties — has informed all Lowcountry history. Fear of black uprising, especially after the ill-fated Denmark Vesey rebellion in 1822, made for a regulation of life unknown outside the South.

For the best overview of slave life, visit The Charleston Museum. Or drive to Middleton Place, another site which, with its landscaped gardens and farm-yard, offers splendid evidence of the world the slaves built. Imagine the daily bustle of slaves around what is now Charleston's Market Area, or in Savannah's waterfront warehouses, now restored.

When you are out and about in the Lowcountry, probably the two most significant things to ponder, when thinking about its past, are the immense *enterprise* that characterized plantations (where they now may be silent and grand, they were once fantastically busy places with dozens of buildings) and the *isolation* the slaves endured there.

The world of the plantation was self-sufficient, marked by dozens of specific activities taking place according to the season: gathering marsh hay for fertilizer, harvesting, clearing and burning the fields, building and repairing, growing food crops, moting and ginning cotton, packing it in the cotton house, taking it to the landing to be shipped on barges. Within that world of action, and responding to its often crushing demands, there arose a culture among slaves, now generally called the Gullah culture, which included elements of their African past. Scholars have identified these remnant "Africanisms" in religious and mythical beliefs, in patterns of speech and dress, in basketry, art, dance, and song. In its totality, Gullah is a way of life that informed — and still informs — the manner in which slaves and their descendants managed their relationship toward white people and kept intact some expression of their own identity.

From the earliest days, black slaves from certain rice-growing regions of the West African coast were prized for their knowledge of that crop's cultivation. Rice-growing is a tricky business. It requires periodic flooding of fields, the design, building, and maintenance of a dike-and-gate system, and hundreds of people, including children, to protect the rice plants from birds, gather it in, separate the grain from the chaff by means of sea-grass "fanner baskets," and clean it with mortar and pestle. In all of these areas, black people were experienced, and they taught what they knew.

Indigo and cotton crops demanded other kinds of hard labor — in preparing the fields with usually nothing more than a hoe and a plow-dragging ox, in building pits to soak the indigo or in chopping weeds to free the cotton plants, in extracting the dye or picking tufts from spiky bolls. Labor was apportioned by "tasks" of land, a task being about a quarter of an acre, for which slaves were responsible. Plantation ledgers were organized around work completed according to this system. In addition, slaves were used as carpenters, black-smiths, cooks, loggers, boat-builders, butchers, and house-servants. While planters left at the onset of "the sickly season" to escape malaria, blacks were immune to this fever and worked through the miasmic heat of summer.

A caste system grew up within the population that served the needs of the plantation master: slaves associated with domestic life were at the top, and field hands were at the bottom. Becoming a black "driver" meant that a slave would work with an overseer to direct crews; it also meant meting out punishment and whippings to fellow slaves. With blacks outnumbering whites by vast majorities, keeping order through work and brutality was essential to the plantation system.

The treatment of slaves varied widely in the Lowcountry. It is important to remember that while the majority of white people in the city and the country owned slaves, only a very small portion of them owned more than a dozen. Some planters bought and sold families; some kept them together, some did not. Some allowed friendships or marriage to occur between plantations; some took skilled slaves to the city and hired them out. Some planters allowed slaves to hunt and fish, keep gardens, raise fowl, and sell eggs. Some gave them staples — molasses, cloth, tobacco, shoes — on a periodic basis.

Slaves who were skilled craftsmen or domestic servants sometime lived in cabins like these at Boone Hall Plantation.

Wade Spees

Slaves lived in cabins or slave rows that shared a common wall and had dirt floors. On the plantations they worshipped at praise houses — usually small, clapboard buildings lined with benches — where services were marked by recitations of the gospel, praying, and the singing of spirituals in which an elder "deaconed out" a line and the worshippers responded in unison. They buried their dead in separate slave cemeteries, dozens of which are in still in use today.

Whatever the specific case, a slaves' identity (and that of his family) was tied to one place, which he might never leave during his lifetime. If ever he did travel it was under a strict pass or ticket system. His fortunes were often tied to one white family, and his heirs to its heirs. Education of slaves was either haphazard or strictly forbidden.

It is not possible to overestimate the way in which the Civil War disrupted the order imposed by the plantation world and the society it held in check. When recovery was to come to the Lowcountry, it would come to the countryside last.

The artistry — and the wealth — that produced the graceful "flying staircase" at the Nathaniel Russell House in Charleston was never to be matched after the Civil War.

Wade Spees

THE CIVIL WAR AND THE YEARS OF POVERTY

If the Lowcountry is seen by visitors as a place rich in references to the Civil War, both physical and spiritual, perhaps it is because there was such a difference in the "before" and "after." The cataclysmic changes wrought by that great conflict are well known.

Perhaps less well known is the fact that even before the Civil War, the Lowcountry already had been undergoing a slow transformation. Historians point to a definite drift of the Lowcountry after the 1820s, from occupying a place at the center of colonial and post-Revolutionary commerce to becoming just one of many prosperous regions in the South.

The Lowcountry's golden age was, in fact, the now-distant time of relative innocence and optimism long before the antebellum era, a time of cosmopolitan outlook and quiet accommodation with the rest of the country that was lost during the overheated days immediately prior to the Civil War. (It has only been in the later years of the 20th century — some might say as recently as the great resort booms, the "second Yankee invasion" — that the Lowcountry has been able to consider itself as reentering the mainstream of American culture.)

The nostalgia for long-lost days, which most every visitor to the Lowcountry feels, is probably for a time more nearly 200 years ago than 140.

By the 1850s, due to a number of factors, including the price and availability of cotton elsewhere, protective tariffs for new industries in the north, and the emergence of the abolitionist movement, the Lowcountry had lost its position of national preeminence. As a result, its outlook became more narrowly regional. Political positions hardened; tolerance for a national view of things receded. The institution of slavery was viewed less as a necessary evil — possibly temporary — and more as a positive benefit, one from which Southerners could not turn back. And there were politicians, like John C. Calhoun, who made an eloquent case for this vision. As Mary Boykin Chesnut wrote in her diary at the time of secession: "South Carolina had been rampant for years. She was the torment of herself and everyone else. Nobody could live in this state unless he were a fire-eater."

Of course, life did go on, populations increased, profits were made. Charleston and Savannah grew, with the addition of magnificent mansions in the Greek Revival style — such as Charleston's Edmondston-Alston House — or the Regency style — such as the William Scarbrough House in Savannah. Small towns like Beaufort raised their own gentry. Nonetheless, planters' societies that might, in the past, have discussed nothing more ominous than crop yields, seed types, and the accounting practices of their agents and cotton factors, now found their attentions turned to defensive matters concerning their slaves, their fortunes, and their state's rights.

S ecession is the fashion here. Young ladies sing for it; old ladies pray for it; young men are dying to fight for it; old men are ready to demonstrate it.

—From a dispatch to the London *Times*, April 1861,
sent from Charleston by English journalist
William Howard Russell

In December 1860, led by Lowcountry Secessionists, South Carolina separated itself from the Union. The following year, Georgia followed suit. Soon, the harbor forts that watched over both cities — Fort Sumter and Fort Pulaski — were battle sites. Both of the forts can be visited today, and the story of their defense is a dramatic one.

Additional glimpses of the Civil War period are poignantly on display at the Confederate Museum in Charleston, with its frayed uniforms and flags, and in the Green-Meldrim House in Savannah, headquarters of General Sherman, who, having completed his victorious March To the Sea in 1864, not only celebrated Christmas in Savannah but also offered the city itself as a gift to President Lincoln.

A less well known chapter of Civil War history, having Beaufort as its center, concerns the efforts on the part of Northern abolitionists to live among the newly freed slaves and prepare them for full "citizenship." The enterprise followed by several months the Union invasion of Port Royal in November 1861. Over the next several years, a hundred or so men and women took up residence in the abandoned plantation houses, managed the plantations for the government, which looked to cotton crops for revenue, and set up schools for slaves young and old in front parlors and cotton houses.

After the Civil War, the Lowcountry, now impoverished, turned in upon itself. It was as if people simply went home and stayed there, hoarding their gentility in their city homes as they might their last pennies, taking in sewing, teaching, and boarding guests. In the country they concentrated on making a living again as farmers, albeit far more modest ones. People were thrown back on their resources — their fishing and hunting and farming — and they made do. For every "Porgy" there were hundreds more: only small numbers of freedmen actually received, and were able to hang on to, land they had been promised.

Although phosphate mining, timbering, and shipyards emerged as centers of postwar activity, the economy was slow to repair itself. An idea of just how poor conditions were, right up until World War II, can be glimpsed in the work of Walker Evans, Marion Post Wolcott, and other photographers sent by the Farm Security Administration to document Lowcountry life.

As it turns out, the legacy of poverty was just as crucial in preserving the built environment of the Lowcountry as prosperity had been, in the early years, for bringing it to life. As early as the 1920s, Charlestonians were organizing to save their old buildings. In 1931, the city passed the nation's first Historic District zoning; some 20 years later, the Historic Savannah Foundation was founded to oppose the demolition of the Isaiah Davenport House.

A kayaker making his way across the marsh and open sea, to Capers Island, near Charleston.

Wade Spees

Ever since, these cities' Historic Districts and properties in the country nearby have been central attractions to generations of tourists. They have provided architects, landscape gardeners, historians — even novelists — with material for inspiration. It is a remarkable testament to the Lowcountry's enduring legacy and powers of regeneration that, despite all this intellectual trawling, the region doesn't seem fished out.

THE LOWCOUNTRY LEGACY

Through all its changes, the Lowcountry landscape has retained its immense allure for those who have lived and traveled here, from roving early settlers to today's nomads of the bus tour. Perhaps this is because a sense of history and a sense of place intersect at so many points in the Lowcountry. There is no high ground here. History itself provides the only vantage point, the only way to detach oneself from an insular sense of place that is always responding to forces — of wind and tide, of society and war — greater than itself.

It was and is a place to be desired. Whether your quest is satisfied by filling a bucket with oysters, or paddling a canoe in the marsh, or visiting an old home accompanied by nothing more than your imagination, the Lowcountry offers a rare chance to enact and to observe the subtle rituals of the past, and to take from them, for yourself, the pleasures they've delivered for so long to so many.

To describe our growing up in the lowcountry of South Carolina, I would have to take you to the marsh on a spring day, flush the great blue heron from its silent occupation, scatter marsh hens as we sink to our knees in the mud, open you an oyster with a pocketknife and feed it to you from the shell and say, 'There. That taste. That's the taste of my childhood.' I would say, 'Breathe deeply,' and you would breathe and remember that smell for the rest of your life, the bold, fecund aroma of the tidal marsh, exquisite and sensual, the smell of the South in heat, a smell like new milk, semen, and spilled wine, all perfumed with seawater.

—From *The Prince of Tides* by Pat Conroy
(Boston: Houghton Mifflin Company)
©1986 by Pat Conroy

CHAPTER TWO
Getting Here, Getting Around
TRANSPORTATION

The first and most important fact about the Lowcountry is that it is mostly water. Land is an illusion, an accident, nothing to count on. Perhaps this is why the old houses of the region's cities and towns — and the dense feeling of permanence they exude — are so wildly venerated, above and beyond their architectural and historic status. While they certainly represented the values of an elite planter class up until the Civil War, they also appear — now, as in the past — lit-

Courtesy of The Charleston Museum, Charleston, SC

The men of Charleston's "Mosquito Fleet" rowed bateaux and gathered oysters from the banks, according to the tide.

erally to triumph over their surroundings, as if daring wind, water, and the harsh storms of hurricane season to teach them the lessons of frailty.

In September 1989, Hurricane Hugo did just that. Walls of water pushed 40-foot boats onto the downtown streets of Charleston. For weeks the drinking water tasted of turpentine, resinous and tannic, as fallen trees decomposed into rivers and leached into the water table, which in the best of times has never been more than a few feet away from the salty sea.

And that was just one storm. Day in and day out, water defines the Lowcountry, its aesthetics, its cuisine, its recreation, the siting of its houses, its economy, its history, its means of transportation. The way people get from place to place today still is determined by a force Lowcountry residents know they can never control, no matter how high bridges are built to accommodate the boat traffic beneath, nor how wide the causeway across the marsh. It takes but one glance at a boat stranded on a mud bar at low tide — as often happens — to realize how dependent the region is on the good graces of the tides.

The tides, which cast the riches of sea life toward shore and offered the first planters the possibility of harnessed power, bestowed on the Lowcountry a natural abundance of marine and bird life, and enabled the cultivation of rice. The settlements that clustered around what we know today as peninsular Charleston, flanked by the Ashley and Cooper Rivers, grew up there to take advantage of the tidal watercourses. Flat-bottomed plantation barges loaded with rice, bales of cotton, and farm produce plied the rivers and creeks to the city harbor. Throughout the Lowcountry, eight-oared bateaux, made on the plantations and navigated by slaves, clove the marsh from one plantation to another, carrying news, goods, and passengers. In Savannah, the river offered both protection to an English colony in the Southern wilderness and a commercial means by which its first English citizens — many of them destitute or castaway — could start their new lives.

For nearly 200 years, water was the best highway in the Lowcountry. Quite often, what roads existed were hardly distinguishable from the water. In 1784, a traveler noted a "common highway" that "as lonely and desolate as this part of the road is, without shade and with no dwellings in sight, it is by no means a tedious road. The number of shells washed up, sponges, corals, sea grasses and weeds, medusae, and many other ocean products which strew the beach, engage and excite the attention."

As time went on, people of the Lowcountry took nature one step further: they made roadbeds of oyster shell, fashioning a crown at the "center line" to facilitate drainage. These were the best roads around, and in some towns like Beaufort they were in use well into the 20th century. An unimproved road, such as you'd find — and still find today — on the Sea Islands, was plowed through fine sand, perhaps a foot deep, rutted and banked. More than one elderly Lowcountry resident can tell a tale of pushing a Model T Ford through this sand, or of watching the ice melt through the sawdust when the iceman got stuck.

Perhaps as a result of the reliance on water travel, as well as the sheer isolation of the plantations and their rural dependencies, a thickly veined series of land transportation routes never really developed in the Lowcountry. Instead there evolved a fleet of small packet steamers that made their way from island to island, picking up passengers, mail, produce, and cotton to deliver in Charleston and Savannah. And ox-drawn carts, or horses, or marsh "tackies" (diminutive horses, something like a Shetland pony) serviced them! When, in 1894, the historian Henry Adams visited St. Helena Island, he traveled first by train, then by carriage over a sand road, then on a shell road, then by foot to the ferry crossing, then over the river to board the steamer *Flora*, which carried him to his destination. Now, at the beginning of the 21st century, the reintroduction of ferry service is being contemplated between Hilton Head Island, Savannah, St. Helena Island and Beaufort.

These days, your car will take you almost anywhere you want to go in the Lowcountry (which, for the purposes of this book, comprises the coastal plain from Charleston to Savannah, from the Atlantic inland about 40 miles). Driving here is convenient, of course, but its seamless ease has displaced an older, deeper feeling — that of reliance on the tides, the whimsy of weather, and navigators who measured the desire to move against what was possible. It might be said that the rhythm of life in the Lowcountry, dubbed the "Slowcountry" by some, was nurtured in those enforced waiting moments; sometimes it seemed wiser to stay put.

Motorists, bicyclists, and pedestrians coexist comfortably in the Lowcountry.

Fortunately, the growth of travel services has produced options to help a modern visitor reclaim this feeling of "down-time," during which you can, in a most modern way, observe your surroundings closely and well. The choices are outlined in this chapter. These days, the boat that takes you in the creek may be a Boston Whaler with a powerful outboard engine, but once you get out on the water, eye-level with the fiddler crabs scudding along the bank, you may as well be riding in an old Lowcountry bateau.

Finally, if you're coming to the Lowcountry from a city, or from someplace where water only runs from the tap, and if you're coming in by plane, take all the time you can to look out the window as the pilot descends. If the plane is circling low, as it often does, notice the watery necklace of islands and savannas, linked by tidal creeks, which make up the Lowcountry. As an abstraction at 10,000 feet, they seem mere daubs of color, surrounded and embraced by water. The truth is, that's the way they really are at ground level, too.

Swamps

Nearly one-third of this vast plain is what the inhabitants call swamps, which are the sources of numerous small rivers and their branches: these they call salt rivers, because the tides flow near to their sources, and generally carry a good depth and breadth of water for small craft, twenty or thirty miles upwards from the sea, when they branch and spread abroad like an open hand, interlocking with each other, and forming a chain of swamps across the Carolinas and Georgia, several miles parallel with the sea coast. These swamps are fed and replenished constantly by an infinite number of rivulets and rills, which spring out of the first bank or ascent.

—From *Travels of William Bartram,* 1791

GETTING TO THE LOWCOUNTRY

BY CAR

Unless your visit to the Lowcountry is limited strictly to Charleston or Savannah or to a self-contained Hilton Head resort — and many delightfully complete visits are — you might consider this trip to be one where having your own car really pays off. The Lowcountry is decentralized; a lot of space separates those "points of interest." What's more, appreciating that very space by finding yourself in it lies at the heart of the Lowcountry experience. That's where you'll find some of the region's subtle treasures: the view of a marsh at sunset, the sight of feeding pelicans as they hit the water, the faded impression of an abandoned oyster-shell road strewn with wildflowers. It is in these very open spaces, in their linked geography, that the sense of times passed and lives abundantly lived will catch up with you and shape your awareness of what the Lowcountry is all about.

From Washington and points north: Travelers from the north can reach the Lowcountry by approaching it on I-95, which roughly parallels the coast. From there, well-marked exits direct you to downtown Charleston (via I-26), to Beaufort (via Highway 21), to Hilton Head (via Highway 278) and Savannah (via I-16). The coastal destinations beyond the big cities, such as Kiawah Island, Edisto Island, Beaufort, and Hilton Head, lie approximately 45 minutes east of I-95. Distance from Washington to Charleston: 512 miles; to Savannah: 616 miles.

From Jacksonville and points south: Like visitors from the north, drivers from the south approach on I-95 and then turn east to the coast. Distance from Jacksonville to Charleston: 241 miles; to Savannah: 139 miles.

From Asheville and points northwest: Take I-40 to I-26, then follow I-26 toward Spartanburg and Columbia. About an hour out of Columbia, you meet I-95. At that point either continue east to Charleston or turn south. Distance from Asheville to Charleston: 265 miles; to Savannah: 297 miles.

From Charlotte: Take I-77 south to I-20 at Columbia; follow I-20 for a few exits to link up with I-26 east. Distance to Charleston: 200 miles; to Savannah: 240 miles.

From Atlanta: Take I-75 to I-16. When it crosses I-95 go north for Charleston, or continue directly to Savannah. Distance to Charleston: 286 miles; to Savannah: 259 miles.

Once you're in the Lowcountry, you will discover U.S. Highway 17, one of the region's oldest roads and still perhaps the most direct, a ribbon of blacktop (mostly two-lane) that threads its way from above Charleston to Savannah (and beyond) through marshes, old rice fields, and bottomland forests. It's worth cutting off I-95 to get there, or to use it exclusively as your north-south highway. Turnoffs that access the Sea Islands to the east (Kiawah, Seabrook,

Edisto, Port Royal, St. Helena, Hilton Head) and the Ashley River plantations (Drayton Hall, Middleton Place, Magnolia Gardens) to the west (along Hwy. 61) are well marked, as are historic sites, parks, and picnic grounds.

BY BUS

Greyhound (www.greyhound.com) serves Charleston, Beaufort, and Savannah and maintains stations in those cities. It also serves points in between, but here the stops are less formal — perhaps as simple as a crossroads store. As a result, if you're planning to do a substantial amount of traveling by bus, you should consult both a detailed map and the bus schedule. Don't expect to find a taxi or rental-car stand — or even a working pay telephone — at every stop.

The service and price to Charleston and to Savannah from various points are roughly equal; in most cases the same bus goes to both cities. Travel times on longer trips may vary up to three hours, according to the number of stops and the specific route, so it's wise to ask about arrival times and whether or not it's a direct trip. (Usually there's at least one "express" trip per day.) Sample listings of weekday prices and frequency of service (both subject to change) from several cities follow. In general, once you purchase your ticket, it is only refundable at 85% of face value; that is, should your plans change and you wish to redeem your ticket, you will be charged a 15% cancellation fee.

To the *Savannah Greyhound Bus Terminal*, 610 W. Oglethorpe Ave. (912-232-2135):

From New York (16–22 hours): Greyhound (800-231-2222) runs five buses daily from the Port Authority at 625 8th Ave. (at 42nd St.). The 2001 one-way fare was $91.50, round-trip $141.

From Washington, D.C. (11–16 hours): Greyhound (202-289-5154) has eight buses departing daily from the terminal at 1005 First St. N.E. The 2001 one-way fare was $79, round-trip $118.

From Jacksonville (3 hours): Greyhound (904-356-1841) departs ten times daily from the station at 10 N. Pearl St. The 2001 one-way fare was $22, round-trip $41.

From Columbia (4 hours): Greyhound (803-256-6465) has four buses departing daily from the station at 2015 Gervais St. The 2001 one-way fare was $27, round-trip $52.

From Charlotte (6 hours): Three Greyhound buses (704-375-9536) depart from the station at 601 W. Trade St. daily. The 2001 one-way fare was $45, round-trip $89.

From Atlanta (6 hours): Four Greyhound buses (404-522-6300) depart from the terminal at 232 Forsythe St. daily. The 2001 one-way fare was $37.45, round-trip $74.90.

BY TRAIN

Amtrak (www.amtrak.com) travels the north-south corridor, making daily stops at North Charleston (4565 Gaynor Ave.; 843-744-8264) about 25 minutes from downtown, Yemassee (about 30 miles west of Beaufort), and Savannah. On the long hauls from major cities like New York, Washington, and Miami, there are generally two trains a day, departing morning and evening and arriving either late the same day or early the following morning. Traveling by night is a nice option for these 8- to 13-hour trips: when you awaken, you're there.

The rates for sleeping accommodations (economy or first-class, which includes meals) are usually tacked on to the lowest coach fare — and that fare varies depending on how far in advance you make your reservations and the availability on specific days. Call Amtrak (800-872-7245) or your travel agent for rates and schedules. Special packages with airlines might be available, as well as discounts if you can restrict your travel to certain days. Reduced fares for families or children are usually offered for summer travel.

If you're staying near Beaufort, Yemassee is your station stop. Make prior arrangements to be picked up; it's a country crossroads with minimum through traffic. The *Beaufort Cab Company* (843-524-4940), the *Yellow Cab Company* of Beaufort (843-522-1121), and *AC Limousine* (843-986-8738) can carry you to town. The 2001 fare was $35.

Some 2001 Amtrak fares from selected cities follow.

From Washington: Trains depart Union Station twice daily for North Charleston, a trip that lasts about 8.5 hours. Coach fares run between $144 and $286 round-trip. With sleeping accommodations the round-trip fares start at $410. Round-trip coach fares to Savannah range from $210 to $366; from $380 to $600 including sleeping accommodations.

From New York: One train departs Penn Station for North Charleston for the 13-hour ride. Coach fares range from $148 to $354 round-trip; with sleeping accommodations, from $480 to $680. There are two trains daily for Savannah. The round-trip coach fares are $148 to $356; starting at $460 for sleeping accommodations.

From Chicago: Travel includes layover and switching trains. One train daily to North Charleston, a 36-hour ride. Coach fares range from $224 to $440 round trip, $440 to $820 for sleeping accommodations. To Savannah, a 30-hour ride, coach fares range from $270 to $444 round-trip; from $640 to $1,120 with sleeping accommodations.

From Jacksonville: Trains depart once a day to North Charleston, twice a day to Savannah. A round-trip coach fare to North Charleston costs between $86 and $150; to Savannah it's $56 to $92.

From Miami: The morning train to North Charleston arrives 13 hours later and costs between $112 and $288, round-trip. There are two trains to Savannah. A round-trip fare costs between $114 and $228.

BY COMMERCIAL AIRLINE

Savannah's modern International Airport confirms a visitor's first impression of the Lowcountry as a place defined by bright light and sharp shadows.

Wade Spees

Travelers bound for the Lowcountry can arrive and depart from *Charleston International Airport* or *Savannah International Airport.*, both of which are very comfortable and easy to navigate. Or they can use *Hilton Head Airport*, which is smaller and handles private planes and commuter shuttle service.

Numerous domestic and international carriers serve the Lowcountry cities, either with nonstop flights or connecting service through the regional hubs of Charlotte, NC, Raleigh/Durham, or Atlanta.

Once you're at the airport, you may want to pick up a rental car (best reserved in advance). For complete information, see the section on rental cars under "Getting Around the Lowcountry."

BY PRIVATE PLANE

If you're flying on your own, contact the following county or regional airports or services:

Beaufort County Airport	843-770-2003
East Cooper Airport	843-884-8837

Hilton Head Airport   843-689-5400
John's Island-Charleston Executive Airport   843-559-2401
Mercury Air Center-Charleston International   843-746-7600
Savannah Aviation   912-964-1022

BY BOAT

*There are historic neighbor-
hoods — and there are
marina neighborhoods.*

Wade Spees

The *Intracoastal Waterway* winds through creek and river, ocean and
sound, from one end of the Lowcountry to the other, making for some of
the most sublime cruising on the East Coast. The region's history of reliance on
water travel, plus the recent development of marinas affiliated with the new
resorts, have conspired to produce facilities of top quality and convenient location. If you're planning a water-based trip, it's best to judge the local options
according to your particular needs — the size of your boat, availability of on-
site repair services, proximity to sightseeing or restaurants or shopping, length
of your stay, your price range, etc.

If you want to make use of the charter fishing, sailing, or tour services based
at marinas, see the **Recreation** section in the appropriate chapter for some
ideas. If your main mode of transportation is by boat, check those listings for
details on berthing facilities and services. You should also consider word-of-
mouth recommendations along the way.

GETTING AROUND THE LOWCOUNTRY

This section will help you decide how you want to travel within the
Lowcountry, for as you plan your trip, the kind of vacation you desire will
really depend on how mobile you wish to be. For example, driving in the

Lowcountry can be fun: the landscape is dead flat, and what hazards there are — ground fog that hangs about headlight-height, wild and brief summer showers— are local phenomena so site-specific that you may come upon them and then pass through them wondering all the time why it's not raining "over there." In this far-flung landscape, if you plan to watch birds, retrace General Sherman's march to Columbia, S.C., or visit rural cemeteries and churches, a car is a must.

On the other hand, if your destination is Charleston or Beaufort or Savannah, their *Historic Districts* are best savored on foot or bicycle, or by joining any one of the dozens of tours offered by city-licensed operators. While these guides offer their commentary on cultural, historic, military, and architectural sites, you can be riding in a horse-drawn carriage, a boat, a minivan, a motorized trolley, a bus — even a surrey with the fringe on top. Inquire if a tour has a theme — African-American history and Gullah culture or ghosts or gardening.

Also ask about combination tickets offered by some vendors and museums. The Best of Charleston (800-540-3919; www.bestofcharleston.cc) and Charleston Heritage Passport (charlestonheritage.org; $29 adults; $19 children) offer discount packages of tickets for the city's mosst popular sites. Knowing the breadth and variety of these services should help you decide if you need a car at all. Some touring options follow at the end of this chapter.

The Shell Road

The only thoroughfare by land between Beaufort and Charleston is the 'Shell Road,' a beautiful avenue, which, about nine miles from Beaufort, strikes a ferry across the Coosaw River. War abolished the ferry, and made the river the permanent barrier between the opposing picket lines. For ten miles, right and left, these lines extended, marked by well-worn footpaths, following the endless windings of the stream; and they never varied until nearly the end of the war. Upon their maintenance depended our whole foothold on the Sea Islands; and upon that again finally depended the whole campaign of Sherman.

—From *Army Life in a Black Regiment*, 1869
by Thomas Wentworth Higginson

BY BUS

Greyhound is your carrier between Savannah and the North Charleston station at 3610 Dorchester Rd. (800-231-2222; 843-744-4247) with a stop in Beaufort (843-524-4646) at 1307 Boundary St. Buses run several times daily and the trip takes about two hours and 45 minutes. In 2001, the one-way weekday fare between Savannah and Charleston was $28. The fare to Beaufort was $12 one-way. From Beaufort to Charleston costs $21 one-way. All fares are doubled for round-trip passage. There is no service to Hilton Head.

LOWCOUNTRY ACCESS

The approximate distances and driving times to Charleston and selected cities are given in the charts below. The distance between Charleston and Savannah is 114 miles, so depending on the direction from which you are travelling, you should adjust accordingly. If you're touring within the Lowcountry, however, stopping along the way between Charleston and Savannah in places like Beaufort, Hilton Head, Bluffton, Edisto, or Walterboro, this trip easily may take a day. In general, traveling to specific Sea Island destinations located to the east of the major cities can add up to an hour to your trip.

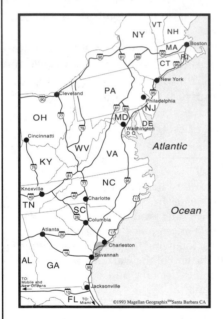

To Charleston from:

CITY	MILES	HOURS
Atlanta	291	5
Boston	929	17
Charlotte	219	4
Chicago	906	15.5
Knoxville	395	7
Miami	590	10.5
New Orleans	784	13
New York	768	13
Washington, D.C.	500	8.5

In *Charleston*, the attractive trolley-like *Downtown Area Shuttle (DASH)* (843-724-7420; www.ridecarta.com) makes regular stops along five routes in the Historic District and greater downtown area. Board at the Visitor Center (375 Meeting St.; 843-853-8000), where you can park your car ($8 per day; $7 with a DASH pass discount). The *DASH* maps and schedules are easy to follow and color-coded by route. All-day shuttle passes cost $2; a three-day pass is $5; single rides are $0.75. Fares for adults over 55 and disabled passengers are $0.25, except at rush hours, and children age six and under ride free. Exact change is required. City buses operated by the *Charleston Area Regional Transportation Authority (CARTA)* service destinations like Kiawah Island, Isle of Palms, Sullivan's Island and Mount Pleasant, some from the Visitor Center, some from nearby stops. Fares begin at $0.75. Bike racks are available at no charge on most of these routes, and take about 10 seconds to operate. For help in planning a trip outside the Historic District call *CARTA* (843-747-0922).

In *Savannah*, there's *Chatham Area Transit (CAT)* (912-233-5767; www.catch acat.org). A free shuttle bus service within the Historic District, with regular stops at the Visitors Center (301 Martin Luther King Blvd.; 912-944-0455), downtown inns and hotels, the waterfront, and many sites of interest. It connects to most bus routes, with fares of $0.75 for regional service throughout Chatham County. Parking adjacent to the Visitors Center in a city lot is $1 per hour until 5 p.m., with your first hour free.

BY TRAIN

Amtrak (North Charleston, 843-744-8264; Savannah, 912-232-4644) runs two trains daily — one in the morning, one in the evening — between Charleston and Savannah, a trip of about 90 minutes. 2001 coach fares were $17–$34 one-way, $34–$70 round-trip.

BY AIR

The quickest way between points in the Lowcountry is by air. The following companies offer a variety of charter, sightseeing, aircraft rental, and emergency services, some of which operate 24 hours a day:

Charleston

Aeroflight	843-559-5626
Carolina Helicopter Services	843-744-6144
Flying High Over Charleston	843-569-6148
Heli-East, Inc.	843-856-4600

Savannah

North-South Airways (groups only)   800-476-9181

Hilton Head

Airstream Aviation Aerial Tours   843-785-7770

Sightseeing tours regularly fly over the Charleston downtown and plantation sites, or across the harbor and Sea Islands. In 2001, tours in a 4-seater plane cost $119 to $149 per person and last one hour and longer. In the Hilton Head, Beaufort and Savannah area, rates for tours lasting from 20 minutes to 70 minutes were $49.95 to $124.95 per person (two-passengers minimum in a six-seater plane). Helicopter sightseeing trips for up to six passengers generally last 30 minutes and cost $550, based on an hourly rate. These vendors may also offer one-way travel within the Lowcountry by prior arrangement for small and large (15–20 people) groups.

BY TAXI OR LIMOUSINE

In the heat of the summer the ice-cold interior of a plush limousine will deliver heavenly relief; or, if modesty suits you better, you may want simply to hire a car and driver for a day. Whether you're touring by the hour or the day, here are some options:

Charleston

Absolute Charleston	843-814-7315
Charleston Connection	843-556-5752
Classic Limousine (Rolls Royces)	843-785-8500
Low Country Limousine	800-222-4771

Beaufort/Hilton Head

AC Limousine&Shuttle	843-986-8738
Lowcountry Adventures	843-681-8212 or 800-845-5582
Lowcountry Limousine&Shuttle	843-525-0800
Yellow Cab	843-686-6666

Savannah

Limousine Elite	912-234-7404
Magnolia Transportation	912-667-4559
McCall's Limousine	912-966-5364

In addition, there are taxi, van, and limousine services at both the Charleston and Savannah airport terminals; you can use these if transportation is not provided by your hotel or resort area. If you're staying in a B&B, the proprietor may be able to make an arrangement for you or suggest a service. The 2001 one-way taxi fare from Charleston International to the city was $18; to the resort islands, $20 per person, for two or more. From the Savannah Airport to downtown costs $18 for one person, $5 for additional riders. If your destination is further afield, say from Savannah to Beaufort (1 hour), expect to pay between $60 and $75. Within the cities, taxis should be called well in advance, for they are sometimes slow to respond, and street pickup is limited.

Alternative transportation in Charleston includes rickshaws, bicycles, and buggies.

Wade Spees

BY BUS, MINIVAN, OR TROLLEY

After all is said and done, the emergence of the "New South" has just as much to do with economics and enlightenment as with air-conditioning. There's no doubt that the comfort and cool of a minivan or bus tour — in which the guide is like your favorite classroom teacher and the atmosphere as fresh as a fine hotel room — has its virtues. The audio is high-quality, the video may be on a laser disc, and extra-large windows offer great views. These tours also travel to sites out of the city limits, such as historic forts and plantations.

But remember that comfort comes at a sacrifice — larger vehicles may not be able to navigate the old, sometimes alley-width streets of Historic Districts, and the pace is swiftly modern. They are a good choice for handicapped passengers, the eager visitor who wants to cover a lot of ground in a day, and groups of six or more. Tours range from one to 2.5 hours, longer for out-of-town sites and scheduled stops at house museums. In 2001, the price per person ranged from $8 to $13 for shorter trips and from $15 to $45 for longer trips, with reduced rates for children.

Charleston

Charleston Tours, Inc.	843-571-0049
Doin' The Charleston	843-763-1233 or 800-647-4487
Gullah Tours	843-763-7551
Sites and Insight Tours by Al Miller	843-762-0051
Sweet Grass Tours	843-556-0664
Talk of the Town	888-795-8199
Taylored Tours	843-830-6375 or 888-449-8687

Beaufort

Beaufort Tour Service	843-525-1300
Gullah & Geechie Mahn Tours	843-838-7516
The Point Tours	843-522-3576 or 800-774-8288

Hilton Head Area

Camelot Limousine and Tours	843-842-7777
Gullah Heritage Trail Tours	843-689-6094
Low Country Adventures	843-681-8212 or 800-845-5582

Savannah

Riding a trolley in Savannah allows a visitor to observe city life in all directions — down the receding street, framed by live oaks, or ahead to landscaped squares.

Wade Spees

Gray Line Bus and Trolley Tours	912-234-8687 or 800-426-2318
Hospitality Tours	912-233-0119
Old Savannah Tours	912-234-8128 or 800-517-9007
Old Town Trolley Tours	912-233-0083
Victorian Lady Tours	912-236-1886

BY RENTED CAR

A rriving by air and then renting a car during your stay is your best option if you plan to explore the Lowcountry. Reserve in advance, particularly in spring. Get a map, the more detailed the better if you're in rural areas. By county, look for Charleston, Dorchester, Colleton, Hampton, Beaufort, and Jasper in South Carolina, and Chatham in Georgia. A new illustrated map/brochure — S.C. Heritage Corridor Region 4 — documents sites of particular African-American interest, and is also useful for the general traveler. The text is thorough and well written. See it online: www.sc-heritagecor ridor.org.

Most of the major car rental companies have cars available at the airport terminals as well as in Charleston, Savannah, Beaufort, and Hilton Head. They include:

Alamo: 800-327-9633 (Charleston International, 843-767-4417; Savannah International, 912-964-7364).

Avis: 800-831-2847 (Savannah International, 912-964-1781; Hilton Head, 843-681-4216).

Budget: 800-527-0700 (Charleston International, 843-760-9025; Savannah International, 912-964-9186; Hilton Head, 843-689-4040).

Enterprise: 800-736-8222 (Beaufort, 843-524-0494; Savannah, 912-920-1093; Hilton Head, 843-689-9910).

Hertz: 800-654-3131 (Charleston, 843-767-4552; Savannah, 912-964-9595).

Thrifty: 800-367-2277 (Charleston, 843-552-7531; Beaufort, 843-522-9996; Savannah International, 912-966-2277).

Visitors approaching Hunting Island State Park near Beaufort are reminded of what residents know from experience.

Wade Spees

From Charleston International Airport: Follow the airport access road to I-26 into Charleston. Any downtown exit will take you to the peninsula. If you're traveling to Sullivan's Island or Isle of Palms, exit at I-526 east. If you're heading to the Ashley River plantations or Folly Beach, take I-526 west. For Edisto or Beaufort, take I-526 west and, when it intersects with Highway 17, go south. Turns for individual Sea Islands are marked.

Miles: 15 to downtown Charleston; 30 to Sullivan's Island and Isle of Palms; 30 to Kiawah and Seabrook; 40 to Edisto; 70 to Beaufort.

Time: 25 minutes to downtown; 40 to Sullivan's Island; 60 to Edisto, 80-90 to Beaufort.

From Savannah International Airport: Follow the access road to I-95, then exit to I-16 downtown. Hilton Head is about a 45-minute drive from I-95. Get on I-95 northbound. Take Exit 8 to Hwy. 278, which becomes the main road on Hilton Head. For Beaufort, follow Hwy. 278 to a left exit on Highway 41, then join SC 170 and follow the signs to Beaufort.

Miles: 11 to Savannah's Historic District; 35 to Hilton Head; 40 to Beaufort.

Time: 25 minutes to Savannah, 50 to Beaufort and Hilton Head.

From Hilton Head Airport: Exit the airport and travel south on William Hilton Parkway, Highway 278. Resort entrances are clearly marked.

BY BOAT

If you can tear yourself away from the authentic seductions of "the built environment," you will be rewarded by views of marshes and marine life that exist in such a pristine state in only a few places in the United States. Even better, you may be overcome by a feeling of wondrous detachment as you see the skylines — and, at dusk, the twinkling lights — of the Historic Districts fade from view.

An excellent area map — from the perspective of water — is available for $9.95 from Coastal Expeditions, Inc. (843-884-7684; 514-B Mill St., Mt. Pleasant, SC 29464; www.coastalexpeditions.com).

Some options for harbor cruises and rides aboard sailboats, pontoon boats and hybrid amphibious craft follow. (For additional options see the **Recreation** sections of individual chapters.) The tours generally last two hours. The 2001 per-person fares ranged from $14 to $30; reduced rates for children.

Charleston

Charleston Explorer Dolphin Tours	843-723-5656
Fort Sumter Tours/Charleston Harbor Tour	843-722-2628
Gray Line Water Tours	843-722-1112 or 800-344-4483
Lowcountry Duck Tours	843-849-0804
Schooner Pride (84' tall ship)	843-559-9686 or 888-571-2486

You can still take in the view of Charleston from a schooner, as passengers did 350 years ago.

Wade Spees

Beaufort

ACE Basin Tours, Inc.   843-521-3099 or 888-814-3129
Islander Cruises   843-524-4000

Hilton Head Area

Adventure Cruises   843-785-4558
Calibogue Cruises   843-681-7925
Cool Stuff (amphibious vehicle)   843-842-3000 or 888-926-6553
Vagabond Cruises   843-842-4155

Savannah

Dolphin Magic   800-721-1240
Old South Ducks, Inc.   912-232-3859 or 888-438-2511
River Street Riverboat Co.   912-232-6404 or 800-786-6404

TOURING WITHIN THE HISTORIC DISTRICTS

BY BICYCLE OR ON FOOT

Discovering the nooks and crannies of the Historic Districts of Charleston, Beaufort, and Savannah, and under your own steam, is the most intimate way to imagine the past. Furthermore, even though homes, churches, and ballast-stone streets have been preserved impeccably, they are still neighborhoods, not museums. Getting out from under the windshield or behind the tinted glass will help you understand the real, living context of these places, in which so much has occurred over time. Besides, it's probably dangerous to smell the jasmine and make a left turn at the same time.

There are bicycles, tandems (for two), and pedal carriages (for two or three people) for rent by the hour, the half-day, the day, or the week. In 2001, the typical hourly rate was $5 for a bicycle, $7 for a tandem, and $15 for a pedal carriage. Personalized tours with a picnic might also be arranged. Helmets, baby-seats, and locks are provided at low or no cost. For the most adventurous (of fittest) cyclist, Carpetbagger tours leads 40–60 mile treks.

Charleston

The Bicycle Shoppe	843-722-8168; www.bicycleshoppe.com
Mike's Bikes	843-723-8025
Carpetbagger Tours	843-762-5747 or 888-879-1879

Beaufort

Lowcountry Bicycles	843-524-9585

Savannah

Cycle Logical	912-233-9401
Savannah Pedicab	912-232-7900

Walking tours are Lowcountry art form. Extolling the virtues of one's city in lacy prose comes naturally. There are many stories to tell, and an abundance of people to tell them.

As guiding has evolved, so have tours tailored to specific interests: architecture, gardening, the Civil War, African-American culture, religious heritage, ghosts, even sites of films or novels set in the Lowcountry. With sufficient advance notice, some private guides will craft a unique tour for your group, or offer bilingual service.

For travelers who wish to explore on their own, the Visitors Centers in Charleston, Beaufort, and Savannah offer guidebooks and maps outlining walking tours in the Historic Districts. (These are useful for bicyclists, too.) Narrated tours on cassette tape (for your car or, with a portable unit and head-phones, for walkers and cyclists) are also available for rent.

Walking tours generally last up to two hours and are scheduled in both morning and afternoon. Ask how large the group can get — smaller is better. Reservations are recommended, in some cases required. In the summer, wear a hat and sunscreen, and you may want to carry water. In 2001, the price per person was $14 to $25, with children under 12 free or at a reduced cost. Since some guides operate from their homes, you may encounter answering machines, not always with the name of the tour identified. Do leave a message with your question.

Here are some ideas.

Charleston

Anna's House and Garden Tours	843-577-5931
Architectural Walking Tours	843-893-2327 or 800-931-7761
Charleston Tea Party Tour	843-577-5896 or 843-722-1779
Charleston Walks	843-577-3800 or 800-729-3420
Civil War Walking Tour	843-722-7033
Ghosts of Charleston	843-723-1670 or 800-854-1670
Tourrific Tours by Sandra Campbell	843-853-2500

Beaufort

The Spirit of Old Beaufort	843-525-0459

Savannah

Ghost Talk, Ghost Walk	912-233-3896 or 800-563-3896
Historic Walking Tours	912-233-0119
Savannah Walks	912-238-9255 or 888-728-9255
Southern Belle Tours	912-898-8744
Tootsy Tours	912-232-0032
Tours by BJ	912-233-2335

BY CARRIAGE

Carriages drawn by horses or mules pull you into the past while your guide tells colorful tales. The companies listed below are some among several. Tours generally last one hour and are scheduled throughout the day and evening. In 2001, the price per person ranged between $10 and $16; children

The carriages haven't changed much and neither have the mules.

Wade Spees

ride at a reduced rate. Customized or private tours are often available if you inquire in advance. In Charleston and Savannah, tours depart from either the company stables or stops at pre-arranged pick-up sites. In Beaufort, tours leave from a lot on Port Republic Street. Call for reservations and meeting sites.

Charleston

Carolina Polo & Carriage Co.	843-577-6767
Classic Carriage Tours	843-853-3747
Old South Carriage Co.	843-723-9712
Palmetto Carriage Works	843-723-8145

Beaufort

Carolina Buggy Tours	843-524-8600

Savannah

Carriage Tours of Savannah	912-236-6756 or 800-442-5933
Magnolia Carriage Co.	912-232-7727
The Point Tours	912-447-1001

"In A Sulky"

I ride right through the morning, from nine 'til four, without suffering from the heat so much as in one trip to town and back on one of our warm, still days at home. I have my white umbrella, there is usually some breeze, often a very cool one; the motion of the sulky puts me to sleep, but the heat of the sun has not been oppressive more than once or twice on this island. If I had attempted to follow all the directions I received before leaving, concerning my health, I should have been by this time a lunatic.

—Charles Ware to his family in Massachusetts, from St. Helena Island,
July 30, 1862

From Letters From Port Royal, 1862–1868, *Elizabeth Ware Pearson, Editor — letters from the Northern abolitionists who went to the Beaufort area in early 1862 to teach the newly freed slaves.*

CHAPTER THREE
A City of Stories
CHARLESTON

Charleston is one of the nation's oldest urban environments. It has been the site of some of the most dramatic and significant events in American history, and it has an architectural inventory that is more varied and abundant than any other city in America. As a colonial city, and then as a regional capital for more than 300 years, it has a continuity of culture.

Wade Spees

The beach provides a naturally dramatic stage for performers from the Anonymity Dance Company.

To a visitor, awareness of this cultural legacy may seem quaint or idiosyncratic. It is, in fact, a meaningful and pervasive sentiment, one that informs the smallest turn of phrase and the largest civic hopes of people who have long viewed their city as a place apart, a place with values so closely held that residents would, and did, die for them. In such a world (Charlestonians have called their home "The Holy City" with only a trace of irony) it is not surprising that when residents talk with visitors about Charleston's history — about its essence — they begin by talking about relationships: those between the races, between and among individuals and families, between the region and the rest of the country.

Compounding this sense of intimacy with the past is its indisputable physical expression in the city's man-made and natural landscape. For while it is one thing to tell a story of times gone by, it is quite another to be able to locate that narrative, and to read it, in an urban setting that still exists and reverberates with meaning. This quality is at the core of the city's cultural identity, more important than buildings or objects, although are plenty of them, too. Charleston is a city of culture because people still believe that a sense of history and of place distinguishes their lives.

Charleston has stayed small — some might say defiantly so — in a way dif-

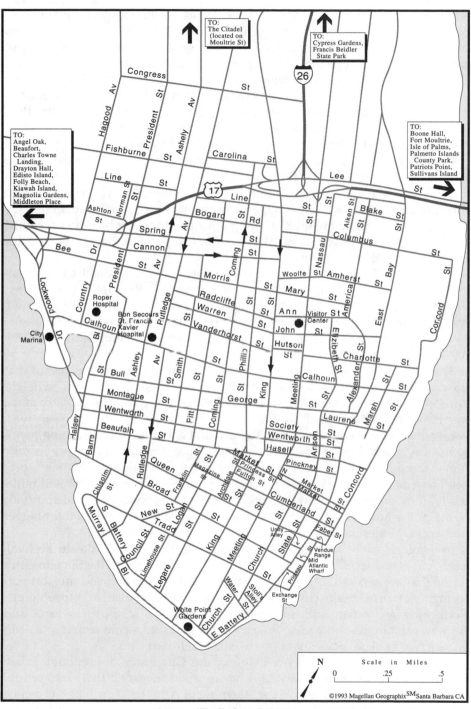

Courtesy of The Charleston Trident Convention & Visitors Bureau (used by permission)

CHARLESTON

ferent from any other region in the United States. Unlike many other American places, it was not compelled to reinvent itself over time. The traditional cultural pleasures to be had in dress balls, small concerts, the cultivation of gardens, card playing, church picnics, and literary societies continued for generations. The life of the plantation, in which families would be absent from the city except in seasonal bursts, heightened the importance of domestic culture: it has been said that without the plantations, set at some distance from each other, there would have been no tradition of Southern hospitality, nor the development of the domestic art of "visiting," so significant to this day.

Most obviously, Charleston stayed the same for so long because it liked what it was. It preferred its provincial insularity to what it perceived as vulgarity elsewhere. Especially in the early years of this century, it was too worn down to do much but carry on in the old ways, its people too habituated to the familiar social roles they inherited long after the society which had assigned those roles had been wiped out. They couldn't step out of their skins, and, for the most part, didn't want to.

But when the time came to protect the life they knew and valued, Charlestonians acted. They did not do so violently, of course, as in the case of Fort Sumter, but by means of political talent, hard work, and a potent sense of what mattered, residents were able to enact the country's first historic preservation ordinance to protect buildings and sites that might have otherwise been destroyed in the name of "progress."

The success of preservation efforts in the ensuing 75 years has meant that the past has been brought forward for all to see: in individual houses, in neighborhoods, and in whole districts. The city has become a colorful tapestry and a magnificent backdrop for all sorts of cultural activities.

Like the historic sections of the city, cultural activities keep brushing themselves up, reinvestigating the old, and cultivating the new. For every historic house there seems to be an art gallery; for every plantation house tour, a presentation on slave life. Where blossoming gardens were once celebrated informally, now programs and walks guide a visitor's appreciation. The spirituals of the praise houses and the blues of the cotton fields are performed for bigger audiences. Modest sailing regattas have become Water Festivals.

Perhaps no event showcases Charleston like the annual Spoleto Festival, held for several weeks in May and June (for information see the Spoleto entry in the **Culture** section). Dozens of operatic, theatrical, dance, and musical performances transform the city. Exhibits of fine art and lecture series proliferate. Performers and artists with international reputations take up residence and flock to restaurants and parks. The city itself sponsors a companion arts festival, Piccolo Spoleto, made up of free events at outdoor sites.

Putting aside all of the activity that enlivens Charleston, it is enough to say that it is a marvelous city because it has escaped the trend that architectural critic Ada Louise Huxtable calls the "theming of America" in which "authentic reproductions" of the past are constructed from scratch based on selected remnants: Charleston has no need to be replaced by a neater version of itself to be understood.

LODGING

An elegant room in a small luxury inn offers all the modern amenities in an authentic historic setting.

Wade Spees

When President George Washington toured the states of the new nation in 1791, he was determined to observe life as it was lived on all levels of society. In the Lowcountry, he accepted the hospitality and enthusiastic graciousness of the planters — he was rowed in their barges by slaves dressed in finery, and took meals in their mansions — but he preferred to spend the night in the "public houses" that existed along the main highways, in the simple places frequented by messengers and mail-carriers, small farmers and merchants. He even paid his own way, when he was permitted.

The public houses of Washington's day are long gone, but the modest style of overnight lodging they offered, of clean rooms, shared bathrooms and communal meals, existed well into the 20th century. It was a custom, like most, that had its roots in necessity: during the years of poverty following the Civil War, taking in guests provided income for families or Confederate widows, who still lived in the commodious old houses.

These days, if you stay in an old home that has been transformed into a glossy bed-and-breakfast — and they are among the most romantic lodging options — the only Confederate widow in evidence will be in a portrait on the wall. They are elegant places, with Jacuzzi tubs and fireplaces: you are likely to hang your clothes in an antique armoire or view from your window walled gardens rimmed with flower beds and dense with camellias and azaleas.

Charleston also has first-rate luxury hotels; several inns and hotels renovated from larger commercial buildings; modest chain hotels; and, on its outskirts, dazzling beach resorts. The lodgings included here represent a sampling of offerings in all of these categories. The list is by no means complete because building and remodeling never seem to stop: two new hotels, Renaissance Charleston and the Market Pavilion, are scheduled to open downtown by spring 2001. Places at the beach — a house in a neighborhood or a villa in a gated resort — are plentiful, and generally handled by agents or through individual resorts.

Each option carries with it unique possibilities for you to consider. Although the distance between Charleston and the beach is not great, if you intend to spend most of your time in the city, to shop and eat out and take part in cultural life, you may not want to travel between 20 and 35 minutes to the beach for a night's sleep. Alternatively, if golf, tennis, boating, and being on the ocean are at the center of your vacation, or especially if you're traveling with children, it might be wise to make a resort or rental home your base, and travel to Charleston by day. Of course, for trips lasting several days, many combinations of lodging are possible.

The hospitality industry is highly evolved here: more than 3 million people visit the area each year. The large hotels provide every amenity you'd expect. The luxury inns outdo each other in finishing touches: chocolates at bedtime, daily newspapers delivered with your breakfast, afternoon tea or refreshments served gratis in gardens, parlors, or courtyards. Even the bed and breakfast units, where a home's owner is your host, offer helpful extras like jogger's maps, a selection of restaurant menus, tips on neighborhood sights, even history lessons from the house-proud.

If you're traveling with children, some hotels and inns can recommend on-site baby-sitting services. You should inquire and make specific arrangements in advance. Some places discourage guests traveling with children; others have rules as to minimum ages and the placement and cost of extra beds in the room. At the resorts, well-staffed activity programs occupy the younger set.

If you have special needs, ask to see if they can be accommodated. Pets, for example, are sometimes allowed; smoking is always regulated, often allowed only on balconies or in courtyards. Wheelchair access, by ramps or elevators, in bathrooms or bedrooms does vary. Off-street parking is usually provided by larger establishments. Confirm the arrangement or fee with smaller ones and private-home accommodations. Ask about — and respect — deposit/cancellation policies, as they are strictly followed in smaller inns. Use the Internet to get a view of some lodging options — website addresses have been included where applicable. For more information, see the *Introduction*.

Rates

Inexpensive	Up to $60
Moderate	$60 to $120
Expensive	$120 to $200
Very Expensive	$200 and up

These rates do not include room taxes or special service charges that might apply during your stay.

Credit cards

AE — American Express	DC — Diner's Club
CB — Carte Blanche	MC — MasterCard
D — Discover Card	V — Visa

HOTELS AND LARGER INNS

Charleston's classic architectural elements — a grand staircase, glittering ornaments, columns — define modern opulence, too, at Charleston Place.

Wade Spees

CHARLESTON PLACE
843-722-4900 or
  800-611-5545.
www.charleston-place.com.
205 Meeting St., Charleston,
  SC 29401.
Price: Expensive to Very
  Expensive.
Credit Cards: AE, D, DC,
  MC, V.

The construction of this luxury hotel some 15 years ago, with its own elegant shops and the cachet to draw other brand names to the neighborhood, signaled a fateful change in the look and feel of downtown historic Charleston. It is a place that is virtually self-contained, hums by day and night with well-dressed tourists and conventioneers, and offers a premium and convenient Charleston address, but not much of a sense of discovery. There are two restaurants, a popular bar, a sensational pool and spa. Its dramatic decorations — a grand curved staircase, a huge chandelier, massive pots of flowers, shiny marble floors, and rooms of polished furniture — make it a destination. Special rate packages, which include tickets to Spoleto performances, are worth looking into.

EMBASSY SUITES-HISTORIC CHARLESTON
843-723-6900 or 800-362-2779.
www.charleston-hotels.net.
337 Meeting St., Charleston, SC 29403.
Price: Moderate to Expensive.
Credit Cards: AE, D, DC, MC, V.

This large hotel chain has managed a fine makeover of the 19th-century Citadel building where generations of Southern boys attended military school. It still looks formidable, with massive, theatrical palm trees, a courtyard, and crenellated turrets, but the outdoor pool and sundeck soften the institutional edges. The two-room suites allow for flexibility (the living rooms have a sleeper sofa) if you're traveling with children or need a workspace, and also convenience: each has its own refrigerator, microwave, and two televisions. Located near the Visitor Center where many tours and trolley service originate.

HARBOUR VIEW INN
843-853-8439 or 888-853-8439.
www.harbourviewcharleston.com.
2 Vendue Range, Charleston, SC 29401.
Price: Expensive to Very Expensive.
Credit Cards: AE, D, DC, MC, V.

Just steps from the Waterfront Park and featuring many rooms with stunning views and harbor breezes, this two-year-old hotel has the right mix of elegance and understatement. There's a minimalist feel to the rooms which emphasizes volume and light over decoration: seagrass/rush carpeting, cream-colored walls, big windows (some with broad slatted "plantation" shutters), perhaps one framed print, and an armoire made by a local woodworking company. Many of the rooms have fireplaces, some have balconies, some have whirlpool baths. A good deal of attention is paid to details here, even in the choice, framing, and hanging of art in the hallways, and it really shows.

KING CHARLES INN
A Best Western Property.
843-723-7451 or 800-247-6884.
www.kingcharlesinn.com.
237 Meeting St., Charleston, SC 29401.
Price: Moderate to Expensive.
Credit Cards: AE, D, DC, MC, V.

A recently renovated choice for visitors on a budget. An outdoor pool is located on an elevated, screened terrace, affording good privacy for an establishment that's in the heart of downtown. It may be modest but the service is attentive, there's parking, and the location is unbeatable.

LODGE ALLEY INN
843-722-1611 or
  800-845-1004.
www.lodgealleyinn.com.
195 E. Bay St., Charleston,
  SC 29401.
Price: Expensive to Very
  Expensive.
Credit Cards: AE, MC, V.

Lodge Alley was one of the first top-notch inns to emerge when the old warehouses on East Bay St. were renovated and it remains lively and popular. Its big outdoor courtyard is a good spot for an afternoon break, and an easy place to reunite if you're traveling in different directions all day; at night there's often live jazz. Inside, 95 rooms run the gamut from modest singles (mostly in the main inn building) to suites; all share a plush, handsome feel. One- and two-bedroom suites offer completely furnished kitchens and can be rented by the night or, in the winter and summer, by the month.

THE MILLS HOUSE
843-577-2400 or
  800-874-9600.
www.millshouse.com.
115 Meeting St., Charleston,
  SC 29401.
Price: Expensive to Very
  Expensive.
Credit Cards: AE, D, DC,
  MC, V.

This is a big, bustling hotel with marble floors and glittering chandeliers where you can relax and people-watch from the cozy "Best Friend Bar" or from a banquette in the lobby. (Nightly entertainment increases the foot traffic.) There are 214 guest rooms decorated with reproduction furniture, loosely Victorian in style to recall the original Mills House Hotel, and 19 larger suites. After a day of walking, you may want to take a few laps in the pool or stretch out on the deck with the newspaper.

**WESTIN FRANCIS
  MARION**
843-722-0600 or
  800-433-3733.
www.westin.com.
387 King St., Charleston, SC
  29403.
Price: Expensive to Very
  Expensive.
Credit Cards: AE, D, DC,
  MC, V.

Newly restored and reopened five years ago, it was a solid 1920s hotel to begin with: wide stairs and hallways, wood paneling, plaster moldings covered in gold-leaf, a lobby with big windows and club chairs, and high ceilings. Today there are 226 guest rooms, including 66 suites of various configurations for extended families. It overlooks Calhoun Square (with great views of Charleston from rooms on the upper floors) and from the snazzy new coffee bar you can watch the goings on in the upbeat College of Charleston neighborhood.

SMALLER LUXURY INNS

ANSONBOROUGH INN
Innkeeper: Allison Fennell.
843-723-1655 or
  800-522-2073.
www.aesir.com/anson
  boroughinn.

This circa-1900 stationer's warehouse two blocks from the City Market was given new life as an all-suite inn, but reminders of its past use — like huge beams and plank floors, and walls of exposed brick — remain to good effect. Each of the 37 suites

21 Hasell St., Charleston,
SC 29401.
Price: Moderate to
Expensive.
Credit Cards: AE, D, MC, V.
A non-smoking inn.

has a wet bar including microwave and mini refrigerator, and varieties of bed sizes so that your suite
can accommodate comfortably everyone in your
party.

BATTERY CARRIAGE HOUSE INN

Innkeepers: Katharine and
Drayton Hastie.
843-727-3100 or
800-775-5575.
www.charleston-inn.com.
20 South Battery,
Charleston, SC 29401.
Price: Expensive.
Credit Cards: AE, MC, V.

The main house at Number 20 South Battery
was built in 1843, and today's visitors stay in
rooms beneath and behind it, in the old carriage
house. South Battery defines the edge of the historic residential district known as "South of
Broad." This is the neighborhood that comes to
mind when most people think of Charleston, a
place of iron gates entwined with jasmine, houses
with massive columns set on high foundations, and
narrow streets. There are 11 rooms, their small
dimensions alleviated by access to a narrow piazza
and a lovely back garden. Continental breakfast
and the newspaper arrive at your door, or you can start your day under the
rose arbor.

FULTON LANE INN

Innkeeper: Michelle
Woodhull.
843-720-2600 or
800-720-2688.
www.charminginns.com.
202 King St., Charleston, SC
29401.
Price: Moderate to Very
Expensive.
Credit Cards: AE, D, DC,
MC, V.
Handicap Access: Two
rooms.
A non-smoking inn.

This inn is located between King and Meeting
Streets amidst the downtown antique and
gallery district. The 27 rooms have a refreshing,
airy, look: sisal, wicker, and muslin decorating
accents; louvered shutters; wall-coverings and
paint in soft, liquid colors like celadon, pale peach,
and lemon. The feel is summer in the Lowcountry
— all year long. You can go simple or go deluxe,
with canopied beds and fireplaces, kitchens, and
cathedral ceilings; all rooms have either one king-
sized bed or two queen-sized beds.

GOVERNOR'S HOUSE INN

Innkeepers: Karen Spell
Shaw and Rob Shaw.
843-720-2070 or
800-720-9812.
www.governorshouse.com.
117 Broad St., Charleston,
SC 29401.
Price: Expensive to Very
Expensive.
Credit Cards: None.

The Governor who lived in the Governor's
House was Edward Rutledge, who at 26 signed
the Declaration of Independence and at 30 was a
patriot under arrest. He may have suffered at the
hands of the British, but the stunning restoration of
this grand home (completed in the last two years)
suggests he appreciated the finer things in life.
There are nine guest rooms in the house — the
nicest among them have 12-foot ceilings and their
own verandah access with rooftop views of the

South of Broad neighborhood — and two suites (one on each floor) in the kitchen house dependency which features its original 1760 fireplace, now converted to gas. With over-the-top marble bathrooms, it's an excellent spot for an indulge-yourself weekend; it's not a place for kids. Ms. Shaw and the Spell family are well-known local innkeepers with an experienced sense of what visitors want and how to provide it.

JOHN RUTLEDGE HOUSE INN
Innkeeper: Linda Bishop.
843-723-7999 or
800-476-9741.
www.charminginns.com.
116 Broad St., Charleston,
SC 29401.
Price: Expensive to Very Expensive.
Credit Cards: AE, D, MC, V.

Tradition has it that John Rutledge (who later signed the U.S. Constitution) built this imposing house around 1763 for his bride, Elizabeth Grimke. The antique furnishings, parquet floors, high ceilings, carved mantelpieces, and rich fabrics that characterize the house today suggest its original opulence, such as might have impressed President George Washington when he visited. Nineteen rooms (17 non-smoking) are offered to guests, either in the main house or in two carriage houses. Suites in the main house include an additional sitting room and fireplace; some have Jacuzzi tubs. Continental breakfast is included and full breakfast is available. The upstairs ballroom, where you will find scrapbooks on the house's history and a collection of antique firearms, is a wonderful place to take tea or sherry.

Tea in the courtyard at Maison DuPre, taken at most any season.

Wade Spees

MAISON DU PRE
Innkeeper: Mark Mulholland.
843-723-8691 or
800-844-4667.
www.maisondupre.com.
317 East Bay St.,
Charleston, SC 29401.

Three restored "single houses" and two carriage houses make up the inn, which is a short walk from the Gaillard Auditorium. There are 15 guest rooms spread throughout, some with private balconies that overlook the garden and courtyard, which are, themselves, among the inn's best features. Imagine yourself here, sitting at a table as the

Price: Moderate to
 Expensive.
Credit Cards: D, MC, V.

light fades and the crepe myrtle blossoms float to the ground, sipping a glass of French wine, taking tea at 4:30, or indulging in a good book. Mrs. Mulholland is a painter and her work, as well as that of other artists, graces the walls. The feeling is European and cozy.

PLANTER'S INN
Innkeeper: Larry Spelts.
843-722-2345 or
 800-845-7082.
www.plantersinn.com.
112 N. Market St.,
 Charleston, SC 29401.
Price: Expensive to Very
 Expensive.
Credit Cards: AE, D, DC,
 MC, V.
Handicap Access: Two
 rooms.

A location at the intersection of N. Market St. and Meeting St. makes this 62-room inn superbly convenient to nightlife, shopping, the Gibbes Art Gallery, and the historic residential areas. You can walk in any direction and find something going on — the closest Charleston comes to having a "big city" feel. The service is superior, the rooms elegant, many with fireplaces and four-poster beds. Continental breakfast is included. An ample side courtyard overlooked by piazzas and a rooftop terrace garden with views of the Historic District make this a top choice. The acclaimed Peninsula Grill restaurant is located here.

**TWO MEETING STREET
INN**
Innkeepers: Jean and Pete
 Spell.
843-723-7322.
www.twomeetingstreetinn.
 com.
2 Meeting St., Charleston,
 SC 29401.
Price: Expensive to Very
 Expensive.
Credit Cards: None.
A non-smoking inn.

This Queen Anne mansion, with its wrap-around porches and rocking chairs has passed the age of 100, but may never have looked better. (Given Charleston, it's young almost to the point of new.) Its oak-paneled sitting rooms and guest rooms are filled with Oriental rugs and period accessories, and highlighted by fabrics and wall-coverings in rich, deep colors. There are nine rooms on three floors, all with private baths (some with Victorian-style tubs), some with private balcony access. Honeymooners and celebrating couples often book a year in advance — especially for those rooms with canopied four-posters needing a special set of stairs to reach. Continental breakfast is served, and there is an elaborate afternoon tea. Minimum stays are required on holidays and weekends. Children over 12 are welcomed.

WENTWORTH MANSION
Innkeeper: Elizabeth G.
 Fisher.
843-853-1886 or 888-466-1886.
www.wentworthmansion.
 com.

Visitors worship Charleston's architecture of the 18th century and antebellum period, but this Second Empire–style mansion (built in 1886 for a cotton baron) will turn your head. For sheer persquare-foot, Gilded Age, extravagance it has no peer: carved plasterwork ceilings, marble fireplaces,

Wade Spees

Rooms at the Wentworth Mansion, a Gilded Age showplace, highlight Charleston style at the turn of the last century.

149 Wentworth St., Charleston, SC 29401.
Price: Very Expensive.
Credit Cards: AE, D, DC, MC, V.
Handicap Access: One room.

Tiffany glass, mahogany paneling, intricately tiled floors, and a cupola accessed by a stairway for the brave which yields a panoramic view of the city. And that's what was there *before* millions were spent on deluxe renovation and antiques. Today there are 21 sumptuous guest rooms and suites, many with separate Jacuzzis and walk-in showers, some with private porches, almost all with fireplaces. A continental breakfast buffet is set on a sun porch; a classic gentleman's library is a late-night refuge. Already one of Charleston's best restaurants, Circa 1886, is in the Carriage House.

BED & BREAKFAST LODGINGS IN PRIVATE HOMES AND GARDENS

A central reservation service, *Historic Charleston Bed and Breakfast* (843-722-6606 or 800-743-3583 or 843-722-9589 fax; 57 Broad St., Charleston, SC 29401) offers some 50 listings of rooms with private baths in homes or their garden dependencies in Charleston's historic neighborhoods. Credit cards (MC, V) can be used to book a deposit, but the balance is usually cash or check only. There are some bargains, especially if you're willing to leave the South of Broad/Market neighborhood, but flexibility and adventure might be the real draw — the chance to feel like a local. Some accommodations are well suited to larger parties, families, or couples traveling together, and they may also have their own kitchen facilities, gardens, and bicycles for you to use. Most, not all, have telephones and televisions. Smoking is rarely permitted inside. Generally the service makes a good match if you have some sense of what you want.

You may also contact individuals directly or book lodgings which are not owner-occupied but not exactly commercial, either. Places of this sort may be as large as four rooms and quite private. Credit cards that are accepted are noted. Otherwise, cash, personal check, or traveler's check are acceptable. Individual websites where applicable are reliable resources. Here are some ideas:

1837 BED AND BREAKFAST (843-723-7166; www.fodors.com/bnb; 126 Wentworth St., Charleston, SC 29401) Nine guest rooms, porches with rockers, full breakfast. College of Charleston area. Moderate. AE, MC, V.

27 STATE STREET (843-722-4243; www.charleston-bb.com; 27 State St., Charleston, SC 29401) Enter your private suite (with kitchenette) through the courtyard of a four-square, circa 1800 house in Charleston's "French Quarter," a block off East Bay St. Expensive to Very Expensive.

36 MEETING STREET BED AND BREAKFAST (843-722-1034; www.36meet ingstreet.com; 36 Meeting St., Charleston, SC 29401) Three guest suites with cooking areas and private baths — one (one bedroom) in an 18th-century home and two (two bedroom) in an adjacent carriage house. Children welcome. Moderate to Expensive. D, MC, V.

4 UNITY ALLEY (843-577-6660; www.unitybb.com; 4 Unity Alley, Charleston, SC 29401) Three suites with bedroom and sitting room, and communal dining area, located just off East Bay St. in the French Quarter neighborhood, a mix of commercial (galleries, fancy restaurants) and residential uses. Expensive. AE, MC, V.

BED, NO BREAKFAST (843-723-4450; 16 Halsey St., Charleston, SC 29401) Two no-smoking rooms with shared bath — a reliable basic value. Off-street parking in Medical University neighborhood. Inexpensive to Moderate. No credit cards.

THE HAYNE HOUSE (843-577-2633; www.haynehouse.com; 30 King St., Charleston, SC 29401) A native Charlestonian and his family are your hosts: six rooms in both a kitchen house and a main house, private baths, and the use of garden, piazza and the main house drawing room and library. No television, full breakfast, great location, kids welcome. Expensive. MC, V.

THE KITCHEN HOUSE (843-577-6362; www.cityofcharleston.com/kitchen.htm; 126 Tradd St., Charleston, SC 29401) Two guest rooms with private baths located in a charming restored outbuilding (circa 1731) next to a colonial herb garden. Expensive. MC, V.

THE THOMAS LAMBOLL HOUSE (843-723-3212 or 888-794-0793; www.lam bollhouse.com/home.htm; 19 King St., Charleston, SC 29401) Open the French doors from your bedroom onto the piazza of this pre-Revolutionary house located steps from the Battery. Private baths, children welcome. Expensive. MC, V.

Charleston Environs

If you prefer to stay outside Charleston, near a plantation or one of the Sea Islands, you'll find plenty to choose from. Here are some possibilities, arranged by location, with separate sections on resort and rental accommodations and beach rental agents.

Kayaks await paddlers outside the Middleton Inn on the Ashley River.

Wade Spees

MIDDLETON INN
Manager: Doyle Gray.
843-556-0500 or
    800-543-4774.
www.middletoninn.com.
4290 Ashley River Rd.,
    Charleston, SC 29414.
Price: Expensive to Very
    Expensive.
Credit Cards: AE, MC, V.
Handicap Access: Some
    rooms.

The Middleton Inn, located on a bluff adjacent to the beautiful gardens at Middleton Place, is about 25 minutes from downtown Charleston. For serenity and privacy, for long walks along the Ashley River or at Middleton Place (admission waived for inn guests), for kayaking and horseback riding, come here. Inquire about weekend packages. Designed by W.G. Clark about 15 years ago, it's handsomely modern on the outside, splendidly understated on the inside. There are 55 rooms in four buildings, each with working log fireplaces, custom-made furniture, soft colors, and large bathrooms. Floor-to-ceiling windows with louvered shutters filter the light and air in the woodland setting. The restaurant at Middleton Place serves lunch and dinner daily.

Folly Beach

CHARLESTON ON THE BEACH (843-588-6464 or 800-465-4329; 1 Center St., Folly Beach, SC 29439) A big (132-room) oceanfront hotel (part of the Holiday Inn chain) with game room, pool, fishing pier, restaurant, and bar. Handicap access and non-smoking rooms available. Moderate to Expensive. AE, D, DC, MC, V.

HOLLIDAY INN OF FOLLY BEACH (843-588-2191 or 800-792-5270; www .hollidayinnfollybeach.com; 116 W. Ashley Ave., Folly Beach, SC 29439) This modest motel, one block from the beach, is as reliable as the chain hotel with the similar name, but it's much more inviting. Moderate to Expensive. AE, D, MC, V.

Isle of Palms

HOLIDAY INN EXPRESS (843-886-3003 or 800-465-4329; www.holidayin-nisleofplams.com; 1126 Ocean Blvd., Isle of Palms, SC 29451) There are 69 rooms, including 18 suites, situated in a great location with all the beach amenities — including microwaves and mini refrigerators. Moderate to Expensive. AE, MC, V.

SEASIDE INN (843-886-7000 or 888-999-6516; www.seasideinniop.com; 1004 Ocean Blvd., Isle of Palms, SC 29451) A new, 51-room hotel, basic but all you need, located next to the Windjammer, the beach area's most popular bar/restaurant.

RESORTS AND RENTALS —CHARLESTON AREA SEA ISLANDS

The Sea Island resort areas around Charleston are 20 to 35 minutes from downtown. They are, by themselves, fully self-contained destinations from which you can travel to the city by day to sightsee and shop, and to which you can return for recreation, dining, and relaxation. You can play golf and tennis and walk on the beach twelve months a year, and swim in the ocean from May to November. Each resort has a well-supervised children's activity program.

What follows here is a list of the *resorts* and an outline of their lodgings. If you are interested in longer stays of a week or more, you may also want to contact some of the *rental agents* who specialize in rental of private beach properties, including villas and houses located both within the resorts and outside of them. Note that rental rates for some especially fancy private homes within the resorts can be as much as twice the average rates quoted below.

Rental accommodations are fully furnished, including washer and dryer, but you should check to see if you need to bring anything, if there are special features like handicap access, or if a fee for cleaning after your departure is included. Deposits are necessary, and if you need to cancel, you must often do so up to three weeks in advance to have your deposit returned. During summer months, minimum stays of three days (in a villa) to a week (in a house) are often required.

The 2001 summer rental prices for a two-bedroom, oceanfront house ranged from $1,100 to $2,500 per week. The farther you are from the beach — by a lagoon or in the woods — the less expensive the rate. January through mid-March, and October through December are generally considered low season and rentals are priced accordingly. The resorts offer numerous packages covering a long-weekend or week's stay to attract golfers, honeymooners, Thanksgiving get-togethers and visitors coming for the tours of historic homes in the fall and spring.

KIAWAH ISLAND GOLF AND TENNIS RESORT
843-768-2121 or
   800-654-2924.
www.kiawahresort.com.
12 Kiawah Beach Drive,
   Kiawah Island, SC 29455.
Price: Expensive to Very
   Expensive.
Credit Cards: AE, D, DC,
   MC, V.

There are many ways to enjoy Kiawah: in the newly renovated 150-room inn, a rambling building with decks, breezeways, ceiling fans, and plenty of places to sit in the shade; in one of some 300 villa accommodations, fully furnished with kitchens, which come in several sizes; or in a private, architect-designed "beach house" which is not, by the way, anything like the faded house on stilts where you played board games in your bathing suit. The beach is private and 10 miles long. Thirty miles of paved bike trails wind around the four golf courses and recreational areas, ultimately linking two distinct resort villages.

SEABROOK ISLAND RESORT
843-768-1000 or
   800-845-2475.
www.seabrookresort.com.
1002 Landfall Way, Seabrook
   Island, SC 29455.
Price: Expensive to Very
   Expensive.
Credit Cards: AE, D, MC,
   V.

Seabrook is a 2,200-acre private country club community now controlled by property owners (there are about 900 permanent residents), which means that it's very low key and means to stay that way. Visitors stay in rented villas or in homes. Its unique asset is its equestrian center, but it also provides resort amenities like golf (two courses), tennis (13 Har-Tru courts), a beach and beach club, pool, and fitness center.

WILD DUNES RESORT
843-886-6000 or
   800-845-8880.
www.wilddunes.com.
5757 Palm Blvd., Isle of
   Palms, SC 29451.
Price: Expensive to Very
   Expensive.
Credit Cards: AE, D, DC,
   MC, V.

Wild Dunes is just 15 miles north of Charleston, a small resort located on the northeast end of the modest Isle of Palms. It's the place to stay if you want beach resort life (two golf courses, tennis, pools, water sports, kids' recreation program, beach club) and the advantage of the city an easy ride away. Sullivan's Island is close by, too. Guests choose accommodations in the 93-room Boardwalk Inn or in fully outfitted villas, townhouses and cottages.

BEACH RENTAL AGENTS

Beachwalker Rentals (843-768-1777 or 800-334-6308; www.beachwalker.com; 3690 Bohicket Rd., Johns Island, SC 29455) Accommodations on Kiawah and Seabrook islands.

Carroll Realty (843-886-9600 or 800-845-7718; www.carrollrealtyinc.com; 103 Palm Blvd., Isle of Palms, SC 29451) Homes and villas by the week, month, or year on Isle of Palms, Wild Dunes, and Sullivan's Island.

Dunes Properties (843-886-5600 or 800-843-2322; www.charlestonbeaches.net; 1400 Palm Blvd., Isle of Palms, SC 29451) Vacation rentals throughout the year at the Charleston-area resorts and on Sullivan's Island, Isle of Palms, and Folly Beach.

Great Beach Vacations (800-247-5050; www.greatbeach.com; P.O. Box 13239, Charleston, SC 29422) For Kiawah, 800-845-3911; for Seabrook, 800-845-2233; for Wild Dunes, Isle of Palms, Sullivan's Island, 800-346-0606.

Island Realty (843-886-8144 or 800-707-6425; www.islandrealty.com; 1304 Palm Blvd., Isle of Palms, SC 29451. Wide selection of rentals and golf packages on Sullivan's Island and Isle of Palms.

Islands West (843-588-6699 or 800-951-2470; www.islandswestrealestate.com; 83 Center St., Folly Beach, SC 29439). Traditional, modest houses at Folly Beach, some villas.

Pam Harrington Exclusives, Inc. (843-768-0273 or 800-845-6966; www.kiawah exclusives.com; 3690 Bohicket Rd., Suite 2-C, Johns Island, SC 29455) Homes and villas on Kiawah.

Seabrook Exclusives (843-768-0808 or 888-718-7949; www.seabrookexclusives. com; 3690 Bohicket Rd., Johns Island, SC 29455)

DINING

Dining is one Lowcountry ritual that remained important, even through hard times. Schoolchildren released for an hour from class and fathers home from the office gathered daily at the midday meal. It honored family, tradition, the art of conversation, and the resourcefulness of the cook. As the extraordinary Southern chef Edna Lewis has said: "The birds are just the beginning. In the South you put everything you have on the table."

Indeed, accounts tell of hunting and fishing parties that delivered marsh hens, dove, quail, and crab by the dozens; that brought in pigeons and deer hunted by torchlight; that landed huge drum, a beast of a fish that pulled at hook and line and dragged a bateau as a whale might. Add to these hunters' trophies the harvest from garden and field — okra, corn, peas and beans, turnips, beets, greens and, of course, rice, first introduced to the Lowcountry in the late 1600s — and you had, and have to this day, a traditional Southern meal, flavored as always with meat marked by "a streak of lean and a streak of fat."

It was not only the natural bounty of the land and the availability of labor for several harvests that led to a Lowcountry dining tradition. The plantation operation and its physical layout — including detached kitchens and smoke-houses — gave rise to a separate world of cooking. Slaves were in charge here and they contributed their own sense of spicing, texture, ingredients, and method. The influence of their African and West Indian heritage, combined with European preferences, produced a distinctive regional style that today is being self-consciously redefined at restaurants like Charleston Grill and Circa 1886, and examined by food writers like John Martin Taylor (reach his marvelous store, now in cyberspace: www.hoppinjohns.com).

The sign that Charleston has come of age may be the prices in the restaurants, but there are still plenty of modest places that serve local specials and are best known to local people. Some of these are listed at the end of the section under "Faster Food."

Here are some suggestions. Many of them have on-line sites where you can check menus and make reservations. The general price range we list is meant to reflect the cost of a single meal, usually dinner, featuring an appetizer, entree, dessert, and coffee. Cocktails, beer, wine, gratuity, and tax are not included in the estimated price.

Dining Price Code

Inexpensive	Up to $10
Moderate	$10 to $20
Expensive	$20 to $30
Very Expensive	$30 or more

Credit Cards

AE — American Express	DC — Diner's Club
CB — Carte Blanche	MC — MasterCard
D — Discover Card	V — Visa

During Spoleto, most Charleston restaurants relax their hours, serving lunch as late as 3 p.m., early supper at 5:30 p.m., and full meals at midnight. The crowds pile up, so make reservations. If you're rushing between performances, enjoy a picnic in the open-air pavilions at the Waterfront Park at the foot of Queen Street, in the shady grove of Washington Square, or on a bench at the Battery.

ANSON
843-577-0551.
www.ansonrestaurant
.com.

Anson practically glows from the street. The cooking technique is last-minute sautéing: the dish arrives at your table sizzling hot, with crispy vegeta-

Passengers on a carriage ride take in all the city's sites and landmarks, including diners at Anson.

Wade Spees

12 Anson St.
Open daily.
Price: Expensive.
Cuisine: American.
Serving: D.
Credit Cards: AE, CB, D, DC, MC, V.

bles, meat, fish, or fowl glistening with juice. The produce comes from local farms growing Charleston "heirloom" vegetables that were cultivated in the 19th century; the rice is "Carolina Gold," growing again after a 100-year hiatus; the lamb, duck, quail, and squab are free-range. There are comfy banquettes and lots of smaller tables for four or six, done up in heavy linens. The fish entrees are fresh from the boat, and the she-crab soup laced with sherry probably the best you'll taste. Dinner starts at 5:30.

BEAUMONT'S
843-577-5500.
12 Cumberland St.
Open daily.
Price: Expensive.
Cuisine: French.
Serving: D; Sat. and Sun. brunch.
Credit Cards: AE, D, MC, V.

Beaumont's is Charleston's version of a restaurant in the Provence region of France. The cuisine and the portions are hearty; the ell-shaped interior is distinguished by exposed brick walls, adorned by family portraits; the tables are inviting and comfortable. It's as if it were Sunday afternoon in the country — every day. Brunch is a favorite, and not just eggs, either: try the calf liver, filet mignon, or creamy pate.

BOATHOUSE ON EAST BAY
843-577-7171.
549 East Bay St.
Open daily.
Price: Expensive.
Cuisine: Seafood.
Serving: D.
Credit Cards: AE, D, MC, V.

A big space whose teak and mahogany paneling and nautical decor recall the small craft and "mosquito fleet" heritage of the harbor. Surprisingly, it's not noisy; and even though it's casual, the food is so good that one's high expectations for it bring an air of formality to dinner. The staples of Lowcountry kitchens plain and fancy — like shrimp and grits or fried green tomatoes — are given a welcome here, as are oysters from far above the Mason-

Dixon line. The raw seafood bar opens at 4 p.m. and is a meal itself. There are steak and salad selections, and a half-dozen pasta dishes, a solid wine list. It gets full — make reservations.

BOOKSTORE CAFE
843-720-8843.
412 King St.
Open daily.
Price: Inexpensive.
Cuisine: American.
Serving: B, L
Credit Cards: MC, V.

Fried oysters, roasted half-chicken, ham-and-eggs, and the blue-plate specials make this a top local choice, especially all-day breakfast on the weekends. Near the Visitors Center, Manigault House, Charleston Museum and Upper King shopping area.

CAROLINA'S
843-724-3800.
www.carolinasrestaurant.
   com.
10 Exchange St.
Open daily.
Price: Expensive to Very
   Expensive.
Cuisine: American.
Serving: D.
Credit Cards: AE, DC, MC,
   V.

Late-night crowds converge at Carolina's, at tables lining the main passageway or in back by the oversized French posters and crowded banquettes. You could have a light meal with Asian flavors (crab wontons with lime ginger sauce), substantial local delicacies (grilled smoked Carolina quail with spicy greens and tasso grits) or just drinks. Perdita's restaurant used to be here, the epitome of old-style Charleston with waiters in livery, and in those days, in its way, it was the place to go. Carolina's gets the scene too, but one look around the room shows you just how far Charleston has come.

CHARLESTON GRILL
843-577-4522.
www.charlestongrill.com.
224 King St., at Charleston
   Place.
Open daily.
Price: Expensive to Very
   Expensive.
Cuisine: New Southern.
Serving: D.
Credit Cards: AE, D, MC, V.

Astonishing menu or manifesto? Acclaimed chef Bob Waggoner makes his convincing case for a Lowcountry cuisine (with some French guidance) that reaches beyond home-grown ingredients and local imaginations. He stuffs the homely hushpuppy with caramelized figs and gives it self confidence. He marries escargot to truffled grits. The entrees are very good, good enough to think about, but you can make a meal of appetizers and salads. The atmosphere is relaxed, a broad, generous clubroom feel, but the diners are here to learn the latest. There's jazz at night, cigars at the bar. Diners come from Beaufort and the further resort islands for the Sunday night "Plantation Suppers" (fixed price around $35) and leave with ideas for their own kitchens.

CIRCA 1886
843-853-7828.
www.wentworthmansion.
   com

The Wentworth Mansion and its carriage house (now expensively restored) were built in the late 19th century; the mission of Circa 1886 is to resurrect some of the dishes popular then. For the recently

141 Wentworth St.
Closed Sunday.
Price: Expensive to Very
   Expensive.
Cuisine: American.
Serving: D.
Credit Cards: AE, D, MC, V.

rich, that was a time to love everything French. Chef Patrick Ramsey honors the sentiment and tweaks it a little. Once common local ingredients like conch, quail, and fresh beets turn up with fruit and sweet accents. There's a vegetarian entree, but big servings of beef tenderloin and lamb chops, too. Desserts like pan-fried angel food cake with fresh berries and peach ice cream speak to waistlines larger than today's. Set in a quiet garden corner, with the garden itself off the beaten track, the lovely building is set up with two rooms (about 50 seats), handsomely decorated with remnant beadboard, heart pine and original stall-door details.

FULTON FIVE
843-853-5555.
5 Fulton St.
Closed Sunday.
Price: Moderate to
   Expensive.
Cuisine: Northern Italian.
Serving: D.
Credit Cards: AE, CB, DC,
   MC, V.

It's said Gian Carlo Menotti chose Charleston for his Spoleto Festival USA because it had a Mediterranean feel, a serene charm as easy to appreciate and as softly worn as stucco walls. Fulton Five wasn't open then, but its romantic setting fits the description. This restaurant, which seats perhaps 40, exudes quiet confidence and lack of pretension, both in the menu and in the decor: green walls that seem murky and lustrous, recessed windows set off by dark brown shutters, brocade fabrics that are velvety to the touch. It's even comfortable to eat here alone. The Northern Italian touches include clams with Tuscan beans, carpaccio, paper-thin veal, risotto dishes, and ossobucco.

GAULART & MALICLET
843-577-9797.
www.gandmcafe.citysearch
   .com.
98 Broad St.
Closed Sunday.
Price: Inexpensive to
   Moderate.
Cuisine: French.
Serving: B, L, D.
Credit Cards: AE, D, DC,
   MC, V.

Known by its nickname "Fast and French," this bistro is the most popular, enduring little place in the Historic District. Seated on high chairs at a counter that juts out into tiny bays, your neighbors are likely to be Broad St. lawyers, Legare St. dowagers, and Queen St. artists (in Charleston, that may describe one family). In keeping with that atmosphere of enlightened tolerance, the smoking policy is: "Ask your neighbor." You'll find platters of pate, sausages, selections of cheeses, and French bread are served; hearty soups; fondues; excellent wine. Vegetarian options. Open late after house tours and Spoleto performances.

HANK'S
843-723-3474.
10 Hayne St.
Open daily.
Price: Moderate to
   Expensive.

In a warehouse in the Market area, in what used to be an eccentric "club" (if you needed to ask you didn't belong), now resides Hank's Seafood, a handsome, self-conscious (the building has been properly "aged" with faux details), good-natured throwback to family seafood houses of the 50s. Except in this incar-

Wade Spees

Hank's is an "authentic reproduction," bringing the weathered look of an old seafood house back downtown. The fine food, on the other hand, is unapologeticly up-to-date.

Cuisine: American; Seafood.
Serving: D.
Credit Cards: AE, D, MC, V.

nation, the shrimp cocktail actually tastes like shrimp, there's not sawdust on the floor, and the grilled fish entrees could come with beurre blanc. Were there rare seared tuna plates with lemon soy broth back then? Not in my town's Clam Box. The servers are fast and wry. So is the menu, with its tattletale map of 50s Charleston on the back.

HIGH COTTON
843-724-3815.
199 East Bay St.
Open daily.
Price: Expensive to Very
   Expensive.
Cuisine: New American.
Serving: D.
Credit Cards: AE, D, MC, V.

Prosperity's high tide of shops and restaurants surged on East Bay St. This is one remarkable piece of sea glass. It's glossy and unabashed, and to use a word of the day, transparent: its intent, apparent in every detail from the smoked meat and home-brewed sauces to the paintings and potted palms is there for a reason, to make you look good and feel good. And who are you? You are looking for venison or red meat or encrusted fish. You know what you like and you've had some fine meals. Come here for a robust dinner (grilling and searing a specialty) and share a dessert soufflé with your friends.

HOMINY GRILL
843-937-0930.
www.hominygrill.com.
207 Rutledge Ave.
Open daily.
Price: Inexpensive to
   Moderate.

What is it about Charleston that an old barber-shop with a tin ceiling in an offbeat neighborhood can be redone so simply, come alive as a full-service restaurant, serve terrific food and not seem to break a sweat? Or burst into irony? The answer is probably the city's deep reserves of

Cuisine: Southern.
Serving: B, L, D, Sat., Sun.
  brunch.
Credit Cards: AE, D, MC, V.

youth, and its appreciation of pleasure, gardens, nice weather, and frame buildings. There is still modesty and grace amidst the excess. A day that starts with butcher-paper tablecloths, thick mugs of coffee, biscuits, and bacon can proceed seamlessly to a turkey club, then move on to linens, catfish and starlight in the walled garden.

JESTINE'S KITCHEN
843-722-7224.
251 Meeting St.
Closed Mon.
Price: Inexpensive to
  Moderate.
Cuisine: Homestyle Southern.
Serving: L.
Credit Cards: AE, D, MC, V.

Plain and simple Southern food, with lots of fried entrees (chicken, oysters, tomatoes, pork) and greens and grits on the side. Unpretentious room right on Meeting St. where, if you get nothing else, you can come for pie and the best sweet tea in town.

LOUIS'S
843-853-2550.
www.louisrestaurant.com.
200 Meeting St.
Open daily.
Price: Expensive to Very
  Expensive.
Cuisine: New Southern.
Serving: D.
Credit Cards: AE, D, DC,
  MC, V.

Louis Osteen, among the first to reinterpret the Southern standards more than a decade ago, is as inventive and voluble as ever. His sensuous, sure hand and intuitive sense of companion tastes bears on obvious and arcane ingredients (mash lima beans, add mint; sauté skate wing, add capers and brown butter; braise sweetbreads with country ham, add old Madeira and new Vidalia onions.) New York designer Adam Tihany designed this bold, signature space. The result, both luxurious and abstract, perhaps reveals Osteen's deeper interest and strength as a chef: a real attention to relationships, not only between flavors but between the cultures of the Old South and the New. His cookbook is a standout, too.

**MAGNOLIA'S UPTOWN/
  DOWN SOUTH**
843-577-7771.
www.magnoliasblossom.com.
185 E. Bay St.
Open daily.
Price: Moderate to
  Expensive.
Cuisine: "Nouvelle"
  Southern.
Serving: L, D.
Credit Cards: AE, MC, V.

This big and breezy place epitomizes the willing-to-please personality of the New South. It's energetic, with a menu that sticks to basic Southern foodstuffs — greens, black-eyed peas, grits, and shrimp — and dresses them up in unusual ways. It's very popular, more visitors than locals during the high season, but has kept its touch and still delivers.

McCRADY'S
843-577-0025.

Named as one of *Esquire* magazine's best new restaurants of 1999, it also deserves a decorat-

2 Unity Alley (off East Bay St.).
Open daily.
Price: Expensive to Very Expensive.
Cuisine: New American.
Serving: D.
Credit Cards: AE, MC, V.

ing award and a good-looking-people-at-the-best-looking-bar award. Whew. Into a burnished in-town setting comes out-of-town style. The original, soft-brick walls are a gorgeous given; wash them with creative, subtle light and the result is an homage to Charleston, and something more. The same is true for the cooking which has classic (French) underpinnings but worldly ingredients and art-world presentation. Lowcountry foodways are not the center of attention here. Diners return for the roasted Chilean sea bass, with velvety leeks, tiny potatoes, and creamy lobster bisque. One friend drove 90 miles just for the foie gras. Some prix fixe options are available.

PINCKNEY CAFE AND ESPRESSO
843-577-0961.
18 Pinckney St.
Open daily.
Price: Inexpensive to Moderate.
Cuisine: American eclectic.
Serving: L, D (Wed.–Sat.), Sun. brunch.
Credit Cards: None.
Special Features: Take-out available.

A pale yellow, flower-bordered cottage with a porch full of tables and chairs that caters to a young crowd and families. The antipasto salad is great for lunch, but the regulars may talk you into the black bean burrito — order both from the kitchen counter. Dinner is full-service and grilled fish, flavored with mint or pecan butters, a favorite. Loads of coffee selections and a variety of sweet desserts to go with them. Sunday brunch omelets recommended.

PENINSULA GRILL
843-723-0700.
www.plantersinn.com.
112 N. Market St.
Open daily.
Price: Expensive to Very Expensive.
Cuisine: American.
Serving: D.
Credit Cards: AE, D, DC, MC, V.

An elegant dining room, sometimes a bit noisy, never overbearing. The room has a great geom-etry, a square place punctuated by pillars and fur-ther softened by walls of dark velvet (no kidding) dressed with 19th-century paintings. The light is suf-fused with soft gold overtones, as if the color had been rubbed on the air. Jell-O would taste good here. You may order "simple" entrees like strip steak, veal chops, or grouper and choose your sauces and sides; or go for the house specials (pan-roasted breast of duck is one). Champagne is always on the menu here. You may also eat in the courtyard or in the bar, tiny and splendid and worth a stop.

SARACEN
843-723-6242.
141 E. Bay St.
Closed Sunday and Monday.
Price: Expensive.

Located in an exotic space, even for a restaurant, the building was established in 1853 as the Farmers and Exchange Bank. Huge arched win-dows, held in place by massive decorated wood-work, reflect architectural styles that have been

Cuisine: French.
Serving: L, D.
Credit Cards: AE, DC, MC, V.

called, all at once, Moorish, Gothic, Hindu, and Persian. The menu changes according to what's seasonally available, but the style is basically French and the results, especially the soups, are sublime. Charlie's Little Bar, a wonderful place upstairs, is where the city's dappled youth often start their eventful evenings.

SERMET'S CORNER
843-853-7775.
276 King St.
Open daily.
Price: Moderate.
Cuisine: North African, Mediterranean.
Serving: L, D.
Credit Cards: AE, D, MC, V.

This restaurant looks and acts like a real bistro, where students, children, grandparents, couples, and solo types feel at home. It's simple and open: big plate-glass windows open onto a busy intersection just north of Saks. The salads are imaginative, many garnished with fruit relish, and there are plain choices for kids and the less-adventurous: paninis, pasta, soups. Live music upstairs at night.

VICKERY'S
843-577-5300.
15 Beaufain St.
Open daily.
Price: Inexpensive to Moderate.
Cuisine: American; Cuban.
Serving: L, D.
Credit Cards: AE, D, MC, V.

A popular place for young locals, with tables and banquettes surrounding a horseshoe-shaped bar, and walls decorated with . . . stuff. Outdoor dining under the umbrellas is cherished; inside it's noisy and friendly. You will probably see the guide who just led your tour (or mother of guide) eating at the next table. Cuban and Caribbean spices warm up burgers, chicken, and pork; black beans and rice, with hot sausage, is the choice of regulars; three dozen varieties of beer wash it all down.

Typically Charleston: a modest storefront is imaginatively transformed into a minimalist bistro with maximum charm.

Wade Spees

VINTAGE
843-577-0090.
14 N. Market St.
Open daily.
Price: Expensive.
Cuisine: New American.
Serving: D.
Credit Cards: AE, D, MC, V.

A new restaurant and wine bar in a wonderful minimalist space (located via passageway) at the foot of the Market, across East Bay St. It has the feel and menu of a bistro for the new millenium — imaginative, pristine, not too fussy. A simple mix of textures, as in poached halibut with crispy celery root cake and creamy spinach, is all you want. There are some 400 wines available, 70 by the glass; on Sunday nights several varieties are paired with offerings on a special, multi-course menu. It's probably a tad too expensive to become a weekly habit, but its intimate, fresh feeling would encourage one.

Charleston Area and the Sea Islands

If you are staying at a Sea Island resort, you will find a variety of dining choices offered in a range of prices and styles; but most of them, like the resorts themselves, are characterized by solid predictability. If you are more adventurous and want to eat with local people, you might try some of the following restaurants.

MUSTARD SEED
843-849-0050.
1220 Ben Sawyer Blvd., Mt. Pleasant.
Closed Sun.
Price: Inexpensive to Moderate.
Cuisine: New American.
Serving: L, D.
Credit Cards: AE, MC,V.

A casual, very popular local restaurant, often packed, but with a nice bar and a simple, robust menu. A hippie feel for year 2001. Lots of pastas, seafood with light sauces, grilled portobello mushrooms, vegetarian specials. Two locations, equally charming. The other is on James Island (843-762-0072).

ROSEBANK FARMS CAFE
843-768-1807.
Bohicket Marina Village, Seabrook Island.
Open daily.
Price: Moderate to Expensive.
Cuisine: Seafood; Southern.
Serving: L, D.
Credit Cards: AE, D, MC, V.

Tucked among the shops of the marina village between Kiawah and Seabrook, and overlooking the berthed boats, this is worth a trip for lunch, if you're exploring, or for dinner to watch an incredible sunset. The seafood comes Cajun style or encrusted with herbs; the pan-fried chicken livers are a specialty. There's always a blue-plate special at lunch. Murals depicting the natural world and the people in it make for a gauzy, tropical island feel — and so do the warm breezes off the creek.

SLIGHTLY UP THE CREEK
843-884-5005.

A mong the many places to eat right at the dock, this is the best. There will be some shrimp trawler traffic, or putt-putts and pontoon boats

130 Mill St., Mt. Pleasant.
Open daily.
Price: Expensive.
Cuisine: Seafood, Southern regional.
Serving: D.
Credit Cards: AE, D, DC, MC, V.

STONO CAFE
843-762-4478.
1956 Maybank Hwy., James Island.
Closed Sun. and Mon.
Price: Moderate to Expensive.
Cuisine: American.
Serving: L, D.
Credit Cards: AE, D, MC, V.

making their way up the creek as you dine (inside or on the patio.) Go for local triggerfish with butter bean ragout or crowder peas. Friendly and casual, easy for children, who will love to watch all the marina-related activity. The country cousin of Charleston's High Cotton.

Holds its own in comparison to the sassier downtown restaurants, but a mellower atmosphere and lots of local people. Emphasis is on fresh and simple entrees, especially at lunch, including pastas with sauces of all kinds, steak, local shrimp, and crab.

FOOD PURVEYORS

BAKERIES/COFFEE HOUSES

Baker's Cafe (843-577-2694; 214 King St.) A busy place especially for Sunday brunch, but ideal for a snack. Located at the head of the King Street antique district.

Fulford & Egan Coffee and Tea House (843-723-4374; 190 King St.) Stop in practically all day (to 11 p.m.) every day for Belgian waffles, homemade muffins and breads, and specialty beverages, including Italian sodas.

Normandy Farm Bakery (843-577-5763; 86 Society St.) Carefully nurtured fermented starter yields incredible french loaves — get them while they're hot. Also focaccia, pastries, and coffee.

Port City Java (843-853-5282; 387 King St.) Smoothies, pastries, coffee, young people. Additional locations at 211 King St. and 261 Calhoun St. (at the Westin Francis Marion).

Saffron (843-722-5588; 333 E. Bay St.) The glass cases filled with daily specials like chocolate-chip scones and pastries, and the racks of fresh bread, could lead to a gourmet picnic; or you can eat here.

CANDY AND ICE CREAM

Charleston Chocolates (843-577-4491; www.charlestonchocolates.com; 190 East Bay St.) It's Valentine's Day year-round here with hand-dipped chocolates and fancy trimmings.

Haagen-Dazs (843-723-9326; 43 S. Market St.) Sometimes it's even too hot in the Lowcountry for ice cream — it's a melted mess after a few licks — but this old favorite stays open after the sun goes down.

Lucas Neuhaus (843-722-0461; 73 State St.) If you're in the Market area and overwhelmed by all the shops and all the merchandise for sale, drop in for one fabulous Belgian chocolate or confection.

PIZZA, SANDWICHES, AND FASTER FOOD

Andolini's (843-722-7437; 82 Wentworth St.) The place for pizza in Charleston. Order as you enter, eat in a high-backed booth or on the back patio.

Cafe Cafe (843-723-3622; 177 Meeting St.) Homemade desserts and breads, sandwiches, Charleston "wraps," lots to drink from gin to ginger ale. Locals go for the daily soup special.

Wade Spees

Many restaurants, like Joseph's, serve meals outside most of the year.

Joseph's (843-958-8500; 129 Meeting St.) A local favorite for breakfast, home-made soups at lunch, and courtyard dining.

Juanita Greenberg's Nacho Royale (843-723-6224; 439 King St.) The four food groups are represented here — hot, fresh, simple. Big burritos, handmade nachos in portions made for two. You can start with a margarita at 4 p.m.

The Kickin' Chicken (843-805-5020; 350 King St.) Fifteen flavors of wings so take plenty of napkins. Salads and sandwiches.

CULTURE

ARCHITECTURE

St. Philip's Episcopal Church, an architectural gem circa 1835, still serves a vital role in Charleston's spiritual and cultural life.

Wade Spees

If you have a serious or layman's interest in architecture, you should approach the riches of Charleston and its environs with a game plan. Is it small rooms and thickly carved mantels of the colonial period you like? The fine lightness of touch and classical decoration introduced by the Adam brothers? Do open-air living spaces afforded by piazzas and walled gardens appeal? Ironwork? Brick or clapboard? Small country churches or city steeples? Interiors or exteriors? Grand plantations or modest rowhouses? Rooms adorned with 18th-century furniture or ones that remain bare, objects in and of themselves? For suggestions on buildings which express these aesthetic considerations, see the **Historic House** listing later in this chapter.

If you're a generalist, start your day (and park your car) at the *Charleston Visitors Center* (375 Meeting St.) where there are lots of maps, helpful docents, and an audio-visual presentation that presents an excellent introduction to the city. From here, you may select a guided tour (for suggestions, see Chapter Two, *Transportation*): carriage tours, city shuttle buses, mini-van tours, and walking-tour guides generally collect and discharge passengers at this site. Sometimes a motorized tour is the most efficient way to review the city's deep inventory of houses — from the famous "single house" (one room wide, standing endways with its door to the street) to double-piazzaed mansions dominating their harborside sites. Or you may head out on your own. Any way you choose, you won't be disappointed.

DANCE

Dance performances take place through most of the year, especially during the Spoleto Festival. Call ahead for schedules and ticket information.

Charleston Ballet Theatre (843-723-7334; 477 King St.).
Robert Ivey Ballet (843-875-9308; 908 Bacon's Bridge Rd., Summerville).

FILM

First-run movie houses tend to be located in malls away from downtown, and they account for most of the region's audiences. In Charleston, the Roxy Theater & Cafe is a gem, with extra-special beverages and snacks — but from time to time, especially during Spoleto, special film series are scheduled in college auditoriums or libraries. Check local newspaper listings or look for handbills posted around town. The new IMAX theatre offers a screen eight stories high, audio booming from every corner, and films well known for their "you-are-there" feeling: the top of Everest, the Zambezi River, in the mist with the gorillas, or underwater with the dolphins.

American Cinema Grill (843-722-3456; 446 King St.).
Charleston Film Society (843-744-2286).
Citadel Mall Cinema I-VI (843-763-7052; 2072 Sam Rittenburg Blvd.).
IMAX Theater of Charleston (843-725-4629; 360 Concord St.)
James Island Cinema Theatre (843-795-9499; 1743 Central Park Rd.).
Mount Pleasant Cinema 1 2 & 3 (843-884-3614; 1001 Johnnie Dodds Blvd.).
Northwoods Mall Cinema (843-569-6794; 2181 Northwoods Blvd.).
Roxy Theater & Cafe (843-853-7699; 245 East Bay Street).

GALLERIES

Many of the galleries featuring the best work of Lowcountry artists are listed in the **Shopping** section. A visit to either of the ones listed below would enhance your appreciation of the region and its 20th-century movement called the Charleston Renaissance. Works on exhibit may or may not be for sale.

Elizabeth O'Neill Verner Studio and Museum (843-722-4246; 38 Tradd St.) The artist, who was in her 90s when she died in 1979, produced etchings, pastels, and pencil drawings of Charleston life that seems long past, including portraits of African-Americans, streetscapes, and steeples. Visiting her studio is like a step back in time. Also home of the Tradd Street Press, which publishes the work of Mrs. Verner, her daughter, Elizabeth Verner Hamilton, and other books of Lowcountry poetry, stories, and local history.

Gibbes Museum of Art (843-722-2706; www.gibbes.com; 135 Meeting St.) The permanent collection presents Charleston from the 18th century to the present. Not to be missed are Charles Fraser's exquisite miniatures of prominent citizens during the city's early days, and interpretations of of 20th-century plantation and rural life, including Alice Ravenel Huger Smith's watercolors, and sketches and woodcuts by Alfred Hutty and Anna Hewyard Taylor. Also, a very fine museum shop. Open Tues.–Sat. 10–5; Sun. 1–5. Closed Mon. and holidays. Adults $6, children $4.

HISTORIC HOMES, GARDENS & RELIGIOUS SITES

It's hard to avoid historic sites in Charleston, but whether or not you visit one, and how much time you spend there will, of course, depend on your interest and schedule, whether you're traveling with children, and whether you have your own car. It may be preferable, for example, to do just one big thing in a day (a boat ride to Fort Sumter, a visit to a plantation garden) plus two smaller ones (see a house museum or church, take a walking tour, picnic in a park).

Distances are not great: to gardens and lighthouses and island sites from Charleston takes about 30 minutes. The sites in the following list are open all year, unless otherwise noted. Admission fees and hours are as of 2000; reduced admission generally applies to children 12 and under, seniors, students and military personnel. Combination tickets offer savings at historic houses and sites: **Best of Charleston** (843-853-2378; www.bestofcharleston.cc; 18 Anson St.) allows you to customize a pass from among nine options; **Charleston Heritage Passport** (www.charlestonheritage.org; available at participating sites and Visitors Center) is good for admission (up to a year) at the Gibbes Museum, two house museums (Russell and Edmonston-Alston) and two plantations (Drayton and Middleton). Cost for adults is $29, children $19.

Keep in mind that the last tours of the day start approximately 30 minutes before closing time. Visitors generally are welcome to enter religious sites, but are asked to observe the worship schedule and related courtesies of visitation as few of the sites offer regular tour services. Handicapped access is sometimes limited in the old buildings and there are usually rules regarding strollers.

AIKEN-RHETT HOUSE
843-723-1159.
48 Elizabeth St.
Mon.–Sat., 10–5, Sun. 2–5.
Admission: Adults $7;
  reduced admission with
  combination tickets to
  selected historic
  properties.

Built in 1817, representing high-style Greek Revival and Rococo interiors, the Aiken-Rhett House is preserved in a somewhat less formal way than other houses. It's full of atmosphere, a little worn at the edges. During the fiercest shelling of Charleston in the Civil War, it was the headquarters of Confederate General P.G.T. Beauregard, a purpose for which it was well suited by virtue of its scale, design, and location off the Battery. The intact workyard is a compelling example of African-American urban life.

AUDUBON SWAMP GARDEN

See "Nature Preserves" in the **Recreation** section.

BOONE HALL PLANTATION
843-884-4371.
P.O. Box 1554, Mt. Pleasant.
April 1–Labor Day,
Mon.–Sat. 8:30–6:30;
Sunday 1–5; in low
season Mon.–Sat. 9–5;
Sunday 1–4.
Admission: Adults $12.50;
children $6.

Of particular interest are the nine mid-18th century brick slave cabins (these housed house slaves and skilled craftsmen, not the field hands), the Gin House, used for processing cotton, and the magnificent avenue of oaks, which runs three-quarters of a mile.

CALHOUN MANSION
843-722-8205.
16 Meeting St.
Wed.–Sun. 10–4.
Admission: Adults $15;
children $7.

You've seen it in the movies and on television, as symbolic as Tara but in the city. High Victorian: ornate plaster and woodwork, 14-foot ceilings, a ballroom with a 45-foot high dome. Built in 1876, when few people had the means to manage such a thing.

CONGREGATION BETH ELOHIM
843-723-1090.
90 Hasell St.
Mon.–Fri. 10–12.

The country's oldest synagogue in continuous use, built in 1840 to replace one that just burned, it is a superb example of Greek Revival architecture.

CYPRESS GARDENS

See "Nature Preserves" in **Recreation** section.

DRAYTON HALL
843-769-2600.
www.draytonhall.org.
3380 Ashley River Rd.
(Hwy. 61, 9 miles NW of
Charleston.)
Mar.–Oct., 9:30–4;
Nov.–Feb., 9:30–3.
Admission: Adults $10
(high season) and $8 (low
season); children $4; free
to members of the
National Trust for
Historic Preservation.

It's a measure of the stunning greatness of this 18th-century Georgian-Palladian dwelling that even as it remains unfurnished, unrestored, unchanged (just stabilized), bare and magnificent, it exists in a class by itself. Built between 1738 and 1742, and set on a lovely Ashley River site, it is one of the most architecturally significant dwellings in America. Managed by the National Trust for Historic Preservation. House tours start on the hour (written tours in French, German, English, and Spanish available), and you are welcome to take the self-guided walking tours of the grounds. The guides are superior — not to be missed even in the pouring rain.

EDMONDSTON-ALSTON HOUSE
843-722-7171.

First built in 1825 by one wealthy man, later enlarged by another, it reveals — in structure, lavish decoration, documents, family furnishings,

www.middletonplace.org.
21 East Battery.
Tues.–Sat. 10–4:30; Sun. &
  Mon. 1:30–4:30.
Admission: Adults $8;
  reduced admission with
  combination tickets to
  selected historic
  properties.

silver, and china — the best of what money could buy. You get a sense that this was the life and lifestyle Southerners fought the Civil War, in part, to protect.

Wade Spees

Growing interest in the Lowcountry's African-American culture and heritage has placed new emphasis on identifying its historic sites and celebrating its community leaders.

**EMANUEL A.M.E.
CHURCH**
843-722-2561.
110 Calhoun St.

The Free African Society, composed of free blacks and slaves in Charleston, was formed in 1791, and by 1818, under the leadership of Morris Brown, this independent congregation built a small church for their services. Denmark Vesey planned his slave insurrection there; when the rebellion failed, the church was shut for 43 years. Reorganization came after the Civil War; this structure was built in 1891.

**EXCHANGE BUILDING/
PROVOST DUNGEON**
843-727-2165.
www.oldexchange.com.
122 East Bay St.
Daily 9–5.
Admission: Adults $6;
  children $3.50.

Even before 1771, when this building was completed, the site on which it stands was used for a variety of public purposes in the young colony. Its commanding location, at the foot of Broad Street, defined both an end boundary for the city, and also, from the water, its point of arrival. In terms of sheer geography it looms large. It's the kind of outsized place that was, and still is, used for huge receptions.

During the Revolution the British held political and military prisoners in the basement.

FRENCH PROTESTANT (HUGUENOT) CHURCH
843-722-4385.
136 Church St.

French Huguenots fleeing religious persecution worshipped in Charleston as early as 1687. This church, built on the site of earlier ones, dates from 1845.

HEYWARD-WASHINGTON HOUSE
843-722-0354.
www.charlestonmuseum. com.
87 Church St.
Mon.–Sat. 10–5, Sun. 1–5. Last tour at 4:30.
Admission: Adults $7; children $4. Discounted admission with combination ticket to other Charleston Museum properties.

Built in 1772 by a rice planter whose son, Thomas Heyward, Jr., signed the Declaration of Independence, this house was also the head-quarters of George Washington during his visit to the Lowcountry in 1791. Its collection of furniture, including several 18th-century Charleston-made pieces and the magnificent Holmes bookcase, is unmatched. The back courtyard still features its dependencies, open to view, and a small garden.

JOSEPH MANIGAULT HOUSE
843-723-2926.
www.charlestonmuseum. com.
350 Meeting St.
Mon.–Sat. 10–5; Sun. 1–5. Last tour at 4:30.
Admission: Adults $7; children $4. Discounted admission with a combination ticket to other Charleston Museum properties.

The outside of this structure is three stories of brick; the inside is something like shaped light. Designed by native son Gabriel Manigault for his brother and completed in 1803, this house, exuding both formality of plan and spontaneity of gesture, shows the nature of beauty and taste favored by elite planters who may have been, as Gabriel Manigault was, educated in Europe and exposed there to sophisticated design ideas and decorating schemes. The furniture is of the period, English, American, and French.

MAGNOLIA PLANTATION AND GARDENS
843-571-1266.
www.magnoliaplantation. com.
3550 Ashley River Rd. (Hwy. 61, 10 miles NW of Charleston).
Daily 8–dusk; shorter hours in winter. Ticket sales end at 5 in winter, 5:30 in summer.

The current building was floated here by barge in 1873, but the entire tract dates back to the time of the Barbadian planters who relocated on the Ashley River. The legacy here is gardens, acres of them, reflecting (in layout and specimen plant-ing) two centuries of horticulture. The gardens include 250 varieties of Azalea Indica and 900 varieties of Camellia Japonica; there are bike and walking paths, a petting zoo, a canoe trail, and picnic areas. You may access an adjacent nature preserve by small train. This is also the site to

Admission to the Plantation and Gardens: Adults $11; seniors and AAA members $10; children 6–12 $5; teenagers $8. Admission to the house costs an additional $6 (children under 6 not admitted to the house). Fares on the Nature Preserve train are adults $5, teens, $4, children $3.

enter the Audubon Swamp Garden (see "Nature Preserves" in **Recreation** section).

MIDDLETON PLACE
843-556-6020 or
800-782-3608.
www.middletonplace.org.
4300 Ashley River Rd.
(Hwy. 61, 14 miles NW of Charleston).
Daily 9–5.
Admission: Adults $15; children $7; House tours always cost an additional $8 per person.

The formal gardens, laid out in 1741 and constructed by 100 slaves over a decade, feature terraces, camellia allées, butterfly lakes, hillside drifts of azaleas, and acres of landscaped paths. The site is so grand that it can be appreciated even when little is in bloom: the geometry of the original plan itself is breathtaking. The adjacent stables and farmyard area evoke the self-suffiency of the plantation era with demonstrations by a potter, weaver, blacksmith, and carpenter. (The animals just hang around on their own.) The main house was sacked by Union forces; tours of a remaining wing honor the Middletons, but the real reason to come here is what's outside. Nice restaurant for lunch and dinner.

NATHANIEL RUSSELL HOUSE
843-724-8481.
51 Meeting St.
Mon.–Sat. 10–5, Sun. 2–5.
Admission: $7.

People have no doubt been admiring this brick townhouse and its garden from the day it was completed (ca. 1808) and with good reason. It represents the high point of the Adam style in the city — its stairway appears to float, a lovely combination of function and fantasy — and it is one of the most thoroughly conceived and exquisitely executed neoclassical dwellings in the nation. The interpretation (it belongs to the Historic Charleston Foundation) is rich and thorough, from the look of table settings to the lives of slaves who made such a household run smoothly.

ST. MICHAEL'S EPISCOPAL CHURCH
843-723-0603.
Meeting St. at Broad St.
Daily 9–4:30.

This church is still the center of many Charlestonians' lives, as it has been since 1761. Research suggests that its stunning white steeple is a close match to the one at St. Martin-in-the-Fields in London, and may have been designed by James Gibbs. It is part of the famous "Four Corners of Law" in downtown Charleston, an intersection that represents, in religious, civic, judicial, and federal buildings, the order imposed on society. There is a tranquil walled graveyard to explore.

ST. PHILIP'S EPISCOPAL CHURCH
843-722-7734.
146 Church St.

Constructed in 1835–1838, facing a central park, and flanked by its graveyard, St. Philip's seems out of the Old World of Europe. The building is sheathed in a mottled, tan stucco material that reflects the gradual shifting in light over the course of a day. The church is open for services Sundays, Wednesdays, and selected Fridays.

THOMAS ELFE WORKSHOP
843-722-2142.
54 Queen St.
Tours Mon.–Fri., 10–12.
Admission: $5.

A meticulously restored Charleston "single house," this dwelling was built before 1760 by the renowned cabinetmaker, who came to Charleston from England in the mid-18th century and left his mark in homes and furniture throughout the city. The carved fretwork that embellishes mahogany tables, chairs, and bookcases makes his work artistically distinctive; his abundant record-keeping has enabled historians to understand his life and times. The small house, panelled in cypress, showcases his artistry.

MILITARY SITES

The presence of the military — invaders and defenders — has enriched the history of the Lowcountry since the time of the American Revolution, and it is still felt today. You needn't be a veteran, or even a Civil War buff, to enjoy the forts, military museums, and rural sites that are so plentiful in the region. Children — with their innate appreciation of danger and adventure and their love of costume — especially seem to twig these sites and installations.

THE CITADEL MUSEUM
843-953-6846.
www.citadel.edu.
171 Moultrie St.
Sun.–Fri. 2–5; Sat. 12–5.
Free admission.

Located on the campus of the Military College of South Carolina, founded in 1842, it tells the history of the school and the Corps of Cadets through documents, photographs, and uniforms. Dress parades take place most Fridays at 3:45 p.m. during the academic year.

THE CONFEDERATE MUSEUM
843-723-1541.
188 Meeting St.
(currently under repair; call

There's a Gullah expression in the Lowcountry that sums up this museum: when you ask someone on the telephone "Is that you?" the person may reply, in a weary tone laced with irony, "That's what's leff' of me." This may be what's left of the old

for information. Limited
tours of the collection,
relocated to 34 Pitt St.,
Sat. and Sun. 12–4).

Confederacy: uniforms, tattered flags, documents,
artifacts, and a fragrant sense of the Lost Cause.

FORT LAMAR HERITAGE PRESERVE
803-734-3893.
(SC Dept. of Natural
Resources/ Heritage Trust
Program).
Fort Lamar Rd., James Island
(Take SC 171 to Battery
Island Rd. Left for approx.
8 miles to Fort Lamar Rd.
Right for approx.5 miles to
small parking lot on left.)
Open daily dawn to dusk.
Self-guided tour; maps
available on site.

The site of the Battle of Secessionville, waged in
the pre-dawn darkness of June 16, 1862, when
Federal troops attacked this Confederate earthwork fort. The battle, involving some 1400 men,
was over in three hours. The walking tour directs
you across what was an open field rimmed by
marsh and woods, around the simple "M" shaped
field fortification, by the magazines, dry moat,
earthworks, and the likely mass grave of Federal
wounded. Off the beaten track: for information call
the number listed above which oversees the rustic
site.

FORT MOULTRIE
843-883-3123 (National
Park Service local office).
1214 Middle St., Sullivan's
Island; 10 miles E. of
Charleston.
Daily 9–5.
Admission: Adults $2;
children $1; or $5 per
family.

The primary site of Charleston's seacoast defense
system, from its first test in the American Revolution, now operated by the National Park Service.
The palmetto-log fort that repelled the British fleet is
gone, but buildings and earthworks dating from
1809 convey the sense of fragility and isolation the
early patriots must have felt. A 20-minute film in the
Visitor Center provides an excellent introduction. It
is also the burial site of the Seminole warrior Osce-
ola who, meeting under a flag of truce, was impris-
oned here in 1838.

FORT SUMTER NATIONAL MONUMENT
843-722-1691.
www.spiritlinecruises.com
(for boat tour information).
Departure from the City
Marina (Lockwood Dr. —
limited handicapped access)
and Patriots Point.
Daily trips year round except
Christmas Day; five or six
trips Mar.–Nov.; fewer in
winter months.
Admission: Adults $11; seniors
$10; children (ages 6–11) $6.

A relaxing ferry trip, which offers splendid
views of the harbor and peninsula, takes you
to the place where the Civil War began. National
Park Service rangers are on hand at the Fort to
answer your questions; there are gun emplace-
ments to explore, and a museum with artifacts to
help you imagine scenes of the siege, which lasted
approximately two years and ended in the abandonment of the Fort by Confederate soldiers. The
entire tour lasts just over two hours.

Fort Sumter, where the stark choice faced by a splintered Union was played out, in bloodshed and historic consequences, in April 1861.

PATRIOTS POINT NAVAL AND MARITIME MUSEUM
843-884-2727.
40 Patriots Point Rd., Mt. Pleasant.
Daily 9–5, to 6 in summer months.
Admission: Adults $11; children $5.50.

The big ones are berthed here — the aircraft carrier Yorktown, the World War II sub Clamagore, the destroyer Laffey, and the cutter Ingham — and on self-guided tours you can see their aircraft, guns, and missiles, as well as views of how personnel lived and worked on board. The view of peninsular Charleston (just over the Cooper River Bridges) from the platform of the Yorktown is unbeatable. Snack bar and gift shop, seating areas for the rest and air you'll need: there's a lot of walking and close quarters.

MUSEUMS

AVERY RESEARCH CENTER FOR AFRICAN-AMERICAN HISTORY AND CULTURE
843-953-7609.
125 Bull St.
Tours Mon.–Sat. 12–5.

Housed in one of the first schools dedicated to educating freed slaves, the center is an archive and library of printed and picture materials and objects related to the heritage of the region's African-Americans. It was built by the Freedman's Bureau at the end of the Civil War to meet the needs of 1,000 eager students who had been receiving instruction from teachers sent by the American Missionary Association and other organizations. Reading room hours are Mon.–Sat., 12–5.

CHARLESTON MUSEUM
843-722-2996.
www.charlestonmuseum.com.

The museum, founded in 1773, is the oldest in America. This means that both the ideas that gave the collection its intellectual underpinnings and the very objects themselves, many from

360 Meeting St.
Mon.–Sat. 9–5; Sun. 1–5.
Admission: Adults $7,
    children $4; combination
    tickets to Museum and
    its historic properties
    available at a discount.

Charleston's oldest families, reflect more than two centuries of the city's self-consciousness. Exhibits interpreting subjects as diverse as flora and fauna, fashion, the art of silversmithing, Native American life, and plantation life, come together to provide a seamless image of a special place. The section on African-American slavery — texts, artifacts, photographs, charts — is superb. Plans are underway to build a special wing for the Confederate submarine *Hunley*, dramatically raised from the harbor in August 2000 (www.hunley.org).

**CHARLES TOWNE
    LANDING 1670**
843-852-4200.
1500 Old Towne Rd. (Hwy.
    171 between I-26 and
    Hwy. 17).
Daily 8:30–5, to 6 in
    summer months.
Admission: Adults $5;
    children $2.50.
Rental bicycles $2/hour.

Consider this 80-acre park an outdoor museum, where the lives of the Lowcountry's earliest European settlers are interpreted in several ways: in a village setting on a 17th-century replica of a typical coastal trading vessel; and in "wilderness," as found in the Animal Forest, where birds and beasts common to the area in 1670 roam in a secured habitat.

Visitors to the Ocean Tank at the new South Carolina Aquarium watch dozens of species of fish, and during feeding time, at least one scuba diver.

Wade Spees

**SOUTH CAROLINA
    AQUARIUM**
843-720-1990.
www.scaquarium.org.
Calhoun St.
Daily 9–5, to 7 in summer
    months; 10–5 Nov.–Feb.

Set on the Cooper River, where its neighbor is a landing for the industrial port of Charleston (a port that sees more than 12 million tons of container cargo pass through each year), the new aquarium provides well-designed displays of the state's aquatic habitat, from the mountain streams of the

Admission: Adults $14;
seniors $12; teens (13–17)
$12; children (4–12) $7.

Upcountry to Lowcountry marshes. More than 10,000 creatures reside here both in the 330,000 gallon Ocean Tank, in living habitat exhibits, and in the hands-on water tables. Interpreted dive programs, where you can watch the fish being fed and learn more about them take place at 11,1, and 3 daily. Kids can spot bottlenose dolphins for themselves from the expansive deck overlooking the river — and there's always a guide to answer questions.

Spoleto Festival USA bursts open in Charleston every spring with dozens of performances, from ballet to a fireworks finale.

Wade Spees

MUSIC

Charleston has a symphony orchestra and chamber groups that play regularly throughout the year, and, of course, it has *Spoleto*, which brings boys' choirs, operatic soloists, and instrumentalists to the city each May and June. The region is rich in indigenous music, too: blues, jazz, spirituals, gospel. As new audiences for these styles develop, concerts to showcase them are emerging. The *Charleston Blues Bash* in February, the *MOJA Arts Festival* in September, and the *Annual Spirituals Concert* in December are some. Often, concerts of gospel music and spirituals take place in conjunction with spring and fall house tours and may be held at a historic site. You should check local newspapers for schedules or, once you arrive in Charleston, contact the organizations below for information.

Charleston Symphony Orchestra (843-723-7528; 14 George St.) Performances under the direction of David Stahl in the Gaillard Auditorium (77 Calhoun St.) throughout the year. Concert series might include selections from the classical repertoire, pops, and chamber works.

Lowcountry Blues Society (843-762-9125) The Society's main event — The Lowcountry Blues Bash — runs for about 10 days every February and features performances at sites all over the city, from small clubs to larger theaters. Some concerts are free, others charge a modest cover, usually under $15. The shows are first rate — musicians come from Chicago, North and South Carolina, anywhere the blues are played.

MOJA Arts Festival (843-724-7305; 133 Church St.) The 16-day festival, whose name is Swahili for "one" or "unity," takes place in the fall and celebrates the African and Caribbean cultural influences on the Lowcountry. It includes many musical performances. Administered by the city's Office of Cultural Affairs.

NIGHTLIFE

Nightlife prospers in the Market Area and East Bay St., where there are dance lounges and noisy student spots, but mellow piano bars at the Charleston Grill, the Mills House, and Charleston Chops are reliably rewarding. Farther afield, on the resort-oriented islands, you will discover the land of "shag," the original, stylized South Carolina dance set to beach music. A list of the better known or easily accessible spots for night owls follows. Cover charges vary widely, depending on the entertainment. Check local newspaper listings when you're in town for special shows.

Charleston Chops (843-937-9300; 188 East Bay St.) Jazz piano bar Tues.–Sat. in this steak-and-seafood restaurant.

Charleston Grill at Charleston Place (843-571-2265; 224 King St.) Jazz trios nightly in a sophisticated, laid-back setting.

Charleston Jazz Club (843-795-1800; 1409 Folly Rd., James Island) Live jazz, rhythm and blues, reggae.

Cumberland's (843-577-9469; 26 Cumberland St.) Band music that's live and loud.

Dunleavy's Pub (843-883-9646; 2213 Middle St., Sullivan's Island) A small place on the corner with a half-dozen or so imported beers and ales on tap and music (acoustic, Irish, small bands) on the weekends.

Indigo Lounge (843-577-7383; 5 Faber St.) An upscale dance club with live Motown performers on the weekends.

Mills House (843-577-2400; 115 Meeting St.) Two lounges, one with a piano bar where you can relax and visit. Good place to gather for an after-dinner drink. Look for Big Band tunes or jazzy guitar.

Mitchell's (843-937-0300; 102 N. Market St.) Latin jazz in a restored warehouse.

Momma's Blues Palace (843-853-2221; 46 John St.) Not a palace, but plenty of blues, acoustic and electric.

Music Farm (843-853-3276; 32 Ann St.) Where the young crowd swarms to dance and mosh.

The Warehouse (843-720-7772; 213 East Bay St.) Punk, ska, reggae, local bands.

SPOLETO

It is said that the first professional dramatic production in America of a play written here was performed in Charleston in the 18th century by a shipwrecked poet, who was washed ashore, as he put it, "full of lice, shame, poverty, nakedness and hunger."

No such description could conceivably apply to the outstanding performers who come to the city for a cultural festival which has put Charleston on the map, nationally and internationally. For 18 days at the end of spring, a time of budding oleander, fading azalea, and unapologetically fragrant magnolias, Spoleto comes to Charleston and Charleston becomes the city it has long imagined itself to be. an artistic mecca where expressions of high culture find their setting among people who believe they understand the meaning of civilized life.

Spoleto gave Charlestonians a chance to prove their claims of having shucked off their provincial preferences, and prove it they have. Emboldened by the artistic vision of Gian Carlo Menotti (who fell in love with Charleston and organized the first festival in 1977), and egged on by an indefatigable mayor, Joe Riley, Charleston's cultural and business communities have consistently — and with full attention — adapted themselves and their city to the idea that first-class art of many kinds can inhabit, enrich, and be enriched by the lively, unique qualities of this old city. Spoleto instilled new vigor, giving rise to building projects and renovations, new restaurants, and shops: it linked the pride in the Lowcountry's past to confidence in its future. It opened the doors of Charleston to the nation.

Spoleto took its name from the town in Italy where, in the 1950s, Mr. Menotti had organized another festival. Spoleto in Charleston was conceived as the counterpart to that venture, though now it stands on its own artistic direction and traditions. In any one season, it offers more than 100 scheduled events, including premieres of opera and dance as well as dozens of chamber music, choral, jazz, and orchestral performances. Performances take place indoors and out — in parks, plantation gardens, amphitheaters, and auditoriums.

If that's not enough, the regular Spoleto events are augmented by some 600 *Piccolo Spoleto* performances (often free), organized by the city's Office of Cultural Affairs (843-724-7305; 133 Church St., Charleston, SC 29401). These events can include organ, choral, and madrigal recitals in churches; mime shows, outdoor concerts, and numerous theater productions.

There are several ways to purchase tickets to Spoleto. The first thing to do is request, by mail or telephone, the festival ticket brochure and guide, a near-tabloid size schedule of events with a pre-printed order form. Contact:

Spoleto Festival U.S.A.
P.O. Box 157
Charleston, S.C. 29402-0157
843-722-2764 / Fax 843-723-6383.
Website: www.spoletousa.org

If you want to order a pre-designed "ticket package" which might include a dance performance, a play, an opera, and a chamber music event spread over several days, order the brochure by mid-November or December. If you're not sure of your schedule, you can order tickets to individual events beginning in January. There is a $6 handling charge for ticket orders.

The variety and number of events can be overwhelming, but poring over the brochure and making plans offers the same pleasurable anticipation that stirs avid gardeners as they read beautiful seed catalogues. Of course, the earlier you can confirm travel arrangements and lodging, the better.

If April 1st comes and you are without tickets but want to attend to Spoleto, you can still do it. With basic Spoleto Festival ticket brochure in hand (see above address) you may order tickets by telephone from 9 a.m.–9 p.m. until the festival's end. Call 843-577-4500 (a ticket agency line dedicated to Spoleto tickets) to order. You may charge to Discover, Visa, or MasterCard. There's a handling charge levied per ticket.

In person, visit the Spoleto Office at 14 George St., which is open year round but extends its hours from April until the festival closes. There are also box offices at all Spoleto venues which handle tickets for the events held there. They are generally open daily during the festival from 10 a.m. until thirty minutes after the final performance of the day.

You can even arrive without tickets, and get lucky. Tickets can be purchased up to one hour before curtain time; remaining tickets go on sale at performance sites 30 minutes before curtain. Chairs or standing room for sold-out performances at the Dock Street Theater and the Garden Theater go on sale at 10 a.m. on the day of performance.

THEATER

By the middle of the 18th century, theatrical performances were well established in the cultural life of Charleston. In the antebellum years theater was but one jewel in the crown of culture, offset by the brilliant setting provided by a society that lived for pleasure and sought it in balls, concerts, seasonal celebrations, and lavish home entertaining.

In this century, it wasn't until 1927 — when DuBose Heyward's novel *Porgy*, the story of a lame Charleston street vendor and his love for Bess, was adapted and performed on the Broadway stage — that drama native to Charleston came alive. Theatrical performances in the Lowcountry still reflect their indigenous stories — they are often showcased during Piccolo Spoleto — but a growing audience also supports new works from nationally known dramatists and selections from the classical repertory. When visiting, call ahead for performance schedules and tickets.

Charleston Stage Company (843-577-5967 or 800-454-7093; www.charleston stage.com; P.O. Box 356) Productions at Dock Street Theatre by a residential theatre group that provide special enjoyment for families, plays like *Cheaper By the Dozen* or *A Christmas Carol*; original work, children's theater, and workshops.

Dock Street Theater (843-720-3968; 135 Church St.) This is a lovely interpretation of a Georgian-style theater, of the sort 18th-century Charlestonians may have patronized. Rebuilt during the Depression within the old Planters Hotel (circa 1809) as a project of the Federal Works Progress Administration, the theater's cypress interiors, intimate box seats, and terrific acoustics make it a wonderful place to attend performances. It's the site of the immensely popular Chamber Music Series during Spoleto and festival plays, as well as a stage for roving companies.

Footlight Players (843-722-7521; 20 Queen St.) An old, established theater company dedicated to community-theater repertory. Six productions each season, from August to May.

RECREATION

W hile guessing what a novelist had in mind in his work can be a risky business, perhaps when DuBose Heyward wrote "It is always Sunday on the Sea Islands," he was thinking that there is, in every day, a piece of Sunday here, a piece of time as yet unscheduled in which to enjoy the best of your surroundings, naturally and simply, with as few complications as possible. This is the definition of recreation in the Lowcountry.

BASEBALL

Charleston RiverDogs (a Class A affiliate of the Tampa Bay Devil Rays) play April through August at Joe Riley, Jr. Park (843-723-7241; www.riverdogs.com; 360 Fishburne St.) Tickets are $4–$8.

BEACH ACCESS

There are hundreds of miles of coastline between Charleston and Savannah and on the barrier islands. At many points the public can reach the coast at designated access sites. Some of these offer changing areas, restrooms, showers, and picnic tables. Others are mere paths in the sand. Some, like the beaches on pristine barrier islands, are accessible only by boat.

The beaches on this coast are flat and wide, without rocks, overlooked by dunes or maritime forest. The surf ranges from placid to roiling (the Washout at Folly Beach is considered a top surfing spot). Lifeguards are not on duty at every beach access point, and swimming may be extremely hazardous. It is not wise to swim in unmonitored areas. Walking on the dunes, picking the sea oats, and driving on the beach are forbidden.

A few suggestions follow for reaching the beach by land or water. For more detailed information about specific access points, contact the chambers of commerce or tourism commissions listed at the end of Chapter Seven, *Information*.

Sullivan's Island and *Isle of Palms* are located north of the city on Hwy. 17 and S.C. 703. The beach at Sullivan's is marked by walkways. You may park along the side of streets. *Isle of Palms County Park* (843-886-3863; 1-14th Palm Blvd.) offers pay parking, restrooms, and changing facilities. Located to the south, off Hwy. 17 on S.C. 171, you can enjoy the fully outfitted *Folly Beach County Park* (843-588-2426; 1010 W. Ashley Ave.) which offers 4,000 feet of oceanfront access, lifeguards, changing rooms, showers, pay parking and a 1,045 foot fishing pier. A bit farther south off Hwy. 17, at the gate to Kiawah Island, is *Beachwalker Park* (843-768-2395; Beachwalker Dr., Johns Island) another well-developed public beach destination with facilities, lifeguards, and pay parking.

SHORE REFUGES

By water, and with advance arrangements, you may visit *Cape Romain National Wildlife Refuge* (843-928-3368; 390 Bull Island Rd., Awendaw, SC 29429) a 64,229-acre site managed by the U.S. Fish and Wildlife Service. The refuge consists of four parts: *Bull Island*, a 5,000-acre barrier island; *Cape Island*, a favorite spot for loggerhead turtles to nest; *Moore's Landing*, the site of ferry services, and an observation pier just right for birders; and *Raccoon Key Island* , a popular spot for shelling.

Coastal Expeditions, Inc. (843-881-4582; ferry information) offers exclusive ferry service to Bull Island, weather permitting. The 2000 ticket prices were $20 for adults and $10 for children under 12. From Mar.–Nov., the ferry makes two round-trips daily every Tuesday, Friday, and Saturday, and one all-day trip on Thursdays. From Dec.–Feb. there's one trip only, on Saturdays. The company also offers pontoon charters throughout the refuge for larger groups.

Another refuge is *Capers Island* — a classic, undisturbed barrier island managed by the *South Carolina Department of Natural Resources*. Contact them (843-762-5000; P.O. Box 12559, Charleston, SC 29412) for general information regarding public use restrictions, instructions for anchoring and beaching boats, and camping permits. You can get there in a sea kayak (guided tour $85/day) offered by *Coastal Expeditions, Inc.* (843-884-7684; www.coastalexpeditions.com; 514-B Mill St., Mt. Pleasant, SC 29464); or on a 40-foot boat with *Barrier Island Eco Tours* (843-886-5000; www.nature-tours.com; P.O. Box 343, Isle of Palms, SC 29421). A 3.5-hour day tour led by a naturalist and marine biologist costs adults $32, children $25; a 2 hour sunset cruise costs adults $25, children $12.

BIRD WATCHING

Sharp eyes and persistence are rewarded with sightings of egret, heron, woodpecker, and wading birds at the Donnelley Wildlife Management area in the ACE Basin.

Wade Spees

The barrier islands mentioned above provide the least-disturbed habitats for birds and wildlife you're likely to find in the Lowcountry; if you're a serious birder, schedule a visit.

But even if you can't make it to the islands, you will not be disappointed in what you can find in more accessible places. Because of its location on the North American flyway and its diverse natural environment, the Lowcountry attracts scores of wading, shore, and songbirds, some of them as unusual as the roseate spoonbill and parasitic jaeger. Woodcocks flock in plowed fields, owls hover in roadside forests, and hawks soar over open grassland. In February, you are likely to see thousands of robins and cedar waxwings swarming in country yards, picking the cherry laurel trees clean.

Local Audubon societies, conducting the annual Christmas count, have reported over 200 types of birds from scrub areas to shorefront. Visitor-friendly sites for birding — where you may find boardwalks, observation areas, and informational slide shows or displays, are listed under **Nature Preserves** later in this chapter.

More informal birding sites recommended by local birders include the following:

I'on Swamp, 15 miles north of Mt. Pleasant off Hwy.17 on U.S. Forest Service Rd. 228. Here spring brings warblers — possibly even the shy Bachman's — and also resident upland birds, including red-cockaded woodpeckers, who make their homes here.

Mt. Pleasant: the area leading to the old **Pitt St. Bridge**. Here sightings of marbled godwits, oystercatchers, grebes, and mergansers have been reported. Activity is best at half tide, especially in fall and winter. A spotting scope is useful here.

Sullivan's Island: around the beach and groins behind **Fort Moultrie**. Here, in fall and winter, you might see peeps or an occasional purple sandpiper.

U.S. Hwy. 17 by the **Ashepoo and Combahee River crossings**. Anhinga, rails, and gallinules nest in the remnant rice fields.

BOATING

CANOEING AND KAYAKING

Interest in these activities has exploded. Guides will lead you along miles of creeks and down rivers; adventurous instructors can teach you how to get beyond the breaking waves into the ocean. Here are some popular locations and names of outfitters. The web address for Charleston-area state parks is www.ccprc.com.

The *Edisto River*, thought to be the nation's longest free-flowing blackwater stream, offers calm waters and great bird and wildlife observation. As you meander along, you're likely to see great blue herons wading by the oak-lined riverbank, or hummingbirds feeding at wildflowers. The trail follows an ancient waterway used by Native Americans and early settlers. *Colleton State Park* (843-538-8206; Canadys, SC; U.S. Rte. 15, 12 miles north of Walterboro, I-95 exit 68) and *Givhan's Ferry State Park* (843-873-0692; Hwy. 61, 16 miles west of Summerville) are along the route. You can put in there, and also camp and picnic. For more information, contact www.travelsc.com.

To inquire about conditions (canoeing and kayaking are not recommended on the Edisto River when the water level is above 7.5 feet) call 843-538-3659. The *Walterboro-Colleton Chamber of Commerce* (843-549-9595; P.O. Box 426, Walterboro, SC 29488) can assist you in renting canoes or kayaks, or securing a guide at certain times of the year.

Nearer Charleston, boats are available for rent at *James Island County Park* (843-795-7275; 871 Riverland Dr.), *Magnolia Gardens* (843-571-1266; 3550 Ashley River Rd.), and *Palmetto Islands County Park* (843-884-0832; 444 Needlerush Pkwy., Mt. Pleasant). The following companies offer kayak rentals, tours, and instruction. The 2000 price for rentals of kayaks, safety equipment, and basic instruction was about $65–$80 per day; $30 per half day. Tours, depending on their length, cost between $45 and $65.

Bohicket Boat: Adventure & Tour Co. (843-768-7294; www.bohicketmarina.com).
Coastal Expeditions (843-884-7684; www.coastalexpeditions.com).
Half-Moon Outfitters (843-881-9472).
Island Outfitters (843-607-9894).
Nature Adventures Outfitters (843-928-3316).
Whitewater Boat Co. (843-406-0034).

JET SKIING

Jet skis (a.k.a. personal watercraft and wave runners) let you navigate in the shallow creeks at a fast, noisy clip. You can rent them by the hour at the following locations. Prices in 2001 were from $50–$75 per hour, depending on whether you take a guided group tour or ride alone.

The City Marina (843-853-4386; www.charlestoncitymarina.com; Charleston).
Sun & Ski (843-588-0033; Folly Beach).
Tidal Wave Runners (843-886-8456; Isle of Palms).

SAILING

Ocean-racing yachts streak across the broad harbors and inlets of Charleston.

Wade Spees

A sailor unfamiliar with Lowcountry coastal waters will encounter dramatic tides and strong currents. If you're interested in renting a sailboat, either for a day's excursion or a sunset cruise, reserve early. It's also wise to check local conditions and discuss your plans with the rental outfitter before you go. (Some boats come with their own skippers if you get nervous.)

Sailboats in a range of sizes are available for hire from the following:

Argo Charters (843-577-8804; 3 Lockwood Dr., Charleston, SC 29401).

Bohicket Boat (843-768-7294; Bohicket Marina Village, Seabrook Island, SC 29455).

The City Marina (843-853-4386; 17 Lockwood Dr., Charleston, SC 29401).

Wild Dunes Yacht Harbor (843-886-5100; P.O. Box 527, Isle of Palms, SC 29451).

If you're towing your own boat, there are dozens of landings (19 in Charleston County — most paved and with landing docks, some more rustic) where you can park your trailer and launch. Parking is free, but unmonitored. Contact the following agencies for listings or maps which show the locations of public boat landings: *Charleston County Parks* (843-795-2628); *South Carolina Marine Resources Division* (843-762-5000; P.O. Box 12559, Charleston, SC 29412); *Lowcountry Resort Islands and Tourism Commission* (843-717-3090 or 800-528-6870; 1 Lowcountry Lane, Yemassee, SC 29945).

BOWLING

AMF Charleston Lanes (843-766-0241; 1963 Savannah Hwy.).
Ashley Lanes (843-766-9061; 1568 Sam Rittenberg Blvd.).

CAMPING

In the old days, a camping expedition usually involved sailing or rowing — or being sailed or rowed — in boats loaded like barges to the uninhabited barrier islands. Upon arrival, the party would set up housekeeping at a "fish camp" for several days. These same spots would be revisited year after year, although they might consist of nothing more than driftwood chairs, a palmetto-log windbreak, and a fire pit. The tradition was rustic, the site well off the beaten track, the experience enhanced by the oft-repeated stories it generated.

Today's visitor can be a happy camper, too (but near running water, toilets, a campground store and gnat repellent) at public campgrounds at the following sites:

Buck Hall, Francis Marion National Forest (843-887-3257; Wambaw Ranger District, P.O. Box 106, McClellanville, SC 29458) 15 sites; hiking trails, boat ramp, fishing.

James Island County Park (843-795-7275; 871 Riverland Dr., Charleston, SC 29412) 125 RV sites, 10 3-bedroom cottages on the marsh, primitive camping area; shuttle service to downtown Charleston, paved trails, fishing and crabbing docks, playgrounds and picnic shelters.

Privately operated campgrounds in the area include:

Lake Aire RV Park and Campground (843-571-1271; 4375 Hwy. 162, Hollywood) 100 sites including full hookups, primitive sites, and camper sites. Seven-acre fishing lake, swimming pool, paddle-boat and canoe rental, showers, laundry, recreation area, bike and foot trails.

Oak Plantation Campground (843-766-5936; 3540 Savannah Hwy.) Full hookups with 15-, 30- and 50-amp. service; 100 tent sites, 150 camper sites, propane, laundry, groceries, bathrooms.

Wood Brothers Campground (843-844-2208or 8446 Ace Basin Pkwy., 37 miles south of Charleston) Wooded and open sites for RVs, campers, and tents; grocery, propane, showers, fishing pond.

DIVING

If you want to use that diver's watch you wear for looks — thick black band, fluorescent numbers, rimmed with rings and buttons — contact these outfitters. Lowcountry creeks and rivers tend to be murky with low visibility, but offshore opportunities (and instruction) are available.

Aqua Ventures (843-884-1500).
Charleston Scuba (843-763-3483).
The Wet Shop (843-744-5641).

FAMILY FUN

The Lowcountry's long summer nights, when dusk comes as late as nine o'clock, mean there's always extra time for that round of miniature golf or walk on the beach. By day, there are waterslides to offer cooling thrill rides. Here are some activities that adults and kids can enjoy together.

Chipper's Family Golf (843-402-9000; 2056 Bee's Ferry Rd.) Two areas lit for night play until 10 p.m.: an 18-hole par 3 course for adults and mini-golf.

Classic Golf (843-881-3131; 1528 Ben Sawyer Blvd., Mt. Pleasant) Miniature golf landscaped and lit for night play.

Frankie's Fun Park (843-767-1376; 5000 Ashley Phospate Rd.) Two 18-hole mini golf courses, go-cart tracks, game rooms, batting cages, and bumper boats. Open daily, 10 a.m.–midnight. A great reward for kids who have been sightseeing all day.

James Island County Park (843-795-7275; 871 Riverland Dr., James Island) The 50-foot climbing wall and 10-foot bouldering wall would attract older kids, while the little ones enjoy the water park with slides and fountains. Rollerblading on miles of paved trails; canoes, paddleboats, and bikes for rent.

Splash Zone at James Island County Park cools kids off in a hurry.

Wade Spees

Palmetto Islands County Park (843-884-0832; 444 Needlerush Pkwy., Mt. Pleasant) Picnic areas and shelters, walking and biking trails, marsh boardwalk, and fishing sites. Bicycles, canoes, and paddleboats are available for rent. Splash Island is a water fun park with slides, pools, and chutes.

Sand Dollar Mini Golf (843-884-0320; 1405 Ben Sawyer Blvd., Mt. Pleasant) Open summer nights until 10 p.m.

FISHING

There's *always* fishing in the Lowcountry, no matter the time of year, and there are as many styles and venues as there are fishermen. They include: fly fishing in the inland flats, fishing from a pier, fishing with bait from small (15'–26') and large (up to 54') craft, fishing off an artificial reef, surf casting from the beach, trolling in the Gulf Stream. Many independent guides and charter services have websites to help you match your interest to their services. Visit them or call for information; there are dozens of options. Reservations and deposits are almost always required (credit cards accepted); check on cancellation and inclement weather policies.

Charter fees include equipment, instruction, fuel (sometimes extra), bait, licenses, and food or drink if applicable. For small craft, the price is generally based on two people, $50 for each additional person (size of party limited by size of boat.) Large craft may include one or two groups fishing together. The 2001 prices for charter boat rentals ranged from $250 for two passengers for a 4-hour excursion to $300 per person for a long day of Gulf Stream adventure. If you head out on your own, an unguided powerboat costs from $30–$80 per hour (capacity is from four to ten people), rental gear extra. You need to purchase a saltwater fishing license if you fish from a boat; not necessary for shore-based fishing or recreational harvest of crab and shrimp. Here are some charter services in the Charleston area:

Like the early bird who gets the worm, the early riser catches the early charter and heads for Gulf Stream fishing grounds.

Wade Spees

Bohicket Boat (843-768-7294; www.bohicketmarina.com; Bohicket Marina, Seabrook Island) Large selection of boats from 14 to 55 feet for inshore bass and trout fishing, jetty fishing, and offshore fishing for shark, mackerel, tuna, marlin. Full-and half-day trips, on your own or with a guide.

Captain Ivan's Island Charters (843-762-2020; www.captainivan.com; 805 Deckhawk Retreat) Captain Ivan Schultz. Thirty-foot, wide beam boat with 21-passenger capacity, full- and half-day excursions to offshore reefs, trips to the Gulf Stream (12 hours).

Carolina Clipper (843-884-2992; Shem Creek, Mt. Pleasant) Captain Randolph Scott pilots a large boat with a snack bar and sundeck, and fully outfitted with gear and bait for Gulf Stream trips. Beginners welcome.

Fish Call Charters (843-509-7337; www.fishcall.com) Fly fishing and inshore light tackle for 1–3 anglers seeking drum, flounder, jack crevalle, trout, and mackerel.

Happyniss Sportfishing Charters (843-884-3225; Mt. Pleasant) Maximum party of six aboard 42-foot Bertram. Full-day for marlin and tuna; half-day for sailfish, wahoo, king mackerel.

FITNESS FACILITIES

Contemporary vacationers may leave their troubles behind, but few of them forget to pack their sweats. Though physical fitness hasn't ranked high among Charleston's pastimes (below hunting, fishing, eating, drinking, visiting, snoozing), the city is accommodating. Favorite places for runners are a loop that includes King St., the Battery and Meeting St., the Waterfront Park, and, for the mighty, round trip across the new James Island connector.

Fitness centers have machines and free weights; some offer day-rates for visitors. Your hotel concierge or bed-and-breakfast host may recommend a personal trainer. Resorts and large hotels have their own facilities or spas. The 2000 fees for daily use ranged from $8–$35.

Earthling (843-722-4737; 334 E. Bay St.).
The Firm (843-723-3476; 77 Wentworth St.).
Lifequest Fitness (843-571-2828; 35 Folly Rd.).
Stella Nova (843-723-0909; 78 Society St.).

GOLF

The first golf course in America was built in Charleston, and the founding of the nation's first golf club in 1786 followed immediately. Courses here, like the great houses or gardens, are designed with natural beauty in mind, built to accommodate the environmental elements, and intended to offer a variety of surprises that keep you interested. **Charleston Golf, Inc.** (843-805-3115 or 800-774-4444; www.charlestongolfinc.com) is a central information and reservation service for tee times, accommodations and discount airfares. Ask for their *Golf Guide*.

Fees vary according to seasonal categories, sometimes nine in all. Lowest rates are usually Dec.–Feb. Carts are required at peak playing times on many courses. For resort play, golf privileges are sometimes extended to non-resort guests: check with your concierge or call the resort directly. Club rentals and instruction are available at all courses. Greens fees/cart rentals reflect 2001 prices and do not include tax.

PUBLIC AND SEMIPRIVATE COURSES

Charleston Municipal Course (843-795-6517; 2110 Maybank Hwy.) Par 72. 6,400 yards. Greens fees during the week: $12 if you walk, $22 with a cart; on weekends, $15 if you walk, $25 with a cart. Twilight rates (after 3 p.m.) are $5. Pro: Richard Trenaman.

Charleston National (843-884-7799; www.charlestonnationalgolf.com; 1360 National Dr., Mt. Pleasant) Par 72. Range: 5,103-yard forward course to 6,975-yard champion course. Fees vary according to nine separate seasonal categories: $32–$60 (weekdays) and $40–$75 (weekends). Pro: Bart Wolfe.

Coosaw Creek Country Club (843-767-9000; 8610 Dorchester Rd., North Charleston) Par 71. Range: 5,064-yard forward course to 6,593-yard champion course. Fees: $40–$59 (weekdays) and $50–$64 (weekends). Pro: Eric Landfried.

Crowfield Golf & Country Club (843-764-4618; 300 Hamlet Circle, Goose Creek) Par 72. Range: 5,682-yard forward course to 7,003-yard champion course. Fees: $26–$38 (local residents) and $35–$45 (non-residents).

Dunes West (843-856-9000; www.golfduneswest.com; 3535 Wando Plantation Way, Mt. Pleasant) Par 72. Range: 5,278-yard forward course to 6,871-yard champion course. Fees: $39–$49 (weekdays) and $49–$85 (weekends). Pro: Devin Zemnickas.

Legend Oaks Plantation (888-821-4077; 118 Legend Oaks Way, Summerville) Par 72. Range: 4,954-yard forward course to 6,974 championship course. Fees: $32–$38 (weekdays) and $42–$48 (weekends). Pro: Steve Smart.

The Links at Stono Ferry (843-763-1817; 5365 Forest Oaks Dr., Hollywood) Par 72. Range: 4,928-yard forward course to 6,616-yard championship course. Fees: $34–$43 (non-resident weekdays) and $29–$33 (resident weekdays); $38–$48 (non-resident weekends) and $33–$38 (resident weekends). Pro: Greg Wood.

Patriots Point Links (843-881-0042; www.patriotspointlinks.com; 1 Patriots Pt. Rd.,Mt. Pleasant) Par 72. Range: 5,562-yard forward course to 6,856-yard championship course. Fees: $40–$50 (weekdays) and $55–$75 (weekends). Pro: Chad Leonard.

Shadowmoss Plantation Golf Club (843-556-8251or 800-338-4971; Hwy. 61) Par 72. Range: 2,700-yard forward course to 6,701-yard championship course. Fees: $24–$34 (weekdays) and $29–$37 (weekends). Pro: Robert Wolfe.

Courses at Charleston-area Resorts

If you are planning a vacation around golf, you might save yourself travel time by staying in resorts or gated communities where the game is the focus. Accommodations range from deluxe hotel rooms to villas and rental homes; renting through the resort yields savings in greens fees. These resorts also have complete recreational layouts which include swimming pools, tennis courts, and marinas. Here's a list of some well-known resort golf courses near Charleston and their 2000 fees.

Kiawah Island (843-768-2121 or 888-854-2924; www.kiawahgolf.com; 12 Beach Dr., Kiawah) Four championship courses have been carved out of Kiawah's gorgeous Sea Island landscape by the game's top designers: Pete Dye, Jack Nicklaus, Gary Player, and Tom Fazio. A fifth course is just off-island. *The Ocean Course* (Par 72. Range: 5,327-yard forward course to 7,371 championship course) is probably the best known: the 1991 Ryder Cup was played here, and it was cited by *Golf Digest* as the toughest resort course in the country. *Osprey Point* (Par 72. Range: 5,122-yard forward course to 6,678-yard championship course) is consistently ranked in the country's top 75 courses. *Cougar Point* (Par 72. Range: 4,944-yard forward course to 6,861-yard championship course) and *Turtle Point* (Par 72. Range: 5,285-yard forward course to 6,914-yard championship course) make good use of Kiawah's unique geography — bracketed by the Atlantic and the River. *Oak Point* (Par 72. Range: 4,671 yard forward course to 6,759 championship course) is part of the resort but located on nearby Haulover Creek. Fees for the Ocean Course are $135–$225 (non-resort guests) and $99–$170 (resort guests). For Osprey, Turtle and Cougar, fees are $95–$160 (non-resort guests) and $63–$125 (resort guests). The fees at Oak Point are $55–$85 (non-resort guests) and $40–$75 (resort guests).

Seabrook Island (843-768-1000 or 800-845-2475; www.theclubatseabrook-island. com; 1002 Landfall Way, Seabrook Island). *Crooked Oaks* (Par 72. Range: 5,250-yard forward course to 6,832-yard championship course, designed by Robert Trent Jones, Sr.) and *Ocean Winds* (Par 72. Range: 5,524-yard forward course to 6,805-yard championship course, a Willard Byrd design) won the resort a silver medal commendation from *Golf* magazine. Visiting players must be resort guests. Fees are $60–$120.

Wild Dunes (843-886-2164 or 800-845-8880; www.wilddunes.com; Isle of Palms) Tom Fazio designed both courses: *The Links* (Par 72. Range: 4,849-yard forward course to 6,722-yard championship course) offers oceanfront golf at its best, wind and water hazards notwithstanding. Fees: $100–$160. *The Harbor* (Par 70. Range: 4,774-yard forward course to 6,446-yard championship course) features challenging holes that are, in some cases, an island apart. Fees: $47–$100. Make reservations up to 90 days in advance.

HORSEBACK RIDING

Wade Spees

Riding at Storybrook Stables.

The first racecourse in the Lowcountry was built near Charleston in 1735, and the South Carolina Jockey Club was founded there in 1758. Equestrian showmanship, hunting, and riding for pleasure are still popular forms of recreation.

If you want to take a trail ride during your visit, call one of the following stables to make advance arrangements. They may take you from a cypress swamp to the Francis Marion National Forest. The prices in 2001 started at $20 per hour.

Charleston Happy Trails (843-559-5427; www.charlestonhappytrails.com; 2729 Bohicket Rd., Johns Island).
Nature Adventures Outfitters (843-928-3316; www.natureadventuresoutfitters.bizonthe.net; P.O. Box 247, Awendaw).
Stono Ferry Stables (843-763-0566; 5304 Stono Ferry Course, Hollywood).
Stono River Stable and Farm (843-559-0773; 2962 Hut Rd., John's Island).
Storybrook Farm (843-571-2820; 1136 Bee's Ferry Rd.).

HUNTING

In the Lowcountry you can hunt a variety of quarry including deer, wild turkey, dove, quail, feral hog, duck, fox, rabbit, woodcock, snipe, and clapper rail. What's more, you can do so during seasons which start as early as late summer (deer) and last through fall and winter until late spring (turkey). The Lowcountry has the longest deer season in the country and is considered the premiere spot on the East Coast to bag marsh hens.

There are six Game Management Areas in the Lowcountry; hunters at work within them are required to have a variety of licenses and permits, to abide by strict size and bag limits, obtain landowners' permission before hunting on private lands, and observe safe and ethical hunting practices in the field. For information, maps, and regulations concerning South Carolina hunting areas, contact the *Wildlife and Marine Resources Dept.* (803-734-3888; P.O. Box 167, Columbia, SC 29202). Outdoor recreation stores that specialize in hunting also provide tips, information, and licenses.

Some of the most popular public hunting grounds in the Charleston area are located in the *Francis Marion National Forest* (843-336-3248; 2421 Witherbee Rd., Cordsville), *Webb Wildlife Center and Palachucola* (843-625-2114; Garnett) and *Bear Island* (843-844-2952; Green Pond).

If you prefer a more managed hunt, consider the guiding, cleaning, and transportation services of plantations that specialize in various kinds of game-hunting, according to the season. Some offer overnight accommodations. For information, contact the *Lowcountry Tourism Commission* (800-528-6870; 1 Lowcountry Lane, Yemassee, SC 29945). *Total Charters* (843-722-2400; www.totalcharters.com) offers fishing and hunting expeditions in the Lowcountry and elsewhere.

The *Southeastern Wildlife Exposition,* which takes place every February in Charleston, is the region's most comprehensive gathering of fishermen, hunters, outfitters, and artists who specialize in subjects of interest to sportsmen. Display sites scattered throughout the Charleston area feature Lowcountry and Western collectibles, crafts, decoys, antiques, and posters. A free shuttle bus service can take you to them. In addition, there are presentations and demonstrations. Write: **EXPO Information,** 211 Meeting St., Charleston, SC 29401; (843-723-1748 or 800-221-5273; www.sewe.com).

NATURE PRESERVES

Many small islands, swamps, or boggy necks nestled in the creeks and riverways of the Lowcountry offer natural camouflage and a pristine habitat to the wildlife that live or migrate there. Some are more developed than others — with boardwalks or marked trails — but none require strenuous activity or advanced knowledge for enjoyment. If you are interested in the ecology of the Lowcountry, the life-cycle of the marsh, the effects of tidal flow on vegetation, and the interdependence of plant and animal life, these sites will give you a feel for the rhythms of the Lowcountry beneath the surface.

Wood storks and egrets share space in local nature preserves and gardens.

Wade Spees

ACE Basin (Access off Hwy. 17 at Green Pond, S.C. 26, Bennett's Point, Bear Island; 843-889-3084) A consortium of private individuals, non-profit organizations, state, and federal agencies have joined together to preserve some 350,000 acres of diverse habitat, including several islands, at the center of the Lowcountry. It is one of the largest undeveloped estuarine sanctuaries on the East Coast. ACE takes its name from the area it embraces: the lands and waters amidst the Ashepoo, Combahee and Edisto Rivers on both sides of

St. Helena Sound, a fishery so rich and pristine it accounts for nearly 10 percent of the state's shellfish harvest. Seventeen endangered species make their home here. Bring binoculars and cameras. ***Bohicket Boat*** (843-768-7294) and ***Cap'n Richards Ace Basin Tours*** (843-766-9664) can take you there by water for $55–$65 per person.

Audubon Swamp Garden (843-571-1266 or 800-367-3517; www.magnoliaplan tation.com; 3550 Ashley River Rd.) Sixty acres of blackwater cypress and tupelo swamp, with trails and footbridges through virgin pine forests, wild flowers, and exotic plants: this is a place that impressed John J. Audubon 150 years ago. Self-guided tour. Admission $5 (adults); $4 (teens); $3 (children 6–12).

Caw Caw Interpretive Center (843-889-8898; www.ccprc.com; 5200 Savannah Hwy. Ravenel, 20 miles south of Charleston. Closed Mon.) You can still see the earth dikes, floodgates, and rice fields that originally marked this former plantation, now home to endangered species, songbirds, and migratory birds. There are seven miles of trails, a swamp boardwalk, and exhibits which highlight the contributions of the African-Americans who worked here long ago. A good stop if you're heading down the coast to Edisto, Beaufort, or Savannah.

Cypress Gardens (843-553-0515; 3030 Cypress Gardens Rd., Moncks Corner. I-26 West to Exit 208, then to Hwy. 52 north) Take a guided tour or paddle a flat-bottom boat yourself through an old rice plantation reserve, now a protected natural swamp garden. A succession of blooms, from the earliest camellia and narcissus to trumpet vine and azalea, brightens the shadowy cypress forest. Open 9–5 daily. Adults $7, seniors $6, children $3, under 5 free.

Francis Biedler Forest in Four Holes Swamp (843-462-2150; 336 Sanctuary Rd., Harleyville. From I-95 take I-26 east to Exit 177, then south on S.C. 453 to U.S. 178. Follow signs east on 178. From Charleston, take I-26 west to Exit 187, then south on S.C. 27 to U.S. 78.) The 11,000-acre sanctuary, managed by the National Audubon Society, contains the largest remaining virgin stand of bald cypress and tupelo gum trees in the world. There's a self-guided boardwalk and Visitor Center, but the point here is to walk quietly and observe well, to absorb what you can on your own without the experience being "packaged" in any way. Open 9–5 daily except Mondays. Adults $5, children $2.50, under 6 free.

POLO

Spectators can pack a tailgate picnic and enjoy Sunday afternoon polo games in September and October, April and May at ***Stono Ferry*** (843-766-6208; 5365 Forest Oaks Dr., Hollywood). Admission charged for some charity polo events.

TENNIS

There are about three dozen public courts in city parks, tennis centers, and county recreation areas, and, of course, manicured layouts at the resorts. Your hotel concierge or bed-and-breakfast host should be able to direct you. Good news for Charleston tennis, the longest-running professional event in women's tennis, the Family Circle Cup (800-677-2293 or www.familycircle-cup.com), has moved here from its longtime home at Sea Pines, on Hilton Head. Matches in April will inaugurate a new facility at Daniel Island.

Charleston Tennis Center (843-724-7402; Farmfield Rd., west of Charleston on Hwy. 17) has 15 outdoor hard courts, lit for night play. $2.50 per hour per person. Visitors should call ahead to check availability, or may reserve by paying in advance.

Some Lowcountry resorts also offer playing-time for non-resort guests on a space-available basis. Fees vary depending on season and time of day. Reservations are required. Inquire about tennis packages.

Kiawah Island (843-768-2121).
Shadowmoss Plantation (843-556-8251).
Wild Dunes (843-886-6000; Isle of Palms).

WINDSURFING

Although the currents and tides make for tricky windsurfing conditions, the Lowcountry's warm water temperature and wide-open spaces have attracted windsurfers for years. Check local forecasts and tides before you go (843-744-3207 is the number for Charleston weather; 843-588-2261 for McKevlin's surf report) and surf in well-known areas. Even experienced windsurfers have found themselves thrust well beyond the confines of, say, Charleston Harbor by the outgoing tide, only to find they have to wait until it turns to paddle or sail in.

Many resorts have windsurfers to rent, or provide instruction first on land, then in sheltered creeks or on a quiet stretch of beach. For more information, inquire at sporting goods shops or call some of the following rental/instruction agencies.

Barrier Island Surf Shop (843-588-6666; 32 Center St., Folly Beach).
Folly Windsurfing (843-795-8872; 878 Folly Rd., Charleston).
McKevlin's Surf Shop (843-886-8912; 1101 Ocean Blvd., Isle of Palms; 843-588-2247; 8 Center St., Folly Beach).

SHOPPING

The time has passed since the port of Charleston was small and accessible, since residents had the pleasure of observing dozens of ships along the wharves and wondering what lay in their holds. Yet such pastimes of commercial life were once commonplace. The anticipation of imports — teas, seeds, books, furniture, china, mail — and the reciprocal sending of an export was a satisfying part of life. If the export represented the result of what plantation slavery had been designed to produce, the import confirmed Charleston's view of itself as a tasteful, cultivated, wealthy society. An ordinary impulse to consume took on meaning as part of a bigger equation.

Today, the impulse is still there, as is the anticipation, but no longer down at the wharves. Now it happens in small places: in glossy boutiques, in shops in old houses, in the open air of a busy corner, in commercial buildings on ballast-stone alleys, under the handsome brick and lattice sheds that line the center of Market St. for several blocks between Meeting St. and East Bay St. The surge in commercial rents due to Charleston's popularity has forced the relocation of several unique and modest stores, the kind of stores that set a tone for a place but don't make a big splash doing so. Seek them out on Queen St., Broad St., Church St., Wentworth St.

ANTIQUES

Several shops with "home" as their theme line upper King Street, just north of Market Street.

Wade Spees

The period of poverty that engulfed the Lowcountry after the Civil War called for living by austere means and resourcefulness. It was not a time when renovating and redecorating was considered possible.

Some residents count this as a blessing: a lot of old houses, and all they contained, were spared the wrecker's ball. In the 1920s, the houses caught the eye of northern decorators and curators, who either imitated their look or purchased them, literally, lock, stock, barrel, and window sash. Later, when the families who had lived in the old houses produced a generation with the means to redecorate them, the urge to adorn them in the old style prevailed. Today, antiques stores throughout the Lowcountry retail this classic look, both in original pieces and in excellent reproductions.

While taste, or a good eye, is hard to define, it seems clear that the very experience of living in Charleston has produced antiques dealers who have absorbed its lessons of enduring beauty. They seem to know what fits — whether it's a pair of simple sterling candlesticks or a stunning chest-on-chest.

A short list of some of the more distinctive antiques shops follows. If you are poking around for something in particular, or a type of thing, ask for it. It's a small world, and dealers should be able to direct you elsewhere.

A'Riga IV Antiques (843-577-3075; 204 King St.) An impressive collection of old scientific instruments and medical kits, some of which can be oddly beautiful as art objects, as well as apothecary jars and ceramic containers that were put to domestic use years ago.

Even fine antiques stores have a relaxed feeling of home.

Wade Spees

Century House Antiques (843-722-6248; 56 1/2 Queen St.) There's a fineness about this shop and the nature of its stock — English and Chinese export porcelain, botanicals, bird prints. It's the feeling you get from being in the presence of an eye that's appreciated beauty for a long time. Behind the Thomas Elfe House.

Charleston Antique Mall (843-769-6119; 4 Avondale Ave. at Hwy. 17, 10 minutes south of downtown.) An interior mall with 20 vendors who sell a mixture of collectibles, antiques and art. Fun to browse for an hour.

Chicora Antiques (843-723-1711; www.chicoraantiques.com; 102 Church St.) A special eye for decorative art from the Federal and Classical periods make this an unusual shop — although there's plenty of mahogany and brass, too.

D&D Antiques (843-853-5266; 190 King St.) Nautical objects and books, including model boats and burgees, fishing creels and antique spinning rods, and a treasure trove of platters, china and serving pieces retired from use in yacht club dining rooms.

Estate Antiques (843-723-2362; www.estateantiquesinc.com; 155 King St.) A superb collection of American antiques, especially Southern and Charleston pieces, and decorative art accessories mostly dating from before 1830. Jim and Harriet Pratt know their merchandise from the inside out and they willingly share their knowledge with even the most committed browsers. The best antique store in Charleston.

Gates of Charleston (843-958-0040; 73 Broad St.) Architectural objects for interiors and a nice selection of pieces for the garden, to use as furniture or as accents to plantings, including old painted ironwork, baskets and vases, and enamel washstands.

George C. Birlant & Co. (843-722-3842; 191 King St.) In business for more than 70 years, selling brass, silver, crystal, and small and large English antiques, which they import directly. Big old-fashioned picture windows open onto the street; inside there's lots of room to walk around. Reproductions of Charleston's own cypress-and-iron "Battery Bench" available.

Historic Charleston Reproductions (843-723-8292; www.historiccharleston.org; 105 Broad St.) Adaptations and reproductions of 18th- and 19th-century furniture, lamps, fabric, brass, wall coverings, and accessories that once graced Charleston homes. High-quality workmanship by companies like Baker Furniture, Scalamandre, and Mottahedeh.

Moore House Antiques (843-722-8065; 150 King St.) Fine American pieces where the styles from England show through, as in Sheraton side tables. Shelves of Chinese export porcelain, Oriental rugs.

Ridler Page Rare Maps (843-723-1734; 205 King St.) Antique maps in a variety of sizes, some as old as the 16th century, many hand-colored.

Shalimar Antiques (843-766-1529; 2418 Savannah Hwy.) A totally unprepossessing place from the outside — it looks like an old motel — but inside, the collection of grandfather clocks, pine tables and beds, primitives, and trunks is pure Southern country.

BOOKS

Local independent book dealers know their stock, particularly as it concerns the history, literature and art of the South, have a good relationship with their customers and their preferences, and thus are a source of suggestions. The national chains, for their part, showcase titles relating to local topics in history, gardening, culture, and photography. There are also several shops for used books and rare and historic volumes.

Atlantic Books (843-723-4751; 310 King St. and 191 E. Bay St.; 843-723-7654.) Thousands of used books on many subjects. Very strong in local history and memoir, military titles, fiction, Civil War, Southern authors.

Audubon Shop (843-723-6171; 99 South Market St.) Field guides galore.

Barnes & Noble (843-572-2322; 7620 Rivers Ave., Charleston); (843-556-6561; 1812 Sam Rittenberg Blvd., Charleston); (843-216-9756; 1716 Town Center Way, Mt. Pleasant) The big book retailer has established itself here with an enormous quantity of books and magazines.

Book Exchange (843-556-5051; 1219 Savannah Hwy.) New and used books and collectible comics.

Boomers' Books (843-722-2666; 420 King St.) Broad selection in fiction, children's, antiques, and architecture.

You could easily spend a quiet hour browsing at Charleston's Chapter Two, a bookstore for children and adults, and you're welcome to do so.

Wade Spees

Chapter Two (843-722-4238 or 800-722-4238; 249 Meeting St.) The best in Charleston, consistently rated among the best in the region. Superb Southern history and art sections, fine magazines, loyal customers who offer suggestions as you browse. A complete inventory of small press-run books of local interest — memoirs, photo collections, family and plantation histories — which will deepen your appreciation of the area. Open late Thursdays and Fridays. Watch for book signings.

Charleston Rare Book Co. (843-723-3330; 66 Church St.) Specializing in Charleston and Lowcountry books, including a good nautical section.

Historic Charleston Foundation Museum Shop and Bookstore (843-724-8484; www.historiccharleston.org; 108 Meeting St.) If you want to know more about regional history and the decorative arts, preservation efforts, architecture, and related topics, stop in here. Also many volumes about historic properties here and elsewhere, as well as an excellent children's section.

Pauline Books & Media (843-577-0175; 243 King St.) A religious bookstore with Bibles and a nice selection for younger readers.

Petterson Antiques (843-723-5714; 201 King St.) If the old books and magazines that sit on carts outside the store don't attract your eye, duck in and cast your gaze to the shelves and cases within. It may take time to find a treasure, but after all, you can never get enough of the atmosphere, which is free.

Preservation Society of Charleston (843-722-4360; www.preservationsociety.org; 147 King St.) The Society's headquarters has an unhurried, old-world feeling, with many books on Charleston history, art, architecture, and culture.

Waldenbooks (843-766-5879; 2070 Sam Rittenberg Blvd.) Best-sellers, good history and military section, coffee-table collections of photographs, regional cookbooks.

CLOTHING

In Charleston, people still wear hats. Not just baseball caps or fedoras, but straw hats, garden-party hats, fishing caps, and velvet berets — hats with attitude. They also dress their children, boys and girls, in smockery and suits. Yet among a population that tends to sartorial conservatism, there is usually a fillip of embellishment to be found, accompanied by the natural confidence to pull it off.

Women will be especially fortunate to be shopping for clothes here. There are several comfortable boutiques (low-key, welcoming, with excellent suggestions) that offer unusual suits and separates in linen, silk, and cotton blends, in a range of styles to suit most ages. Given the temperate climate, this is the place to find shawls and patterned sweaters rather than tweeds and down.

The following suggestions do not list clothing stores that are part of a national chain, although those to be found in Charleston include Polo, Laura Ashley, Gap, Victoria's Secret, Saks Fifth Avenue, and Talbot's.

A.J. Davis & Co. (843-577-3088; 296 King St.) Men's clothes, plain and cheerfully sporty, and accessories.

Berlin's (843-722-1665; 114 King St.) Men's and women's clothes in traditional styles and top quality brands. Since 1883.

Bits of Lace (843-577-0999; 212 King St.) Fine lingerie and other little fancy things for women.

Bob Ellis Shoes (843-722-2605; 332 King St.) Vast selection of fine footwear for men and women and a sales staff that keeps bringing out the boxes.

Christian Michi (843-723-0575; 220 King St.) For women, high fashion from top European and American designers. It's as if a small section of SoHo left Manhattan for life in the provinces.

Copper Penny (843-723-2999; 311 King St.) If you saw it in *Vogue* or *InStyle*, it's here, too. Up to the minute fashion and accessories (even if they seem a little too edgy for Charleston.)

Eighty-Two Church (843-723-7511; 108 Church St.) If this store were anywhere but in the "South of Broad" district, it would probably be a museum by now. A lovely selection of hand-smocked dresses for girls to size 14, bonnets, clothes for newborns, christening outfits, sweaters, cotton rompers, and seersucker playsuits. Boy's clothing to size 6. Very nice baby gifts, too. A Charleston treasure run by an extended family.

Ellington (843-722-7999; 193 King St.) If you're returning to office life after a break and need something unusual and spiffy, or if you don't dress up much but like to wear a finely tailored piece when you do, look here for clothes with elegant, modern lines and solid construction.

Granny's Goodies (843-577-6200; 301 King St.) Antique and vintage clothes for men, women, and children: poodle skirts, Hawaiian shirts, gloves and gauze, fur-trimmed opera capes, boas. Great selection and guaranteed laughs.

M. Dumas & Sons (843-723-8603; 294 King St.) Even the wallpaper here is riding to hounds. The original source for what has become an "American Country" look.

RTW (843-577-9748; www.rtwcharleston.com; 186 King St.) A boutique for women who delight in gorgeous fabrics, sweaters that tumble with color, one-of-a-kind shirts, hats, scarves, and accessories, and who like to dress with a sense of individuality and esprit. A rare find in any city.

Worthwhile (843-723-4418; www.shopworthwhile.com; 268 King St.) This wonderful, crazy store defies easy categorization: it's ironic (could be a 5&10 for yuppies, lots of small beautiful objects for the house) but sweet (flax and linen clothes for women, goofy baby hats). Cotton sweaters, T-shirts and leggings, nightclothes.

CRAFTS

The Lowcountry's *sea grass baskets* are a regional specialty, and if you're interested in them, you won't have far to look. The basket weavers are out every day where *Meeting Street* and *King Street* meet *Broad Street* and in the *Market Area*. Prices vary for items as small as keepsake decorations or as large as fanner baskets and hampers. You're welcome to watch the process, which incorporates palmetto strips and pine straw with the pale grass. Other weavers sell their work at stands located north of Charleston on *Highway 17*.

American Originals (843-853-5034; www.americanoriginals.cc; 153 East Bay St., second floor) Contemporary crafts by local and national artists whose artistry and high standards shine through in glass, pottery, jewelry, pictures, textiles, and more.

Cabbage Row Shoppe (843-722-1528; 110 Church St.) For needlework canvases, threads, yarns and patterns, and old Charleston accents and design ideas, come here.

Ceramics Cafe (843-722-7687; 432 King St.) Just behind the Visitors Center, a paint-your-own pottery studio in which you select a piece (from dozens available), paint it with glaze, and get it fired. It's one way to see if Charleston's beauty inspires. Wine and coffee available to stimulate your imagination.

Charleston Crafts (843-723-2938; 87 Hasell St.) Crafts and exhibits by members of this local co-op, who are considered superior in their fields, be they weavers, sculptors, or photographers.

People, Places & Quilts (843-937-9333; 1 Henrietta St.) Folk art, quilts and quilting supplies, patterns, and sewing notions.

FARMS AND FARMERS' MARKETS

The Lowcountry growing season lasts from February to the first frost in November, with many crops being planted more than once. A visit to the outdoor market at Hutson St. (one block north of *Marion Square*) on Saturday mornings between April and November may yield anything from fresh basil to watermelon. Farmstands on the Sea Islands have an enormous range of produce, their own and other farmers', as well as jellies, relishes, shrimp, and fruit. Three near Charleston are: *Stono Farm Market* (843-559-9999; 842 Main Rd., John's Island); *Leland Farms* (843-559-1296; 4801 Maybank Hwy., Wadmalaw Island) and *Rosebank Farms* (843-768-9139; 3953 Betsy Kerrison Parkway, John's Island).

The *Charleston Tea Plantation* (843-559-0383 or 800-443-5987; 6617 Maybank Hwy., Wadmalaw Island) where American Classic Tea is grown, is unique in the nation. You may stroll out to the tea fields or watch a video on the harvesting and curing process. Open weekdays from 10 a.m. to 4 p.m. (Take Hwy. 17 to SC 171. Turn east toward Folly Beach and soon after, turn south on SC 700, Maybank Highway. The plantation is located at nearly the end of this road.)

GALLERIES

The recently organized Charleston Fine Art Dealers Association, whose members run eight galleries in Charleston, is a force for appreciation of both the work of the Charleston Renaissance artists of the 20th-century and of the New Renaissance artists in the Charleston of the 21st. Their Fine Arts Annual each November, held in association with the Gibbes Museum, consists of lectures and gallery receptions designed to educate and celebrate the enduring work of local and regional artists. There are also galleries for strong contemporary art from national artists, as well as places where the collections are more intimate reflections of Lowcountry light and life. You can browse some Charleston galleries online at www.artnet.com.

Audubon Gallery (843-853-1100; www.audubongallery.com; 177 King St.) Fine new and antique wildlife prints, duck and bird decoys and carvings, original paintings and watercolors. Artists of the Southeastern Wildlife Exposition show their work here all year.

Bernie Horton Gallery (843-958-0014; 111 Church St.) Here are the colors of the Lowcountry, from the fluorescent green of the summer marsh and the pink and purple at sunset, to the white boots of clammers. Originals and limited edition giclee reproductions of the countryside and the people and animals who live in it.

Carolina Fine Paintings and Prints (843-723-2266; 188 King St.) Antique prints by masters such as Audubon and Catesby, pre-1945 American art, and contemporary realistic art by local artists: Stephen Chesley, Margaret Peery, Jim Smeal, Anna Onufer, Craig Crawford, and Johnson Hagood, who is often in the shop, gracious and well informed. Featuring the work of the Charleston Renaissance: Alice Ravenel Huger Smith, Anna Heyward Taylor, Alfred Hutty, and others.

The Charleston Renaissance Gallery (843-723-0025; www. artnet.com/hicklin. html; 103 Church St.) Located in a beautifully restored post-Revolutionary brick building, Robert Hicklin's gallery is at the forefront of renewed interest in Charleston's 20th-century art history — and it's worth going to for the education it offers. West Fraser's city scenes and Lowcountry landscapes, some in oil, some in watercolor, are showcased, as are 19th century paintings and sculptures.

Coleman Fine Art (843-853-7000; 45 Hasell St.) Members of the gallery include a number of artists working in a realistic style in oils and watercolors as well as the paintings of portraitist and illustrator Mary Whyte. Smith Coleman III, who owns the gallery, also restores damaged works of art and makes lovely frames.

Eva Carter Gallery (843-722-0506; 132 East Bay St.) Abstract oils, works on paper, and sculpture.

Gallery Two Queen (843-853-8512; 2 Queen St.) Marty Whaley Adams is a prolific artist who works in many media; here you'll find her colorful, vivid paintings of still lives and Lowcountry landscapes. Also textile art by Paige Hathaway Thorn.

Jerald Melberg Gallery (843-965-5000; 8 Vendue Range) Representing contemporary American art in a variety of styles, from glass to textiles, including artists Dale Chihuly and Wolf Kahn; considered one of the best in the South.

John Carroll Doyle Art Gallery (843-577-7344; 54 Broad St.) Doyle is one of the painters in the "new" Charleston Renaissance, capturing people in intense moments (like blues harmonica players) and teasing that intensity out of landscapes and animals.

Martin Gallery (843-723-7378; 57 Queen St.) Contemporary art and elegant craft work, including jewelry incorporating precious stones and sculpted gold.

Nina Liu and Friends (843-722-2724; 24 State St.) Wonderful contemporary art in media such as fabric, collage, ceramic, paper, and glass, that can be startling, magical, and strong. The owner is an artist with a fine eye.

Robert B. Fraser (843-884-5717; 953 Covenant Sq., Snee Farm, Mt. Pleasant) Specializing in sporting and southern art, and in contemporary and early-20th century Charleston artists.

Wells Gallery (843-853-3233; 103 Broad St.) Contemporary art of nationally recognized artists such as Susan Mayfield West, John Carroll Doyle, Betty Anglin Smith, and Rhett Thurman. A good stop to see how the Lowcountry experience is being realistically brought to life.

GIFTS

The African American Gallery (843-722-8224; 43 John St.) A large gallery with unique gifts representing work by African-Americans in many media, including original paintings, prints, wearable art, crafts, and framing services.

Fifty-Two Five (843-722-3525; www.corporaterocksucks.com; 75 Wentworth.) New/used records, cds, videos, along with a great selection of posters and tee shirts. A shop with brains and attitude. Unique in the city.

Karen Vournakis (843 723 3921; 125 King St.) Evocative, dreamy hand painted photographs of Charleston and the Lowcountry.

Quadrupeds (843-534-1700; 106 Church St.) A tiny shop run by a young designer whose eye, which would make a whole room go bright, is apparent here in a selection of sublime Japanese ceramics, boxes, toile clutches, textiles for the table, and doggie things. But you cannot take the Jack Russell home.

Queen Charlotte Antiques (843-722-9121; www.queencharlotte.com; 173 King St.) Quirky pieces for the garden (small enough to carry), old sconces, wooden bowls, and little accent pieces which convey the look of old Charleston.

Riverrun (843-723-0200; www.riverrun-charleston.com; 6 Beaufain St.) An Irish specialty shop located on a side street just north of Charleston Place that has Nicholas Mosse pottery, photographs, and Irish books, tweed caps, and linens.

The Smoking Lamp (843-577-7339; 189 East Bay St.) Everything for the smoker, including unique boxes, pipes, and other comforts for a maligned modern species.

GOURMET AND HEALTH FOOD STORES

Aloha Natural Foods (843-849-5521; 628 Coleman Blvd., Mt. Pleasant) Organic produce and juice bar, books, herbs, face, and body products.

Carolina Wine and Cheese (843-577-6144; 54 1/2 Wentworth St.) Fresh German bread, excellent deli meats, coffees and teas, wine, of course, and all the makings for home-brewed beer.

Hoppin' John's (800-828-4412; www.hoppinjohns.com) Chef John Martin Taylor's wonderful shop is no more — he's taken it on-line. A marvelous selection of Lowcountry foodstuffs like his signature grits, cornmeal and corn flour (order early, demand outpaces supply), chow chow, pickles, real hoppin' john for New Year's, and salty Virginia country ham.

Olde Colony Bakery (842-722-2147; www.southerntreats.com; 280 King St.) The source, since 1919, for benne wafers and other regional southern treats.

Raspberry's (843-556-0076; 1331 Ashley River Rd.) Natural, unprocessed foods including grains, herbs, bulk flour, and organic produce. Vitamins and body care items, too.

Uncork (843-577-9303; 333 King St.) Very fine wines and snacks, and lots of ideas for bottles under $10.

HOME FURNISHINGS/KITCHENWARE

Blink (843-577-5688; www.thinkblink.com. 62-B Queen St.) The owner, and the gifted eye behind the wonderful ceramic, glass, metal, and fabric objects in this tiny shop, is Mary Leonard. Nothing in Charleston compares — perhaps nothing south of SoHo.

Like many shops in Charleston, Blink is an expression of unique taste and a celebration of modern style that challenges and complements its historic setting.

Wade Spees

Charleston Gardens (843-723-0252; www.charlestongardens.com; 61 Queen St.) Furnishings, accessories (botanical prints, old posters, lamps, pots) and books, as well as serious gardening tools and live topiaries. A beautiful, rather serious place, with a back garden courtyard.

Details (843-723-5300; 115 Calhoun St.) Objects both new and found, assorted in size and function and usefulness. Use them to create a corner of interest in a plain house (good wedding/housewarming ideas here) or to calm down a city apartment.

fred (843-723-5699; 237 King St.) Clean, spare design in black and white and stainless steel: kitchen basics, cutlery, towels and racks, mechanical wonders. A great local favorite.

Homestore Carolina (843-853-2319; 319 King St.) Cookbooks, gifts, ceramics, table settings that bring Provence or Tuscany to your sunny rooms.

Indigo attracts locals and visitors with its amazing variety of whimsical, decorative and practical items – from a flying pig to a pocket knife.

Wade Spees

Indigo (843-723-2983; indigohome.com; #4 Vendue Range) Fred and Beth Moore's creative lives, interests, and taste converge here in a selection of patterned tablecloths and painted mats, iron sculpture, handmade frames, ceramics, little metal animals like crabs and bunnies. A spirited, joyful store.

Le Creuset (843-723-4191; 221 Meeting St.) Famous French enameled cookware at factory prices. (The factory, and another store, is located off I-95 at Yemassee if you're heading south.)

Metropolitan Deluxe (843-722-0436; 164 Market St.) The idea of an old mercantile store, updated. Several large rooms are piled high with household goods, from the opulent (velvet upholstery, leather boxes, brass lamps, high-count cotton sheets) to the funky (wire baskets, painted benches, canvas chairs, fresh flowers.)

Studio Marc Howard (843-722-2762; www.studioliving.com; 314 King St.) Lush, multi-colored leather pillows, museum-store desk accessories, modern clocks, high-tech floor lamps.

SPORTING GOODS AND CLOTHING

Bicycle Shoppe (843-722-8168; 280 Meeting St.) Rent or buy bikes, or choose from cases full of bike hardware and gadgets.

The great outdoors beckon at Half Moon Outfitters, with its wet suits and river shoes, kayaks, backpacks, and durable outerwear.

Wade Spees

Half-Moon Outfitters (843-853-0990; 320 King St.) The most durable and fashionable outdoor wear (like Patagonia) is here, plus coats, tents, packs, camping supplies, and the best advice on local outdoor adventuring to be found in the city.

King Street Skates (843-723-5811; 433 King St.) All the brands of skateboards and the fashion stuff that goes with the sport.

Outdoor Outfitters (843-763-9115; 1662 Savannah Hwy.) A one-stop shop if you're going to be in the woods, the marsh, or on the water.

CHAPTER FOUR
An Old City, A Modern City
SAVANNAH

It's no secret that the preservation of the great places of the Lowcountry, including the city of Savannah, occurred less as a result of enlightened social policy than from post-Civil War impoverishment. Indeed, the many years of slow growth and stalled expectations treated Savannah as they did Charleston, and to this day the cities share similar assets including vibrant, architecturally intact, downtown historic districts; a heritage that reflects the diverse contributions of genera-

Wade Spees

The Waving Girl statue on River Street, expressing the sadness of farewell, is a memorial to the lives of lighthouse keepers and the safe passage their watchfulness provided for generations of sailors.

tions of residents; and a culture enriched by unique musical, religious, culinary, and artistic contributions.

Yet in several subtle ways, Savannah today is a far more complex and interesting *modern* city than Charleston is. For whatever historic reasons, and they run deep, it seems to have achieved an unusual sense of detachment. For every bold statement claimed about its history or beauty, there will be lurking on the lips of someone nearby a counter-claim, a small sarcasm. (Once upon a time during the cotton boom, Savannah madly envied New York City for its commercial muscle; 160 years later the two cities share a liking for gesture and attitude.)

This trait was evident even during the Civil War. Legend has it that General W. T. Sherman spared Savannah because the city was beautiful, the women were gracious, and the parties were just what he needed at the end of his blazing "March To the Sea" campaign. He took up residence, was indeed feted, and, in a remarkable telegraph of 1864, offered the unmolested city to President Lincoln as a Christmas gift.

Well, Savannah is still beautiful, and they're still partying. (This quality, and the world it describes, is revealed with great skill in the best book on Savannah, John Berendt's 1994 work, *Midnight in the Garden of Good and Evil.*) The blend of reverence and hilarity, of high-mindedness and getting by, gives the city its character. In fact, as time passes, it becomes more palpable. When the local minor league baseball team renamed itself the Sand Gnats (the top choice in a city-wide poll), it chose for its slogan *"Bite Me."* The city literally shuts down every St. Patrick's Day to accommodate 24 hours of revelry. Clearly, this is not Charleston, a city thought by some Southerners as being "wrapped too tight." Savannah doesn't mind having been thought of as too sleepy or too indifferent to capitalize on its own potential.

By the time that national economic and social development did recommend change — after World War II, after a manufacturing and military base undergirded the economy, after federally mandated integration — Savannah residents with the means and interest to do so were faced with reconciling their historic cultural identity, on which they relied so deeply, with a post-war world which placed increasing value on money, mobility, and a celebration of things modern and new. The time had come to set the ongoing physical and intellectual activities associated with historic preservation, neighborhood renovation, and tourist attraction on a larger and more public stage. This they did, and in the process became what might be called curators of their own collection, a collection whose very display case — the old city — is a work of art.

Originally laid out in an orderly, compact grid, downtown Savannah retains this geography today. It is defined by 22 handsome squares that function as vest-pocket parks, are embowered and rimmed with native flowering species, and are linked by narrow cross streets or broad parkways divided by columns of trees. It is the nation's largest registered Urban Historic District, containing some 1,200 buildings of architectural and historic significance. These include blocks of magnificent townhouses, many 19th-century places of worship, and several examples of Regency architecture popularized in this country by an Englishman, William Jay.

Some sections deserve particular note. One is the old City Market area, which has been transformed into a pedestrian streetscape, with shops, galleries, restaurants, and clubs. Another, the Victorian District, features large wooden houses faced with decorative moldings, fretwork, and porches, and many gingerbreaded bungalows. On the riverfront, the site of the old Cotton Exchange, brick warehouses and cotton factor's offices are filled with commercial and tourist-related attractions. From here, ferries zip across the Savannah River to Hutchinson Island, to the new International Trade and Convention Center and Westin Savannah Harbor Resort. Most recently, Broughton Street, a main commercial avenue that had fallen on hard times, has been transformed by new galleries, shops, theaters, restaurants, and a hotel.

The restoration and adaptive re-use of private and institutional buildings continues in very imaginative ways. The Savannah College of Art and Design (www.scad.edu) has itself redone more than 40 sites. As in Charleston, visitors

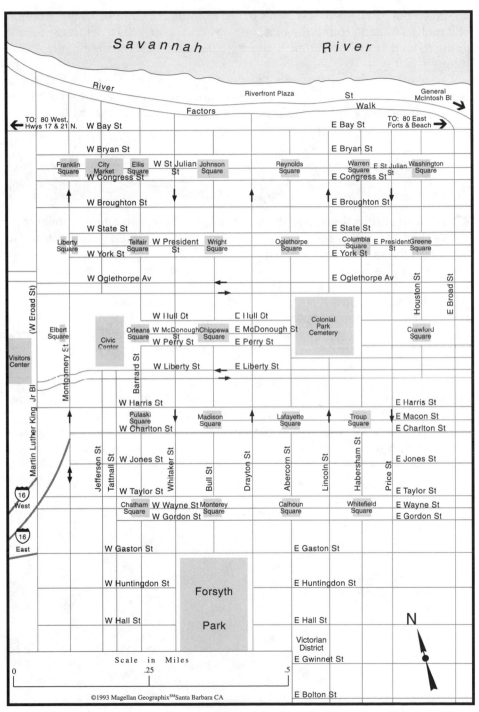

Courtesy of The Savannah Area Convention & Visitors Bureau (used by permission)

SAVANNAH

are given the privilege to feel as residents: nothing is frozen in amber. There is still motion in and around the most awe-producing architectural icons: people going to work, to school, home to lunch, to the market, just hanging out, or visiting.

The ways in which Savannah chose to survive have served it well. It has withstood General Sherman and Forrest Gump. Relishing its contradictions as it does, it faces the future with an extraordinary cultural and historic landscape, and a population with the sass and ginger pop to really enjoy it.

LODGING

Savannah and its Sea Island neighbor, Tybee Island, offer a range of accommodations, from upscale inns to funky beach villas. Tybee is closer to Savannah than Charleston's beach areas are to that city (about 20 minutes by car), and unlike Savannah's other nearby resort islands, it is not a gated community.

Like Charleston, Savannah had its tradition of providing guest accommodations in city mansions whose owners had rooms to spare. As more visitors came to the area, "tourist homes" and "guest houses" sprang up to serve the mainly Northern clientele who flocked in springtime to see Savannah's gardens and experience its faded charm.

The only thing you'll find faded in Savannah today is a shirt that's been left out in the sun too long. Splendid inns, some of which are listed below, have emerged as old houses have been renovated and cityscapes renewed.

The caveats invoked in earlier chapters hold true here: reservations are recommended, especially in the "high season" of spring, when a two-night's minimum stay is the usual practice; cancellation policies and room deposits are

Savannah's newest hotel, the Westin Resort, is accessible by an updated version of the region's oldest form of transportation: the small boat.

Wade Spees

standard; rules exist regarding smoking on the premises and guests under age 12; access for handicapped persons can be problematic (carriage houses with ground-floor access are usually a good bet.) Don't hesitate to ask the innkeeper about these restrictions when inquiring about reservations. *Historic Reservations* (800-791-9393; www.savannahinns.com) offers an overview of accommodations and a reservation service for rooms in luxury inns and private homes in the Historic District. *The Savannah Area Convention and Visitors Bureau website, www.savannahvisit.com*, provides information and some links to accommodations of all sorts in the city.

The same range of rates applies in Savannah as in other Lowcountry places. They are:

Inexpensive	Up to $60
Moderate	$60 to $120
Expensive	$120 to $200
Very Expensive	$200 and up

These rates do not include room taxes or special service charges that might apply during your stay.

Credit Cards

AE — American Express	DC — Diner's Card
CB — Carte Blanche	MC — MasterCard
D — Discover Card	V — Visa

HOTELS AND LARGER INNS

HILTON SAVANNAH DE SOTO
912-232-9000 or
    800-426-8483.
www.hiltonsavannah.com.
15 E. Liberty St., Savannah,
    GA 31412.
Price: Expensive.
Credit Cards: AE, DC, MC,
    V.
Handicap Access: Yes.

This is a wonderful location in the heart of the Historic District, a short walk to the riverfront. Some of the 246 rooms have private balconies, many are non-smoking, many have great views of Savannah's splendid squares. Pool and health club.

HYATT REGENCY SAVANNAH
912-238-1234 or
    800-233-1234.
2 W. Bay St., Savannah, GA
    31412.

A 346-room hotel, with the trademark Hyatt atrium lobby and glass elevators, towers over the riverfront with an unparalleled view of the ship and tugboat traffic. There's an indoor pool and shopping arcade, and you're steps away from busy River Street. Best location for River Boat excur-

Price: Expensive to Very
  Expensive.
Credit Cards: AE, DC, MC,
  V.
Handicap Access: Yes.

sions, the ferry to Hutchinson Island, or the day-
trip ferry to Daufuskie Island and Hilton Head.

THE MARSHALL HOUSE
912-644-7896 or
  800-589-6304.
www.marshallhouse.com.
123 East Broughton St.,
  Savannah, GA 31401.
Price: Expensive to Very
  Expensive.
Credit Cards: AE, D, MC, V.
Handicap Access: Some
  rooms.

This thoroughly renovated hotel opened again
in 1999, nearly 150 years after it was built in
bustling, downtown antebellum Savannah. It's still
right downtown, of course, and the Broughton
Street area is bustling again, having undergone a
recent commercial revival. (Some rooms facing the
street can pick up the sounds of late night traffic).
The Lucas Theatre is one block away, and Chad-
wick's, the hotel's bar, draws a crowd to hear jazz
combos Thursday to Saturday nights. There are 68
rooms, some suites among them with separate
sleeping areas. It's been modernized with all the
amenities, but the heart-pine floors and understated decor make the high-tech
assets fit right in.

THE MULBERRY INN
(A Holiday Inn property).
912-238-1200 or
  800-465-4329.
www.savannahhotel.com.
601 East Bay St., Savannah,
  GA 31401.
Price: Expensive.
Credit Cards: AE, MC, V.
Handicap Access: Yes.

Right across the street from the commercial
riverfront, this 145-room inn (including suites
with wet bars) blends the close attention found in
smaller inns with the full services of a hotel.
Informal piano concerts set the tone for afternoon
tea, and complimentary hors d'oeuvres are served.
There's an outdoor pool and heated rooftop Jacuzzi.
Special package rates are often available.

**WESTIN SAVANNAH
  HARBOR RESORT**
912-201-2000.
Fax: 912-201-2001.
www.westinsavannah.com.
One Resort Drive,
  Savannah, GA 31421.
Price: Expensive to Very
  Expensive.
Credit Cards: AE, D, DC,
  MC, V.
Handicap Access: 14
  rooms.

Savannah's new luxury resort complex is located
on Hutchinson Island, just across the Savannah
River from the Historic District, a two-minute
water taxi ride or a brief car trip over the Talmadge
Bridge. From here the views of Savannah and the
river traffic are stunning, especially from the 55
Club level rooms, some of which feature balconies.
It's a huge place (16 stories, 403 guestrooms) with
conventional and technological amenities, from
blow dryers to dual-line phones with dataports.
Also on the site is the Greenbrier Spa with a menu
of treatments to choose from, a fitness center, tennis courts, a par 72 golf course, clubhouse, marina,
two pools, bar, grill room, and restaurant.

LUXURY INNS

Teatime in the parlor at The Ballastone Inn renews the Southern custom of visiting.

Wade Spees

BALLASTONE INN
Innkeeper: Jean Hagens.
912-236-1484 or
  800-822-4553.
Fax: 912-236-4626
www.ballastone.com.
14 E. Oglethorpe Ave.,
  Savannah, GA 31401.
Price: Expensive to Very
  Expensive.
Credit Cards: AE, MC, V.
Handicap Access: Limited.

At Christmas, the Ballastone Inn looks like a scene out of Dickens — holly, magnolia leaves, native mistletoe, and garlands of smilax carry its grand front parlor back in time to 1838 when the townhouse was built, when English taste influenced the city. The decor echoes this high-style period in rich colors (like chocolate-toned walls), drapes and furnishings, but updated for comfort. There are 16 rooms, including three deluxe suites — many of them with Jacuzzis and fireplaces, and a courtyard you may not want to leave. A handsome full-service bar on the first floor is a wonderful amenity, one of the coziest nooks in the city. A full Southern breakfast is included.

EAST BAY INN
Innkeeper: Ronnie Jones.
912-238-1225 or
  800-500-1225.
www.eastbayinn.com.
225 East Bay St., Savannah,
  GA 31401.
Price: Expensive.
Credit Cards: AE, D, DC,
  MC, V.
Handicap Access: No.

This modestly appointed place sits at a great location, across the street from the busy retail and nightlife hub of River Street. There are 28 guest rooms in this circa-1853 cotton warehouse, each furnished with queen-sized, four-poster beds, reproduction antiques, and coffee-makers. Continental breakfast is included, and children under 12 stay free. Look into vacation packages with special rates.

ELIZA THOMPSON HOUSE
Innkeepers: Carol and Steve Day.
912-236-3620 or 800-348-9378.
www.elizathompsonhouse.com.
5 W. Jones St., Savannah, GA 31401.
Price: Expensive to Very Expensive.
Credit Cards: AE, MC, V.
Handicap Access: Limited.

This 25-room inn gives off a sense of family warmth amidst beautiful old objects. It was one of Savannah's first luxury bed-and-breakfast inns. Its spacious courtyard and fountain and its wonderful location (on a brick-paved street embowered by oaks and lined with iron-balconied townhouses) still fulfill the expectations of visitors who come in search of the cities of the "Old South." Sign up for the special walking tour.

Staying downtown in a luxury inn puts visitors steps away from Forsyth Park for an early morning run.

Wade Spees

FORSYTH PARK INN
Innkeepers: Hal and Virginia Sullivan.
912-233-6800 or 800-484-6850.
www.forsythparkinn.com.
102 W. Hall St., Savannah, GA 31401.
Price: Expensive to Very Expensive.
Credit Cards: AE, D, MC, V.

This is a modest, quiet inn with 10 rooms, including a courtyard cottage that can accommodate up to four, but might best be used for a romantic weekend getaway for a busy couple. The main house is a Victorian-era mansion, with inlaid hardwood floors and furnished with period antiques, reproductions, and four-poster beds. The baby grand piano in the entrance hall seems right in scale with the tall ceilings and long windows. Continental breakfast is included.

THE GASTONIAN
Innkeeper: Anne Landers.
912-232-2869 or
800-322-6603.
www.gastonian.com.
220 E. Gaston St.,
Savannah, GA 31401.
Price: Very Expensive.
Credit Cards: AE, D, MC, V.
Handicap Access: 4 rooms.

This Regency/Italianate residence complex dating from 1868 has lost little of its imposing feel. Period-appropriate decor and muted colors take a visitor back to the post-Civil War era when "the Old South" was becoming "the New South." Each of the 17 suites has a gas fireplace; many have four-poster beds and some have Jacuzzi tubs. There's a sun deck with a hot tub, too. Local people often reserve months in advance for special occasions. The Carriage House suite, with its own balcony and kitchen, is a favorite for honeymooners. Full Southern breakfast.

GRANITE STEPS
Innkeepers: Donna and
Randy Sparks.
912-233-5380.
www.granitesteps.com.
126 E. Gaston St.,
Savannah, GA 31401.
Price: Very Expensive.
Credit Cards: All major.
Handicap Access: One
suite.

Built in 1881 in the Italianate style and still featuring massive moldings and mantels from the period, this inn is probably the highest-end accommodation in Savannah. The rooms are enormous (even the bathrooms, all but one with a Jacuzzi spa) and elegantly furnished with heavy drapes, quality reproductions, gas fireplaces, and large-screen televisions. The handicapped suite has an entrance off the courtyard, where guests may also relax. Other common areas include a parlor, sunroom, library, and elaborate dining room with a table for 14. Nightly "cocktail hour" is generous in time, wine, and hors d'oeuvres. Children aged 12 and over are welcome. Strict cancellation policy and cancellation fee.

HAMILTON-TURNER INN
Innkeepers: Charlie and
Sue Strickland.
912-233-1833 or
888-448-8849.
www.hamilton-
turnerinn.com.
330 Abercorn St., Savannah,
GA 31401.
Price: Expensive to Very
Expensive.
Credit Cards: All major.
Handicap Access: One
room.

This 10,000 square-foot house was a character in John Berendt's book, *Midnight in the Garden of Good and Evil* (home of the eccentric "Mandy") and a must-see for fans of the book. Even on its own, it's an amazing place, built in the Second Empire style in 1873, totally renovated in 1998 by a local family and furnished with Empire, Eastlake, and Renaissance Revival antiques. There are 17 rooms and suites in the four-story house and carriage house, many with private balconies, whirlpools, and fireplaces. Full breakfast and afternoon tea are served in a grand dining room.

THE KEHOE HOUSE
Innkeeper: Melissa Exley.
912-232-1020 or
800-820-1020.

This restored Victorian mansion has had several lives: this is its grandest. There are 15 guest rooms (many with private balconies) and several grand public rooms adorned with huge urns of

123 Habersham St.,
    Savannah, GA 31401.
Price: Very Expensive.
Credit Cards: All major.
Handicap Access: Elevator
    from street level.

fresh flowers in the main building, and three additional rooms in the townhouse across the courtyard. Everything here is scaled to fin-de-siècle oversize: the ceiling moldings, the valances, the draperies, the armoires, the library tables, even the banisters and paneling. Not a corner's been cut in refurbishing, nor is there any stinting in guest services: a concierge is on duty 24 hours; there's off-street parking; a full breakfast is served in the double parlor; and a complimentary cocktail hour rounds out the day.

MAGNOLIA PLACE INN
Innkeepers: Rob Sales, Jane
    Sales, and Kathy
    Medlock.
912-236-7674 or
    800-238-7674.
www.magnoliaplaceinn.
    com.
503 Whitaker St., Savannah,
    GA 31401.
Price: Expensive to Very
    Expensive.
Credit Cards: AE, MC, V.

This late-19th century inn of 15 rooms faces Forsyth Park, which offers a view and sense of restfulness in addition to being a great place to jog. It has one of the nicest looking interiors of all the Savannah inns, partly because the materials were carefully chosen, including many lovely Oriental objects and fabrics, but also because the rooms are not overstuffed. Praise has come from those who like the bathroom soak-tubs and the many fireplaces; others have valued its sense of privacy. It's comfortable without being folksy, sophisticated without being stiff. There's a lot of repeat business and word-of-mouth referral. Continental breakfast is included; children 12 and older are welcome, pets are not.

BED AND BREAKFAST ACCOMMODATIONS IN HOMES / PRIVATE SUITES

Listing services and brokers can provide accommodations in private homes or in stand-alone lofts and townhouses in the Historic District. Credit cards are accepted for some — but not all — lodgings; deposits required, usually seven working days in advance, with penalties or charges for cancellation. Handicap access is available; some hosts allow pets. Rates are Moderate to Very Expensive. Can be a budget choice, or an option for extended families or friends travelling together.

The Manor House (800-462-3595; www.manorhouse-savannah.com.) An inn with additional guest accommodations downtown and at the beach.

R.S.V.P. Bed and Breakfast Reservations in Savannah (800-729-7787) A reservation service that matches your needs to its list of accommodations in historic inns and homes.

RESORTS AND RENTALS — TYBEE ISLAND

Tybee Island pleasures can be as simple as finding a sand dollar on the beach.

Wade Spees

S avannah's main beach is Tybee Island, a place of character (and characters) and informality, with shops, bars, and a down-home feeling. Don't be surprised if you're invited to your neighbor's beach party. Condo complexes and inexpensive motels are typical lodgings. For information and ideas, contact: *Tybee Visitors Center* (800-868-2322; www.tybeeisland.com. 506 Strand Ave., Tybee Island. GA 31328).

BEST WESTERN DUNES INN
912-786-4591 or
888-678-0763.
1409 Butler Ave., Tybee
Island, GA 31328.
Price: Moderate.
Credit Cards: AE, D, DC, MC, V.
Handicap Access: Yes.

A slightly revised version of the chain motel. Some of the 32 rooms have kitchenettes, some king-sized beds and Jacuzzis. It's simple, clean, close to the beach, and has a swimming pool.

HUNTER HOUSE BED AND BREAKFAST
Innkeeper: John Hunter.
912-786-7515.
1701 Butler Ave., Tybee
Island, GA 31328.
Price: Moderate.
Credit Cards: AE, MC, V.

F our rooms in a circa-1910 house at the beach — sounds like an old-fashioned vacation. It's one block away from the water, 20 minutes from downtown Savannah. Each room has queen-sized beds and a private bath. A fancy restaurant on the premises.

**SAVANNAH BEACH &
RACQUET CLUB**
800-864-7985.
www.sbrctybee.com.
1217 Bay St., Tybee Island,
GA 31328.
Price: Moderate to
Expensive.
Credit Cards: MC, V.

Modest one-to-three bedroom condo lodgings with pool, tennis, and beach access, available by the night, week, or month. Typical rates in summer (six–eight people) from $844/week; Spring Vacation week (March/April) from $985/week.

17th STREET INN
912-786-0607 or
888-909-0607
12 17th St., Tybee Island,
GA 31328.
Price: Moderate.
Credit Cards: MC, V.

Eight rooms with private entrances and full kitchens, with a deck for all guests with grills and plenty of room for families. Clean, friendly, funky, right near the beach. Air mattresses and pull-out beds can be provided for kids at modest additional cost.

RENTAL AGENTS AT TYBEE ISLAND

Solomon Properties (912-786-5468 or 888-756-2694; 211 Butler Ave., Tybee Island, GA 31328) Weekly and monthly rentals of properties at Lighthouse Point, Savannah Beach and Racquet Club, and private homes, including townhouses and villas.

Tybee Island Rentals (912-786-4034; www.tybeeislandrentals.com. 203 First St., Tybee Island, GA 31328) Some 120 properties are available for rent by the week or month, with a two-night minimum stay.

DINING

"Nothing helps scenery like ham and eggs."
— Mark Twain

By the end of the American Revolution, visitors to Savannah were impressed with the abundance and variety of its foods, the sophisticated way they were prepared by slaves, and the splendid manner in which meals arrived at the table. Lavish, at-home dining had established itself as a mark of high social position.

The art and pleasure of dining stayed home-based for many years after that, well into this century. There were few places to dine out and few reasons to do so. The culture centered around home, family, the connections of friends and neighbors, and a convivially shared history. You could conduct your business in a restaurant but not your social life.

Savannah's many restaurants show how that has changed. Today, the city is filled with plain and fancy places to eat. The local population, including hundreds of students, are eager to dine out, and have the means to do so; visitors arrive with high culinary expectations. While there may be fewer no-frills lunch counters and cafeterias, there are plenty of informal cafes, taverns, and beachside bistros to take their place. Don't discount Tybee Island (listed in *Savannah Area* section) as a dining destination: it's not just fried seafood anymore.

The hours and prices of restaurants listed below have been checked as close to the date of publication as possible, but a call ahead to confirm is always wise. The general price range we list is meant to reflect the cost of a single meal, usually dinner, featuring an appetizer, entree, dessert, and coffee. Cocktails, beer and wine, gratuity, and tax are not included in the estimated price.

Dining Price Code

Inexpensive	Up to $10
Moderate	$10 to $20
Expensive	$20 to $30
Very Expensive	$30 or more

Credit Cards

AE — American Express	DC — Diner's Club
CB — Carte Blanche	MC — MasterCard
D — Discover Card	V — Visa

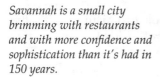

Savannah is a small city brimming with restaurants and with more confidence and sophistication than it's had in 150 years.

Wade Spees

Delicatessens, sweet shops, and bakeries are listed below larger restaurants; gourmet and health-food stores are listed under **Gourmet Food** in the **Shopping** section of this chapter.

BISTRO SAVANNAH
912-233-6266.
309 W. Congress St.
Open daily.
Price: Expensive.
Cuisine: American,
    Southern.
Serving: D.
Credit Cards: AE, MC, V.
Reservations
    recommended.
Handicapped Access.
Special Features: All food
    available to go.

The Bistro draws a mix of residents and visitors staying at the downtown B&Bs. Repeat customers come for the homemade soups and desserts, the house smoked pork, greens, and hot pepper cornbread, and the casual, upbeat atmosphere. The menu is full of fresh market specials featuring organic produce. The "small plates" feature warm salads, and roasted garlic, squeezed on goat cheese with Vidalia onion relish. Extensive wine list, specializing in California vineyards.

Wade Spees

Café Metropole is a typical Savannah blend: a French bistro located in an Art Deco bus station with an art gallery on site and outdoor dining.

CAFE METROPOLE
912-236-0110.
109 Martin Luther King Jr.
    Blvd.
Closed Wed.
Price: Moderate.
Serving: L, D.
Credit Cards: MC, V.
Special Features: Take-out,
    especially the bread.

The outside doesn't look promising — it's the former bus depot — but inside the funky style of industrial-strength Art Deco (perhaps the first bus station so designed) works its charm. One long wall is given over to exhibit space that might include painting, sculpture, photographs, while the one opposite is pierced by the old bus bays with their rolling, retractable doors. Tables for four spill across the floor between them and out to a patio. Good bistro food, the best bread in Savannah. A building redo that succeeds in style and substance.

CITY MARKET CAFE
912-236-7133.
224 W. St. Julian St.

This popular and unpretentious restaurant covers a lot of bases well. The menu includes pasta, sandwiches, rotisserie chicken and ribs, ice-cream

Open daily.
Price: Moderate.
Cuisine: American.
Serving: L, D.
Credit Cards: AE, CB, D,
   MC, V.
Handicapped Access.

CLARY'S CAFE
912-233-0402.
404 Abercorn St.
Open daily.
Price: Inexpensive.
Cuisine: American.
Serving: B, L, D,
Credit Cards: AE, MC, V.
Wheelchair accessible
   seating.

sundaes and fountain concoctions, Coke in the bottle and 16 brands of beer. The place itself seems full of fizz: brick walls, a black tin ceiling, starched tablecloths, and indoor and outdoor dining. The staff is unfazed by children and won't even blink if you order a hefty grilled sandwich for dinner while your companion has beef tenderloin and fine wine.

A bacon-and-egg sandwich on wheat and coffee is a typical order at Clary's, a downtown eatery where your cup stays refilled and breakfast waffles can set you up for the day. At lunch, the Greek salad is big enough to share, or if you're hungry you might try the chicken potpie which includes salad and a roll. Top it off with a root beer float. *Midnight in the Garden of Good and Evil* fame sent the crowds here, but the diet-busting food makes it worth the trip.

From the front porch at Elizabeth on 37th, it's hard to believe you're in urban America.

Wade Spees

ELIZABETH ON 37TH
912-236-5547.
105 E. 37th St.
Closed Sun.
Price: Expensive to Very
   Expensive.
Cuisine: American;
   gourmet Southern.
Serving: D.
Credit Cards: AE, MC. V.
Reservations
   recommended.

Chef, author, and James Beard Award winner Elizabeth Terry created her restaurant using superior seasonal products and signature flavorings to great acclaim. She's passed the restaurant on, but diners can still count on elaborate meals in the sumptuous setting of an old mansion. Take your time and enjoy the formality. Favorites include thick cuts of grilled meat encrusted with herbs, local fish, and Southern standards like seafood soups.

45 SOUTH
912-233-1881.
20 E. Broad St.
Closed Sun.
Price: Very Expensive.
Cuisine: Continental;
   gourmet Southern.
Serving: D.
Credit Cards: AE, MC, V.

A softly lit place, lots of dark green in the decorating, almost like a row house, with elegant tables situated in three sections and a small bar. The service is here in abundance — a waiter to refill your water glasses; another to grind the pepper. Soft breadsticks give way to well-dressed food, especially the crab cake appetizer with roasted red pepper remoulade, or scallops of veal with garlic potatoes and spicy mustard. Quiet and romantic.

The line forms outside The Lady & Sons.

Wade Spees

THE LADY & SONS
912-233-2600.
www.ladyandsons.com
311 W. Congress St.
Open daily.
Price: Inexpensive.
Cuisine: Country Southern.
Serving: L, D.
Credit Cards: All major.

The lunch buffet offers the full "groaning board" Southern specialties like fried tomatoes and shrimp grits — a smart choice if you're having a late evening meal and plan to be walking and touring for the rest of the day. The chicken pot pie is a popular entree — or you can make a meal of appetizers and sides like fried okra. The restaurant's cookbook shares its kitchen secrets. The modest restaurant can get quite crowded: check in and then wander around the City Market until your table's ready.

MRS. WILKES'
   BOARDING HOUSE
912-232-5997.
107 W. Jones St.
Open Mon.–Fri.
Price: Inexpensive.
Cuisine: Southern.
Serving: B, L.

This is truly homemade cooking served as it would be at home: the diners seated around large tables, with heaping platters of fried chicken, baskets of biscuits, and bowls of slaw, vegetables, red rice, and black-eyed peas or green beans placed before them. You take the dishes to the kitchen when you're done. It's located in the basement of

Credit Cards: None.
Handicapped Access.

THE OLDE PINK HOUSE
912-232-4286.
23 Abercorn St.
Open daily.
Price: Expensive.
Cuisine: Southern.
Serving: D.
Credit Cards: All major.

OLYMPIA CAFE
912-233-3131.
5 East River St.
Open daily.
Price: Inexpensive to
  Moderate.
Cuisine: Greek.
Serving: L, D.
Credit Cards: All major.

SAPPHIRE GRILL
912-443-9962.
www.sapphiregrill.com.
110 W. Congress St.
Open daily.
Price: Expensive to Very
  Expensive.
Cuisine: American.
Serving: D.
Credit Cards: AE, MC, V.

an old red-brick house, but you'll recognize it by the line forming at mealtime.

Located in an elegant 18th-century mansion which has been designated a National Landmark, here the Declaration of Independence was read in Savannah for the first time. There's a quiet dining room upstairs, and a more lively one downstairs, the *Planters Tavern*, where two fireplaces (roaring in winter), live piano music featuring Gail Thurmond, a ballad singer, a welcoming bar, and a full dinner menu attract the regulars. This is one of the most popular places downtown to have a cocktail or relax after dinner — that is, if the diners release their tables. The seafood and lamb are recommended — but then, so are the architectural details, designed by Thomas Jefferson.

River Street is not the most subtle stretch of Savannah, with its bars and gift shops and crowds, but it's lots of fun, and this is its best restaurant. Savannah's population of Greek descent, proud of its deep roots in the community and its civic contributions, make this a casual, friendly place. There are, of course, Mediterranean appetizers like tzadiki and dolmadakia, and gyros and kabobs, as well as traditional Greek dishes like lemon chicken and mousaka. If you hear servers and diners shouting "opa" it means another order of flaming cheese appetizers was a hit.

A sharp, stylish, restaurant on three floors serving a first-rate dinner. Located in the City Market area, it is modern and sleek — bare hardwood floors, wooden blinds, white tablecloths, and lots of brushed metal. The bar, along one side, can get crowded and create a lot of traffic, and the restaurant tends to be noisy. Nonetheless, it's a special place. There's always an excellent choice of beef or duck, several pan-seared or grilled fish dishes, and foie gras added to any plate. Signature appetizers are the shrimp and arugula and fried green tomatoes with chevre croutons.

Suits, strollers, and students mix congenially at Vinnie Van GoGo's in Savannah's City Market.

Wade Spees

VINNIE VAN GOGO'S
912-233-6394.
317 W. Bryant St.
Open daily.
Price: Inexpensive.
Cuisine: Pizza, Italian.
Serving: L (Sat., Sun); D
(from 4 p.m.)
Credit Cards: None.
Special Features: Delivery
by bicycle courier to
downtown area.

Calzones and thin-crust pizza by the slice or pie (14" or 18") made from dough prepared on the premises during the day and rolled and tossed while you watch from the counter. These cooks are having fun. Nineteen toppings including healthy vegetables. Large selection of imported beers and a concoction called spodeeodee (cheap red wine, 7-Up, splash of orange soda), which sells by the glass or pitcher as fast as they can mix it up. Eat on the patio — you're surrounded by art students— and get sense of a new population that has enlivened the old city.

Savannah Area

**CRAB SHACK AT
CHIMNEY CREEK**
912-786-9857.
www.thecrabshack.com.
40 Estill Hammock Rd.,
Tybee Island (second
right past Lazaretto
Creek Bridge).
Open daily.
Price: Moderate.
Cuisine: Seafood.
Serving: L, D.
Credit Cards: MC, V.

As informal as your own back porch: wooden tables inside and out, beer in the bottle, sandy feet welcome. The food is strictly off-the-boat and not fried: raw bar selections, delicious, fat crab served in cakes or blended with spices and cheese, and Lowcountry boil, a platter including shrimp, corn, potatoes, and sausage. Located at a bend on the creek, the view is premium Lowcountry, enjoyed from the home-made Tiki Bar or from the deck, where "Crab Shack chandeliers" (made from old baskets) light up the night. The old bait shop has been converted to a funky gift shop: visit it while waiting for your table (you can be notified by beeper).

GEORGES'
912-786-9730.
1105 East Hwy. 80, Tybee
   Island.
Closed Mon.
Price: Expensive to Very
   Expensive.
Cuisine: American Fusion.
Serving: D.
Credit Cards: All major.
Reservations highly
   recommended.

Georges' is nothing to look at from the outside, (Tybee's not even chic in a shabby way yet) and there's no view to speak of, but this handsome, mellow restaurant places easily in Savannah's top three. Sometimes the food has Asian influences like wasabi, sesame seasonings, or ginger rice, but not always. The reduction sauces flavored with fig, mango, apricot, or pomegranate are subtle and smooth, encouraging the rack of lamb or seared yellowfin tuna they're paired with. The standout appetizer is duck liver salad and a martini. Wines average about $30 per bottle from a good and varied list. If you appreciate a meal that is itself a destination, make time to come here. Dress is upscale casual.

NORTH BEACH GRILL
912-786-9003.
41-A Meddin Dr. (by the
   Lighthouse) Tybee
   Island.
Price: Inexpensive to
   Moderate.
Cuisine: Seafood; Caribbean.
Serving: L, D (no Thursday
   lunch).
Credit Cards: AE, MC, V.

Take an old beachside snack bar (where you could have rented surf boards and umbrellas and bought a hot dog), screen it in, add island spices and African beer, and you're getting close to describing this place. It's very small, informal, and nonchalant, serving jerk chicken, salmon, and pork (sandwiches or plates), Cuban pot roast, crab with asparagus, and plantains. Success hasn't spoiled it one iota. (The owners have a new hit in Georges', see above).

THE BREAKFAST CLUB
912-786-5984.
1500 Butler Ave., Tybee
   Island.
Open daily (6 a.m.–1 p.m.).
Price: Inexpensive.
Cuisine: Southern.
Serving: B, L.
Credit Cards: MC, V.

Get a feel for the kicked-back life of Tybee here among locals sitting at booths and tables set close together in this small, unpretentious place. You might run into the shrimpers coming in or the early anglers and birders just setting out. If you want to get a jump on the day, or take a quiet walk on a deserted morning beach, this is a great place to start.

FOOD PURVEYORS

On Saturdays from 8 a.m. to 2 p.m., the City Market becomes an open-air Farmers' Market, with selections from the garden, the field, the sea, and the oven. There are good bargains: bread from the Metropole and inexpensive shrimp among them. Great treats are also available at the following locations.

If you can climb to the top, the Tybee Island Lighthouse offers a great view.

Wade Spees

BAKERIES/COFFEEHOUSES

Ex Libris (912-525-7550; 228 Martin Luther King, Jr. Blvd.) Three floors of books, art supplies, and overstuffed sofas to sit on and sip your coffee after you browse.

Express Cafe and Bakery (912-233-4683; 39 Barnard St.) An upscale Art Deco-style bakery created in the shell of a downtown storefront. Opens early. The breads and desserts are homemade; omelets are light and fresh. Light lunches include soups and sandwiches.

Gallery Espresso (912-233-5348; 6 E. Liberty St.) Coffees, rum cakes, outdoor tables and indoor art exhibits. Longtime favorite of artsy locals.

Gryphon Tea Room (912-525-5880; 337 Bull St.) A real Edwardian-style, over-decorated, high-ceilinged cafe, with tile floors, stained glass, dappled light and potted palms. Treat yourself to afternoon tea.

Savannah Coffee Roasters Cafe (912-232-5282; 7 E. Congress St.) Pastries and simple snacks, lots of overstuffed chairs, and no one particularly bothered if you're eating, sipping, and reading slowly. On Johnson Square.

CANDY AND ICE CREAM

Byrd Cookie Co. (800-291-2973; www.byrdcookiecompany.com. 6700 Waters Ave.) A local institution since 1924. Delicious cookies and gourmet desserts made on site. Tours available.

Peaches and Cream (912-233-3131; 5 E. River St.) Frozen yogurt and French ice cream on the waterfront.

Savannah's Candy Kitchen (912-233-8411; 225 E. River St.) The largest candy store in the South, where you can see the candies made and have some sent home.

DELIS AND FASTER FOOD

A seat in a Savannah restaurant is a window on a world.

Wade Spees

Brighter Day (912-236-4703; 1102 Bull St.) A family-run health-food store featuring a full line of natural foods and health-care products as well as excellent sandwiches to go or to eat there, breads, and organic produce.

Good Eats (912-447-5444; 606 Abercorn St.) Beautiful fresh salads and wonderful bread. Inexpensive, ready-to-go lunches.

606 East Cafe (912-236-5113; 319 W. Congress St.) Creative sandwiches (grilled ham, marinated olive salad, and melted mozzarella served on grilled Greek pita bread) and vegetarian wraps, a peel-your-own shrimp patio. The whole place is slightly funhouse.

Soho South Cafe (912-233-1633; 12 W. Liberty St.) A cafe inside an art gallery. The setting adds to the modernist/gourmet atmosphere with sandwich choices like portobello mushroom or crabcake.

Sushi Zen (912-233-1188; 41 Whitaker St.) An intimate, minimalist setting where you can get sushi, American sandwiches, and creative "lunchbox specials."

CULTURE

ARCHITECTURE

Appreciating architecture in Savannah is a little like being a parent: you can read about it, you can hear it described fully and well, you can understand why people do it, and you can give it a rational and historic context. But you haven't begun to feel its power until you face it for yourself, four-square, on a lazy walk in the city.

It is not necessary to arrive and hit the ground running. Whether or not you visit every historic house and church, or mentally catalogue its interior detailing, is not that important. You can buy an exquisite book for that (see Chapter Seven, *Information* for suggestions, or visit a bookstore listed under **Shopping**). What's special about this region is that you can experience architecture in drifts, in vistas, as a harmonious whole that came into being as a response to the natural conditions of climate and the studied ones of prevailing fashions.

Further, the very settings of these built gems bear appreciation for their scale and for the surviving scale of the environment around them. This you can experience only by being there.

Savannah's architectural inventory includes Federal-period mansions and townhouses; buildings designed by William Jay, the Regency-period architect who delighted in fancy scrollwork and a free-hand imposition of Greek motifs; grand antebellum homes; and a whole district of Victorian homes (made of both wood and masonry). Whatever their specific style, the older buildings downtown seem to share a formal and restrained design, often colored from a muted palette of greys, greens, and tans, and echoing the geometry of Savannah's squares.

A good place to start is the *Savannah Visitors Center* (303 Martin Luther King, Jr. Blvd.) where you can join a tour or get a good overview of the city's history.

When you're out and about, you will find that local people appreciate your interest and are happy to chat. But since all but a few of the historic homes are privately owned, remember that while photographing is fine, entering gardens or taking you car up the driveway is not. For such closer looks, visit the area's many house museums where well-briefed and accommodating docents can answer your questions. In addition, there are annual tours of private homes and gardens, sponsored by local preservation organizations or churches. They usually take place in March and October, last all day, and range in price from $15 to $40. Contact the Historic Savannah Foundation (912-233-7787).

DANCE

Ballet South (912-691-2900; 5501 Abercorn).

FILM

Carmike Cinemas (912-353-8683; 511 Stephenson Ave.).
Eisenhower Cinemas (912-352-3533; 1100 Eisenhower Dr.).
Savannah 10 Cinemas (912-927-7700; 1132 Shawnee St.).
Tara Cinemas (912-925-2135; 12319 Largo Dr.).

Victory Square Cinemas (912-355-0110; 3001 Skidaway Rd.).
Wynnsong 11 Cinemas (912-920-1227; 1150 Shawnee St.).

GALLERIES

The Telfair, Savannah's art museum, has educated generations of viewers with classic and contemporary art.

Wade Spees

The Savannah College of Art and Design (called SCAD locally) has greatly raised the profile of the city as an arts center. Frequently changing exhibitions of work are on display in college buildings throughout the city. Find schedules at www.scad.edu or call 912-525-4950. A glance at *The Georgia Guardian* will turn up undiscovered or short-run shows. Here are some places to look at art — it may or may not be for sale.

Beach Institute (912-234-8000; 502 E. Harris St.) Established in 1865 by the American Missionary Association to educate the newly freed slaves of Savannah, the Beach continues to be an African-American cultural center which features exhibits of arts and crafts. Of special interest is the collection of hand-carved wooden sculptures, including likenesses of Presidents, by acclaimed folk artist and Savannah barber Ulysses Davis. Open Tues.–Sat. 12–5. Admission is $3.50.

Ellis Gallery. (912-234-3537 or 800-752-4865; www.rayellis.com. 205 W. Congress St.) Paintings, watercolors, bronzes and prints of golf and traditional maritime scenes by Ray Ellis, perhaps the best-known of Lowcountry artists. Also, books of his work and notecards.

Exhibit A Gallery (912-525-5180; 342 Bull St.) The original gallery of the Savannah College of Art and Design, featuring work by students, faculty, and occasional guests. Open Mon.–Fri. 9–5:30; Sat. 10–4.; Sun. 1–6.

Jack Leigh Gallery (912-234-6449; 132 E. Oglethorpe St.) Photographs taken over the last two decades of the rural and coastal South, including beautiful photo essays on oystering, shrimping, and boating.

John Tucker Fine Arts (912-231-8161; 5 W. Charleton St.). This handsome gallery on Madison Square features several shows each year of established artists whose work sometimes reflects Southern themes.

RAF Gallery (912-447-8807; www.rafgallery.com; 5 W. York St.) Specializing in displays of contemporary art glass, bronze sculpture and two-dimensional art pieces.

HISTORIC HOMES, GARDENS & RELIGIOUS SITES

A distinguishing quality of longtime Lowcountry residents is that they are, to slightly alter the words of the Rolling Stones, "practiced in the art of perception"; that is, they know how to see and how to honor, over the generations, what they see. In Savannah, this means that historic sites — be they mansions, gardens, forts, or houses of worship — are cared for in a personal way. A site is valued not just because it is important and beautiful (though they all are), but because it has given meaning to the community. Structures that could be classified as monuments are familiar touchstones. Such an attitude puts flesh on the bones of historic preservation rhetoric.

And it's not just buildings that are treated well: Savannah's squares and cemeteries are testimonials to public beauty. Observing the years of care that have been lavished on Savannah's historic places — from efficient, Federal-style frame dwellings to vast Romantic Revival warehouses — is one pleasure that will come naturally to every observant visitor.

ANDREW LOW HOUSE
912-233-6854.
329 Abercorn St.
Mon.–Wed., Fri.–Sat.
　10:30–4:00; Sun. 12–4;
　closed Thurs.
Admission: Adults $7;
　students $4.50.

A city house in the high style, although adapted to the rigors of Savannah's summer heat by means of jalousied rear porches. By 1849, when it was built, Savannah was in its prime: this is how the wealthy cotton merchants lived. It was from this house that Juliette Gordon Low founded the Girl Scouts and where she died in 1927.

**CONGREGATION
　MICKVE ISRAEL
　TEMPLE**
912-233-1547.
20 E. Gordon St.
Open Mon.–Fri. 10–12 and
　2–4.

The Gothic-style synagogue was built in the 1870s, more than 100 years after the congregation was established. The museum and library house the oldest Torah in America, as well as letters, books, and historical documents.

**FIRST AFRICAN
　BAPTIST CHURCH**
912-233-6597.
23 Montgomery St.
Open Mon.– Fri. 10–2.

The oldest continually active church for black worshippers in North America, and the birthplace of the Civil Rights Movement in Savannah. Within the church (circa 1861) is a small museum and archive.

The Gift

To His Excellency President Lincoln, Washington, D.C.: I beg to present you as a Christmas-gift the city of Savannah, with one hundred and fifty heavy guns and plenty of ammunition, also about twenty-five thousand bales of cotton.

— W.T. Sherman, Major-General. From Savannah, Dec. 22, 1864.

GREEN-MELDRIM HOUSE
912-232-1251.
1 W. Macon St.
Tues.,Thurs.– Fri.10–4; Sat. 10–1.
Admission: Adults $5; students $3.

Used as headquarters by General W.T. Sherman during his 1864 Christmas occupation of Savannah, this Gothic Revival mansion on Madison Square was considered the city's most expensive house when it was built in 1850. The exterior ironwork and porches are the best example of the style in the city.

HISTORIC RAILROAD SHOPS
912-651-6834.
601 W. Harris St.
Mon.–Sat. 10–4, Sun. 1–6.
Admission: Adults $2.50, students $2.

This National Historic Landmark is a collection of 13 structures first built in 1850 and used as a railroad manufacturing and repair facility. Today you can see the roundhouse and turntable, a 125-foot brick smokestack, antique steam engines, diesel locomotives, and rolling stock.

ISAIAH DAVENPORT HOUSE
912-236-8097.
www.davenportsavga.com.
324 E. State St.
Mon.–Sat. 10–4:30, Sun. 1–4:30 (last tour at 4).
Admission: $5.

The proposed demolition of this landmark (built in 1820 by a master-builder from Rhode Island for his family) to salvage the brick and make way for a parking lot galvanized Savannah preservationists. That was 1954, and the effort marked the birth of the Historic Savannah Foundation. Today it's a museum adorned with furnishings and decorative arts of the Federal Period. There's a lovely garden out back and an excellent museum shop.

JULIETTE GORDON LOW GIRL SCOUT CENTER
912-233-4501.
142 Bull St.
Daily (except Wed.)10–4; Sun. 12:30–4:30.
Admission: Adults $6; children $5.

A Regency townhouse decorated in postbellum period style, this building commemorates the childhood of the founder of the Girl Scouts, who was born here in 1860. Gift shop with special things for Scouts.

KING-TISDELL COTTAGE
912-234-8000.
www.kingtisdell.org.

This charming, original Victorian cottage (circa 1896) houses a museum of the black history and culture of Savannah and the Sea Islands. Walking or driving tours on the Negro Heritage

514 E. Huntingdon St.
Tues.–Fri. 12–4:30;
Sat.–Sun. 1–4.
Admission: Adults $1.50;
children $0.75.

Trail, highlighting events and significant sites that pertain to black history, can be arranged in advance.

**LAUREL GROVE —
SOUTH CEMETERY**
912-651-6772.
At the western end of 37th St.
Open daily. Tours by appointment.

The South Cemetery of Laurel Grove was dedicated in 1852 for the burial of "free persons of color" and slaves. Many of the city's most famous African-Americans are buried here.

Wade Spees

The Owens-Thomas House is a magnificent example of Regency architecture, a style that came to Savannah in the first decades of the 19th century.

**OWENS-THOMAS
HOUSE MUSEUM**
912-233-9743.
124 Abercorn St.
Mon. 12–5, Tues.–Sat. 10–5;
Sun. 2–5. Last tour at 4:30.
Admission: Adults $7;
seniors and AAA members $5; students $3; children (6–12) $2.

Designed in 1816 by Englishman William Jay and considered the best example of his Regency style for an urban villa, this house contains a collection of European and American decorative arts and has a formal garden. The Carriage House is the site of one of the few discovered slave quarters in the Historic District, and its collections offer insight into the lives of urban African-American slaves.

**RALPH MARK GILBERT
CIVIL RIGHTS
MUSEUM**
912-231-8900.
460 Martin Luther King, Jr. Blvd.
Mon.–Sat. 9–5.
Admission: Adults $4;
children $2.

Dr. Gilbert, who died in 1956, was a leader in early efforts to gain educational, social, and political equality for African-Americans in Savannah. This new museum features state-of-the-art interactive exhibits focusing on the history of the Civil Rights Movement in Savannah.

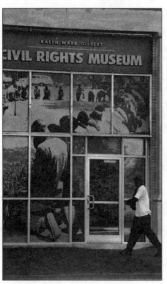

Savannah's Civil Rights heritage is honored in a museum named for a local activist, Ralph Mark Gilbert.

Wade Spees

SECOND AFRICAN BAPTIST CHURCH
912-233-6163.
123 Houston St.
Open Mon.–Fri. 10–2, Sun. 1–3. Tours by appointment only.

The church was established in 1802, and was the site of two historic occasions: General W.T. Sherman's reading of the Emancipation Proclamation to the newly freed slaves and, nearly a century later, Dr. Martin Luther King's delivery of his "I Have A Dream" sermon.

WORMSLOE HISTORIC SITE
912-353-3023.
7601 Skidaway Rd., Isle of Hope.
Tues.–Sat. 9–5, Sun. 2–5:30.
Admission: Adults $2; children (6–18) $1.

The tabby ruins, an avenue of oaks, and artifacts excavated from the site are all that remain of the colonial plantation built by Noble Jones, a physician and carpenter who came with the first settlers on the ship *Anne* and survived to establish the Georgia colony. An audio-visual show and interpreters of colonial life make the period vivid for visitors.

MILITARY MUSEUMS & SITES

A strategic upriver location and an abiding sense of history that predates the American Revolution make Savannah rich in military history. The island forts and lighthouses, in particular, recall both the sense of estrangement felt by soldiers stationed there and the effort they made to create a community in an isolated setting.

FORT JACKSON
912-232-3945.
1 Fort Jackson Rd., 3 miles
from downtown.
Daily 9–5.
Admission: Adults $2.50;
seniors and students $2.

The oldest standing fort in Georgia, Fort Jackson saw action during both the Revolution, when an outbreak of malaria forced its abandonment, and the Civil War, when it was central to the Confederate network of river batteries. A self-guided tour takes you to military exhibits in the fort's casemates. Special military history programs enliven the fort several times each year.

**FORT McALLISTER
HISTORIC PARK**
912-727-2339.
www.gastateparks.org.
3894 Fort McAllister Rd.,
Richmond Hill (24 miles
south of Savannah, exit
15 on I-95).
Tues.–Sat. 9–5, Sun. 2–5.
Admission: Adults $2;
children $1.

The fall of Fort McAllister, on the Ogeechee River, signaled the end of Sherman's "March To The Sea." By that time it had already outlasted other forts due to its earthen walls, which, unlike the popular masonry equivalent, could be swiftly repaired after a round of bombardment. There are self-guided tours, rangers on hand, and a good, small museum. Picnicking in the park is popular, but bring insect repellent.

Massive and moated, Fort Pulaski at the mouth of the Savannah River survived 30 hours of Federal bombardment before succumbing in 1862.

Wade Spees

**FORT PULASKI
NATIONAL
MONUMENT**
912-786-5787.
Cockspur Island, Hwy. 80
east, about 30 minutes
from Savannah.
Daily 8:30–5:15, to 6:45 in
summer months.
Admission: Adults $2; ages
16 and under, free.

A young officer named Robert E. Lee had his first military assignment here, soon after the fort was built. It's a masterpiece of engineering, a huge and heavy brick building, surrounded by a moat, sitting on an unstable marsh. And yet during the Civil War, rifled cannons blasted holes in the masonry of such forts, and they became obsolete. Interpretive programs explain life at the fort during the Civil War, and you are free to roam its ramparts. An excellent selection of books is available at the gift shop.

**MIGHTY EIGHTH AIR
FORCE HERITAGE
MUSEUM**
912-748-8888.
www.mighty8thmuseum.
com.
175 Bourne Ave., Pooler.
(Take exit 18 off I-95,
then E on U.S. 80, then
left on Bourne Ave.).
Open daily 10–6; last tickets
sold at 5:15 p.m.
Admission: Adults $7.50;
children (6–12) $5.50;
under 6 free. Discounts
for seniors and military.

A new museum dedicated to the men and women who served in the "Mighty Eighth" Airforce (formed in Savannah in 1942) during World War II. Exhibits also track later engagements, such as Operation Desert Storm, supplemented by photos and film presentations.

**TYBEE ISLAND
MUSEUM and
LIGHTHOUSE / FORT
SCREVEN**
912-786-5801.
30 Meddin Dr., Tybee
Island, 18 miles E of
Savannah.
Closed Tuesday. Check
seasonal hours.
Admission: Adults $3;
children $2 (Museum);
Adults $3; children $3
(Lighthouse).

L ocated within Fort Screven, which was acquired by the Federal government in 1808 and used as a post through World War II, the Museum and Lighthouse offer visitors a glimpse of life at a beach outpost over the years. The museum has an assortment of objects, Native American and Civil War weaponry, as well as illustrated newspaper accounts of the Civil War and memorabilia. A lighthouse has marked this site since 1736. Today you can climb this 19th-century version (over 150 feet tall) for a wonderful view of the river.

MUSEUMS

**OATLAND ISLAND
EDUCATION CENTER**
912-897-3773.
711 Sandtown Rd.,
Savannah.
Mon.–Fri. 8:30–5, second
Sat. of each month
(special programs) 10–5.
Admission: $1 donation.

C hildren will love walking the woodland trails of this 175-acre preserve, where they can watch for animals. Sheep, goats, ponies, and swans may cross your path; bald eagles and hawks soar overhead. There is a farmyard, too.

**SAVANNAH HISTORY
MUSEUM**
912-238-1779.
303 Martin Luther King, Jr.
Blvd.
Daily 8:30–5.
Admission: Adults $3;
children (6–12) $1.75.

T wo sight-and-sound presentations, displays, and objects relating to Savannah's history are housed in the old Central of Georgia railway depot train sheds, by the Visitors Center. The Black Soldier exhibit highlights the 1st South Carolina Volunteers and the 178,895 black men who fought in the Civil War.

SAVANNAH SCIENCE MUSEUM
912-355-6705.
4405 Paulsen St.
Tues.–Sat. 10–5, Sun. 2–5.
Admission: Adults $4.50; children $2.50.

If you want to see one of the Southeast's largest collections of amphibians and reptiles, living and dead, comprehensive collections of shells, rocks, minerals, and a wonderful pressed herbarium of indigenous plants — or if someone in your party actually prefers this kind of exhibit to a house museum (gasp!) — spend time here. There's a great planetarium, too.

SHIPS OF THE SEA MUSEUM
912-232-1511.
41 Martin Luther King, Jr. Blvd.
Tues.–Sun. 10–5.
Admission: Adults $5; students, seniors $2.

Ship models, a magnificent dollhouse-style construction of a huge 19th-century ship, and ships-in-bottles tell the exciting story of maritime adventure, war, commerce, and exploration in the world's oceans, from the time of the Vikings forward. Located in the William Scarbrough House, a Regency jewel with a lovely garden.

TELFAIR MUSEUM OF ART
912-232-1177
121 Barnard St.
Open Tues.–Sat. 10–5, Sun. 1–5, Mon. 12–5.
Admission: Adults $6; seniors and AAA members $5; students $2; children (6–12) $2.

Savannah's main art gallery, housed in a Regency-style mansion, with a permanent collection of American and European Impressionist paintings, and frequent exhibits of modern art. A Moshe Safdie-designed modern addition is under construction.

UNIVERSITY OF GEORGIA MARINE EXTENSION SERVICE AQUARIUM
912-598-2496.
30 Ocean Science Circle, Skidaway Island, 14 miles from downtown.
Mon.–Fri. 9–4, Sat. 12–5. Closed Sun.
Admission: $1.

This is a working research lab and facility, but visitors are welcome to visit the aquarium and exhibits, which depict the underwater marine and plant life of coastal Georgia. Fossils of sharks' teeth and whale skulls are prominently displayed. A self-guided visit takes about an hour. Afterward, you can picnic. From here it's but a short hop to Skidaway Island State Park (912-598-2300) where you can walk through a maritime forest, birdwatch, and observe the teeming life of the marsh.

MUSIC

Savannah Symphony Orchestra (912-236-9536 or 800-537-7894; 225 Abercorn St.) The orchestra presents regularly scheduled symphony performances; chamber music ensembles often play on Sunday afternoons at the Telfair Academy.

NIGHTLIFE

Club One Jefferson (912-232-0200; www.clubone-online.com. 1 Jefferson St.) If you're looking for Chablis, who sang and carried on the "Midnight" this is the spot.

Doc's Bar (912-786-5506; 10 16th St., Tybee Island) A funky, fun beach bar.

Kevin Barry's (912-233-9626; 117 W. River St.) Irish bar serving sandwiches. There's live Irish music most weekends.

Lion's Den (912-232-9000; 15 E. Liberty St.) A jazz lounge in the DeSoto Hilton with known and less well established jazz bands and soloists. The patrons know their music — sophisticated but relaxed.

Savannah Blues (912-447-5044; www.savannahblues.com. 411 W. Congress St.) Urban blues, an arty/student crowd. Live music starts at 10 p.m.

THEATER

City Lights Theatre Company (912-234-9860; 125 E. Broughton St.) Productions in a small 75-seat theater; "Shakespeare-in-the-Park" in Washington Square in spring.

Lucas Theatre (912-232-1696; 32 Abercorn St.) An old movie palace, just renovated in 1998, features films, musical performances, and theatricals.

Savannah Theater Company (912-233-7764; 222 Bull St.) Seasonal productions of contemporary drama, musicals, and comedy.

SCAD'S Trustee's Theater (912-525-5015; www.trusteestheater.com; 206 E. Broughton St.) A former Art Deco movie house transformed by the Savannah College of Art and Design into a glittering 1105-seat performance art hall, featuring movies, plays, and dramatic readings.

The Trustees Theater is a newly renovated Art Deco showplace operated by the Savannah College of Art and Design.

Wade Spees

RECREATION

BASEBALL

The area's professional farm team is the Savannah Sand Gnats (912-351-9150; www.sandgnats.com. Grayson Stadium, 1401 E. Victory Dr.) When at home, they play games weeknights at 7:15, and Sundays at 3 p.m. Admission is $5 for adults, $3 for children.

The waves break long, low, and slow at Tybee Beach, offering good opportunities for surfers, skimboarders, and swimmers who ride the waves right up into the soft sand of the wash.

Wade Spees

BEACH ACCESS

The only accessible beach on Georgia's northern coast, *Tybee Island* lies 18 miles east of Savannah on Hwy. 80.

Ossabaw Island is a barrier island 20 miles south of Savannah. There are five campsites, and the minimum stay is two nights for groups of four or more. Transportation and fresh drinking water are available. Contact 912-233-5104 for information and reservations.

Wassaw Island, located east of Savannah and Skidaway Island, can be reached by private or charter boat arranged through the U.S. Fish and Wildlife Service, Savannah Coastal Refuges Office (912-944-4415; 1000 Business Center Dr., Suite 1, Savannah, GA 31405). Within its 10,000 acres, there are more than 20 miles of inland island trails to explore and a seven-mile beach to walk.

BIRD WATCHING

The best spots for birding around Savannah are part of the Savannah National Wildlife Refuge System, a complex of seven coastal parks that provide habitat on the beach and dunes as well as in abandoned rice fields, swamps, creeks, and estuarine systems. Get to *Tybee Island North Beach* by parking at the Tybee Island Museum (see listing above in **Military Museums and Sites**). *Skidaway Island State Park* (912-598-2300; www.gastateparks.org; 52 Diamond Causeway, Savannah, GA 31411) is separated from the Atlantic to the east by salt marsh and to the south by Wassaw Island. This unique geography attracts a wide variety of songbirds, as well as large ospreys and bald eagles. To get there take Exit 164 off I-16 west of Savannah and head south. It will become Diamond Causeway. *Harris Neck National Wildlife Refuge* (912-652-4415) is an old World War II Army airfield that supports a large colony of wood storks and dozens of nesting wading birds. Take U.S. 17 south to Harris Neck Rd. and travel 6.5 miles to the refuge entrance. Get a map at the Visitor Center and drive along the 4-mile Laurel Hill Wildlife Road for a good introduction to the area, which includes fresh-water marsh, river-bottom hardwood swamp, and tidal rivers and creeks. Contact the Georgia Dept. of Natural Resources (912-994-1438; www.dnr.state.ga.us; 116 Rum Creek Drive, Forsyth, GA 31029-6518) and ask for the pamphlet and map of Georgia's Colonial Coast Birding Trail.

BOATING

CANOEING AND KAYAKING

Access points along the Savannah River allow you to travel through tidal creeks leading into the *Savannah National Wildlife Refuge* (912-944-4415). For outing ideas, guided tours, and maps, you might call one of the companies listed here. In 2001, the price for three-hour kayak lessons started at $75 per person and skills workshops ranged from $45–$85 per person. A typical three-hour guided day trip cost $45 per person. Daily kayak rentals started at $20 for a single, $40 for a double. Half-day and full-day trips on the Ogeechee River, including shuttle service, cost $35 per canoe.

Isle of Hope Marina (912-354-8187; 50 Bluff Drive, Savannah, GA 31411)
Ogeechee Park Rentals (912-748-5996; Hwy. 80, Eden, GA)
Sea Kayak Georgia (912-786-8732 or 888-529-2542. www.seakayakgeorgia.com. P.O. Box 2747, Tybee Island, GA 31328).

SAILING

For sailors unfamiliar with Lowcountry waters and tides, renting a sailboat or having a lesson is a good way to get acquainted with local conditions. For saltwater experiences in the creeks and bays, contact *Sail Harbor Marina* (912-897-2896; 618 Wilmington Island Rd.). Prices vary according to season, length of sail lesson or charter, and type of boat. The *Savannah Sailing Center* (912-231-9996; at Lake Mayer Community Park, Montgomery Crossroad and

Sallie Mood Drive) offers lessons for $20 an hour in the calm setting of the 35-acre lake, which may be easier for a beginner to negotiate.

BOWLING

Major League Lanes (912-925-0320; 115 Tibet Ave.).
Victory Lanes (912-354-5710; 2055 E. Victory Dr.).

CAMPING

River's End Campground and RV Park (912-786-5518 or 800-786-1016; www.gocampingamerica.com; 915 Polk St., Tybee Island, GA 31328) 126 sites, full hookups, tent sites, and cabin rentals.

Skidaway Island State Park (912-598-2300; www.gastateparks.org; 52 Diamond Causeway, Savannah, GA 31411) A 533-acre park with 88 tent, trailer, and RV sites; laundry, pool, bath house, nature trail, and interpretative walks and programs.

DIVING

Diving Locker and Ski Chalet (912-927-6603; 74 W. Montgomery Crossroads).
Hammerhead Scuba (912-961-7966; 23 Ramsgate Rd.).

FAMILY FUN

A dip net, bait, a bucket, and some time are all you need to catch supper.

Wade Spees

Island Miniature Golf (912-898-3833; 7890 Hwy. 80, Whitemarsh Island) On the way to the beaches and boat landings; a good stop on the way home.

The Playground (912-925-7529; 1127 Fulton Rd.) An indoor playground with a dozen activity areas. Admission is $4 to $6.

Putt-Putt Golf Course (912-355-4795; 202 Mall Blvd.) Three courses, lit for night play, open to midnight.

FISHING

Tybee Pier.

Wade Spees

The waters off Savannah provide a variety of fishing experiences. Inshore, there's fishing in shallow waters and in narrow creeks when the tide is right; offshore, there are bigger game fish in the Gulf Stream. Some guides specialize in the art of saltwater fly-fishing.

A good place to plan a fishing trip is at a marina (see Chapter Two, *Transportation*), although some sporting goods stores may have recommendations (see **Shopping**, below). Non-commercial saltwater fishing does not require license; non-resident freshwater fishing does. Contact the Wildlife Resources Division's Savannah office (912-651-2221) for information on licenses and regulations, or talk to your guide. Licenses are available at most sporting goods stores and bait shops.

A listing of some of the many *Charter Boat Services* available follows. Most boats are fully outfitted with supplies and bait, but check in advance, especially if you have questions about bringing your favorite rod — an option for fly-fishing — or if the length of the trip requires food. Always bring sunscreen, a hat, and a windbreaker. The 2001 prices for half-day trips (generally 1–3 passengers for inshore fishing; 4–6 for offshore fishing) started at $200. A 15-hour trip to the Gulf Stream costs about $1000.

Lazaretto Creek Marina (912-786-5848 or 800-242-0166; www.tybeeisland.com; 1 Old Hwy. 80, Tybee Island) A full-service marina offering inshore trips for 4 people (20 for an extra person) to Gulf Stream expeditions

Miss Judy Charters (912-897-4921; 124 Palmetto Dr., Savannah) Deep-sea fishing and trolling, and Gulf Stream trips with Captain Judy Helmey.

The Restless (912-351-0755; 602 Early St., Savannah) Captain Flash Clark guides inshore fishing (light tackle and fly) by the full day (up to 9 hours) or half-day. Minimum of two passengers.

Salt Water Charters (912-598-1814; 111 Wickersham Dr., Skidaway) Captain Bob Morrissey. Inshore and deep-sea fishing for bass, grouper, and other species by full day or half day.

Savannah Light Tackle Fishing Co. (912-355-3271; www.sltfishing.qpg.com; P.O. Box 3666, Savannah) Captains Greg Davis and Matt Williams offer inshore and near-shore fishing (four-person limit) by the full and half-day, and barrier island tours (six-person limit).

Tybee Island Charters (912-786-4801; P.O.Box 1762, Tybee Island) Inshore and deep sea fishing; sightseeing tours. Six people maximum.

FITNESS FACILITIES

Coastal YMCA (912-350-5480; 6400 Habersham Pkwy.) This facility honors YMCA memberships from other parts of the country and, in any case, your first visit is free. Childcare is available.

Downtown Athletic Club (912-236-4874; 7 E. Congress) Step training, aerobics, spa facilities, classes, and fitness machines.

Tybee Island YMCA (912-786-9622; 204 E. 5th St., Tybee). A new facility, open daily.

West Broad St. YMCA (912-233-1951; 1110 May St.) Recreation center, gym facilities.

GOLF

Bacon Park Golf Course (912-354-2625; Shorty Cooper Drive) Par 72. 27 holes; 6,700 yards. Lighted driving range; putting green. Fees for 18 holes: $22–$26.

Henderson Golf Course (912-920-4653; www.hendersongolfclub.com. 1 Henderson Drive) Par 71. 18 holes; 6,700 yards. Lighted driving range; putting green. Fees: $35 (weekdays); $42 (weekends). Cart included. Pro: Cindy Jones.

Savannah Inn and Country Club (912-897-1612; 612 Wilmington Island Rd.) Par 72. 18 holes; 6,876 yards. Driving range and putting green. Fees: $32.80 (weekdays); $48 (weekends), including cart. Pro: Charlie Dobbertin.

Southbridge Golf Club (912-651-5455; www.southbridgegolf.com. 415 Southbridge Blvd.) Par 72. Rees Jones–designed 18 holes, 6,990 yards. Driving range, putting green, and a full staff of teaching pros onsite. Fees: $38 weekdays; $44 weekends and holidays. Twilight play $29–$35. Cart included. Pro: Michael Butler.

HORSEBACK RIDING

L ocal stables can accommodate riders of varying skills, and it's best to call in advance to arrange lessons, trail rides, or workouts in the ring. The 2001 prices ranged from $30–$50 per person for 90 minutes of riding time, depending on the setting. Here are some places to contact for more information:

Norwood Stables (912-356-1387; 2304 Norwood Ave.).

Triple B Ranch (912-964-6698; 60 Triple B Rd.).

HUNTING

A s in other regions of the Lowcountry, land quarry in the Savannah area include a variety of waterfowl, turkey, and various sizes of game. Familiarize yourself with specific hunting seasons, license requirements, and bag limits by visiting an outdoor recreation store (see the listing in **Shopping**) or contact the *Game and Fish Division* of the *Georgia Dept. of Natural Resources* (912-727-2112; www.dnr.state.ga.us; 22814 Hwy. 144, Richmond Hill, GA 31324).

Some of the most popular public hunting grounds in the Savannah area are located in the *Webb Wildlife Center* and *Palachucola* (843-625-3569; Hampton and Jasper Counties), *Turtle Island* and *Victoria Bluff* (843-844-8957; Jasper and Beaufort Counties), and in the *Savannah National Wildlife Refuge* (912-652-4415).

NATURE PRESERVES

S ome of the most accessible, and user-friendly preserves in the Lowcountry are located within 30 minutes of Savannah. They include:

The Bamboo Farm and Coastal Gardens (912-921-5460; Canebrake Rd. off Hwy. 17) A 46-acre educational and research center that started more than 100 years ago when a local bamboo fancier was given three Japanese giant timber bamboo plants and cultivated them on her property. Today there are more than 100 types of plants, flowers, and trees growing here, and more than 200 species of bamboo, under the direction of the University of Georgia.

Harris Neck National Wildlife Refuge (912-652-4415; Take I-95 Exit 67 to US 17 South, and travel approximately one mile to Harris Neck Rd.) The refuge entrance is 6.5 miles on the left, and signs direct you to the driving and biking trails which wind through this 2,700 acre area of freshwater impoundments, saltmarsh, forest, and field.

Pinckney Island National Wildlife Refuge (912-652-4415; Hwy. 278 at foot of Hilton Head bridge) A 4,053-acre complex of small islands and hammocks set in the marsh. Only Pinckney Island, interwoven with 14 miles of trails, is open to visitors. A good place to spend an hour walking and birding.

Savannah National Wildlife Refuge (912-652-4415; Take I-95 Exit 5 to Hwy. 17 south; 8 miles south of Hardeeville) The refuge consists of 25,608 acres spread across land once used for growing rice. Get a map at the Visitor's Center and drive along the five-mile Laurel Hill Wildlife road for a good introduction to an area which includes fresh-water marsh, river-bottom hardwood swamp, and tidal rivers and creeks. Hiking trails (39 miles in all) are well marked, many of them following the path of the old rice dikes.

Victoria Bluff Heritage Preserve (Sawmill Creek Rd., off Hwy. 278, 3 miles from the Hilton Head bridge) This beautiful parcel of some 1,000 acres on the Colleton River has long been eyed for residential or industrial development, but local residents secured its protection as a passive recreation area.

TENNIS

Seven city parks in and around Savannah have a total of 47 courts, and nearly all are lighted for night play. The custom at public parks is first-come, first-served. The locations are: *Bacon Park* (Skidaway Rd.); *Daffin Park* (1500 E. Victory Dr.); *Forsyth Park* (Gaston St. & Drayton St.); *Lake Mayer Park* (Montgomery Crossroad & Sallie Mood Dr.); *Stell Park* (Bush Rd.); *Tybee Memorial Park* (Butler Ave.); *Wilmington Island Community Park* (Lang. St. & Walthour Rd.)

SHOPPING

Savannah's River Street attracts shoppers and strollers by day; by night it's the center of the city's nightlife.

Wade Spees

There's not much you can't buy in Savannah, from collard greens off a truck to a gilded armoire. There are galleries displaying the work of students from the Savannah College of Art and Design; boutiques with unique accessories to dress up your house; bookstores with rare and current volumes; places to buy old prints, sea charts, and maps; and antiques stores by the dozen. In fact, antiques stores might be considered the city's specialty. The Lowcountry habit of preservation has meant that English and American antiques and accessories of an earlier day, purchased during the boom years, have remained in the old houses. Today they are trickling out to local dealers, as tastes change and there are other options for decorating.

The region's temperate, multi-crop climate means you can buy lettuce, collards, potatoes, tomatoes, watermelon, and peaches most of the year. The man with the bags of boiled peanuts may knock at your door only in summer, but most everyone else can, and does, peddle their goods year round.

There are, too, right in the city and certainly out in the country, stores that are old and vibrant centers of community life, places of shelves that bear small quantities of many things, of dangling fly-paper, squirrel nut candies, pickled eggs, moon pies, single beers, and icees. They are too modest to claim National Register status; they'll never be etherized, either. Drop in for a local newspaper and a "Co' Cola."

There's particularly good strolling and shopping along Whitaker Street, Broughton Street, and Barnard Street (City Market area). Check these websites for more information: www.savannahcitymarket.org. and www.shopping 31401.com.

Parking downtown can be difficult. Make use of Municipal Parking garages at City Market and Bryan Street (at Abercorn). Discount parking passes are sold at the Visitors Center, at the Bryan Street garage and at several hotels and inns.

ANTEBELLUM ARTIFACTS

Blatner's (912-234-1210; 47 Abercorn St.) Civil War era military items, old bottles, glassware, and silver.

Pinch of the Past (912-232-5563; 109 W. Broughton St.) Architectural fragments and vintage house parts, including doorframes, columns, mantels, lighting fixtures, and hardware.

ANTIQUES

There are antiques of probably every period and style in the city — or a dealer will find you what you want. Whether you live in a sleek, minimalist apartment or a farmhouse, you're likely to find a piece that works. A man was quoted in the paper as saying: "We love old things. It makes life easier because you don't have to like the new ones."

Many antiques stores are as small as one room, but they overflow with a sense of taste and style.

Wade Spees

Arthur Smith Antiques (912-236-9701; 1 W. Jones St.) Four floors of rooms filled with antique tables, rugs, armoires, beds, and side pieces. It helps to know what you want.

Francis McNairy Antiques (912-232-6411; 411 Abercorn St.) The loveliest antique shop in Savannah. Fine antiques, many of Southern origin, and many small pieces. If you don't buy one item you can educate yourself here.

Mode (912-234-3161; 226 W. Broughton) Lots of sleek, early 20th-century pieces for city dwellers, and some funky 19th-century ones, too. Many lamps.

Phillip Dorian Hunter (912-232-7212; 124 E. Jones St.) European and 20th-century American furnishings and accessories. Sometimes you find nice old fabric.

Pierce Antiques (912-238-3525; 101 W. Jones St.) American country furniture and primitives, transfer ware and toys.

V. & J. Duncan (912-232-0338; 12 E. Taylor St.) You could browse through the files and piles of prints, maps, old advertising art, and illustrations here for hours. A comprehensive, well-organized collection of fine antique material.

BOOKS

Savannah has an unusual number of little bookstores, many specializing in certain areas. Don't overlook the small ones.

Barnes and Noble (912-353-7757; 7804 Abercorn St.) As you would expect, a thorough inventory of Savannah books and many coffee-table size volumes on architecture and related subjects.

"The Book" Gift Shop (912-233-3867; www.midnightinsavannah.com. 127 E. Gordon St.) Headquarters for *Midnight in the Garden of Good and Evil* fans, the base for tours, a mini-museum of the book that changed Savannah.

E. Shaver Booksellers (912-234-7257; 326 Bull St.) Right downtown and great for browsing. If some topic of Lowcountry history has captured your interest, you'll find something on the topic here. Twelve rooms of new and rare books, history, fiction, children's section, and excellent art books.

Books are stacked floor to ceiling at Ex Libris, a bookstore that also sells art supplies. It attracts browsers from all over the Lowcountry, SCAD students, and visitors. There's a coffee bar and tables where you can crack the spine of your latest acquisition.

Wade Spees

Ex Libris (912-525-7550; 228 Martin Luther King, Jr. Blvd.) This three-story book store provides course books and supplies for students at the Savannah College of Arts and Design, and it is also full of treasures for the avid reader.

Printed Page (912-234-5612; 211 W. Jones St.) A selection of rare and scarce books for bibliophiles and book lovers looking for a special title. By appointment.

Waldenbooks (912-352-2750; 7804 Abercorn St. and 912-927-1408; 14045 Abercorn St.) Good selection of popular titles and books of regional interest. Nice children's and nature-oriented titles.

CLOTHING

There is grunge and retro fashion in Savannah, but it's still the South, after all, and there are plenty of small-scale dress shops (selling more than dresses these days) which are thriving and up-to-date in their sensibility. Mens' styles tend toward the casual and outdoorsy, given the weather.

Gaucho (912-232-7414; 250 Bull St. and 18 E. Broughton St.) Jewelry, leather, flowing scarves and both rustic and romantic clothes for women. The Designers' Room at the new Broughton St. location features new artists' work every season.

Jezebel (912-236-4333; 25 E. River St.) Light-hearted and good-looking dresses, casual wear for women.

Terra Cotta (912-236-6150; 34 Barnard St.) Elegant, soft cottons for the bed and bath, simply cut, stylish casual wear.

CRAFTS

Arts & Crafts Emporium (912-238-0003; 234 Bull St.) Some 300 American crafts-people have their work for sale here.

Bull St. Station (912-236-4344; 151 Bull St.) Model railroad supplies and other accessories, kits, and tools for hobbyists of all kinds.

Gallery 209 (912-236-4583; 209 E. River St.) Thirty of the region's finest artists and craftsmen show here. Their works include batik, fiber, glass, pottery, wood, paintings and sculpture, displayed in a 19th-century cotton warehouse.

Palmetto Point Gallery (912-238-3435; 11E. Park Ave.) Handcrafted work by regional artisans — you never know what you'll find but you'll enjoy the experience.

Village Craftsmen (912-236-7280; 223 W. River St.) Original arts and crafts are still being created by members of this 25-year old co-op gallery. You'll see jewelry, books, quilts, decorative painting, and much more.

GALLERIES

If you'd like to see local artists at work, drop by the *City Market Art Center*, a downtown art colony located upstairs (there's elevator access, too) at 308 and 309 West St. Julian St. Also, pick up a copy of *The Georgia Guardian*, the newspaper of the Savannah College of Art and Design: look for announcements of student and faculty shows in the College's many galleries. Other galleries worth checking out include:

East End Gallery (912-233-9244; 507 E. River St.) Featuring the work of eight accomplished local artists, one of whom is always in the gallery to talk about art.

Friedman's Fine Art (912-231-6600; 28 W. State St.) A collection of the region's best representational artists is on exhibit here, but there's also fine art framing and a large selection of antique botanical and maritime prints for sale.

Gallery Elan (912-232-5180; 306 W. Congress St.) Work by Lori Keith Robinson and Vicci S. Waits.

Gallery Lumiere (912-236-7720; 124 E. Oglethorpe St.) Excellent contemporary art from artists who work locally and internationally.

Myrtle Jones King Studio (912-234-3313; 122 W. Gaston St.) Pastel works by an artist who's been working for more than 50 years and who treats some Savannah scenes as Turner treated London.

Pei Ling Chan Garden for the Arts (322 Martin Luther King, Jr. Blvd., at West Harris St.) This walled garden, with individual sections reflecting African-American, English, French, and Asian cultures, is the backdrop for sculpture exhibits. There is a small amphitheater used during theatrical productions. A nice place in the thick of downtown to have a quiet moment.

GIFTS

Cottage Shop (912-233-3820; 2422 Abercorn St.) Linens for bed and table, stationery, lamps, and crystal.

Davenport House Museum Shop (912-236-8097; 324 E. State St.) Gifts with a Savannah theme and a Lowcountry flavor in the first house restored by the Historic Savannah Foundation.

Harry Barker (912-527-2700; www.harrybarker.com; 411 E. Liberty St.) A store for pets who have needs you never imagined.

Owens-Thomas House Museum Shop (912-233-9743; 124 Abercorn St.) A superior gift shop in a recently renovated ground-floor space with a great selection of art and architecture books, travel books, small clothing items, and prints.

GOURMET FOOD

Hunter Horn Plantation Co. Store (912-355-1812; 7202 White Bluff Rd.) The store specializes in spiral-sliced, honey-glazed hams, but also carries baked chickens for take out (the best in the city), and sells many varieties of salads and other deli items by the pound.

The Market at Jones and Whitaker (912-231-1006; 401 Whitaker St.) Fresh French bread delivered daily, as well as kitchen and house accessories in the French style.

Parker's Market (912-233-5000; 222 Drayton St.) The hippest recent rehab downtown, a 24-hour market on the site of a 1930s filling station, featuring 350 wines and microbrews, fresh herbs, fresh cookies and pastry daily, custom blended coffee.

Sophisticated Palate (912-355-6160; 238 Eisenhower Dr.) Gourmet foods including wines, cheeses, canned goods, and coffees; also the tools to make your cooking gourmet, too: pasta machines, coffee grinders, small appliances, and the like.

HOME FURNISHINGS/KITCHENWARE

Edison Lighting (912-4471008; 407 Whitaker St.) Antique reproduction lighting which could give you ideas for some upgrades at home. Small, nice atmosphere — you'll never go to Home Depot for lights again.

The Gypsy Moth (912-232-6800; 311 W. St. Julian St.) Folk art, birdhouses, funky wooden medallions and sculpture, Day of the Dead mementos, wooden animals, and rugs.

Kitchen Kaboodle (912-238-3474; 31 Barnard St.) Coming here will motivate you to make your kitchen more efficient and beautiful, and it will change your buying habits (see above listing).

Marco (912-234-4164; 38 Barnard St.) Walking by, you might first spot the wooden furniture, then the painted frames, then the chandelier in neon — eclectic and unusual.

Molly Wright Gallery (912-651-0115; 108 E. Harris St.) A studio with hand-painted floorcloths, furniture, and accessories, sturdy as workhorses but fresh and useful.

Off The Wall (912-233-8840; 206 W. Broughton St.) The best looking pieces of painted furniture, funky accessories, and found objects are not art on the wall in this gallery, but called "decoration" — and they're fun.

SPORTING GOODS AND CLOTHING

Most of the following stores not only have athletic equipment and accessories for sale, but they rent equipment, too. Call ahead to check on the availability of rental goods, or to reserve them in advance of your stay.

Bicycle Link (912-233-9401; 22 W. Broughton).

North End Surf Shop (912-786-8823; 1207 Hwy. 80, Tybee Island).

Pro Bass Outfitters (912-354-3377; 6608 White Bluff Rd.).

Rec-Arts Outdoor Clothing and Gear (912-201-9393; www.rec-arts.com.15 E. Broughton St.).

Star Bike Shop (912-927-2430; 127 E. Montgomery Crossroads).

Thompson's Sports Shop (912-920-0977; 8110 White Bluff Rd.).

Wilderness Outfitters (912-927-2071; 105 Montgomery Crossroads).

CHAPTER FIVE
Sea Island Gems
BEAUFORT, EDISTO, AND BLUFFTON

> *A place that ever was lived in is like a fire that never goes out. It flares up, it smolders for a time, it is fanned or smothered by circumstance, but its being is intact, forever fluttering within it, the result of some original ignition. Sometimes it gives out glory, sometimes its little light must be sought out to be seen, small and tender as a candle flame, but as certain.*
>
> —Eudora Welty, 1944

The fields, creeks, sandy roads, and spreading marshes of the rural Lowcountry, the place where Lowcountry history began, have once again become its center of attention. All along the coast, from Charleston to Savannah, there is an increasing awareness of what the culture of the country-side, expressed in a life-time of habits and ritu-als, has meant to the two great cities that bookend the region and present themselves, to today's visitor, like magnificent finished products.

Wade Spees

Beaufort's cotton boom gave rise to magnificent homes.

Perhaps the shift in emphasis from urban to rural is simply nostalgic, spurred on by a wishful return to the basics. Perhaps it has come because coastal development is accelerating. Typical Lowcountry spaces — fields rimmed by live oaks and stands of pine — are no longer simply evocative "open space": they are potential building sites. Or maybe the mood has shifted because another shape has emerged from what was a familiar picture — like in those clever drawings, where it is sometimes the vase that appears before your eyes, and then it is the facing profiles.

The Lowcountry's alternative view, the rural view, can be seen most clearly in the areas around Beaufort — Lady's Island, St. Helena Island, and Port

Royal — on Edisto Island, and in the little village of Bluffton. Before the Civil War they were as imposing, in their own small incarnations, as Charleston and Savannah: they boasted luxurious houses, profitable plantations, hundreds of slaves. Planters sent their children to be educated abroad. But all that changed one day, the day in 1861 that Federal troops arrived to occupy the Sea Islands. All at once, these self-satisfied and self-conscious towns receded from the foreground view into the rural background.

It took years for them to recover, but recover they have. Furthermore, they seem to have done so with a unique sense of the importance of celebrating both views of themselves — the part of them that was prosperous, worldly, and city-like, and the part of them that struggled for decades to make do with the essentials. It comes as no surprise that they are places where vistas, boughs, and fields are valued as much as brickwork, eaves, and intersections.

Today, rather than rely simply on one picture of themselves, these places celebrate the less apparent patterns in their composition: the landscape of "vernacular" homes of farmers and fishermen; the old market roads; the remains of a wharf; the praise houses and plantation neighborhoods; the plantation cemeteries; the creek landings and fishing holes; the "rabbit-box" stores and packing houses. The appreciation of what's plain has brought a proud recognition of how resourceful country people were.

To a visitor, this means that there is more to seek out and understand, and many more chances to do so. The most mundane memories and the most idealized ones are spilling forth from the vault of the past. Their blending is what gives the Lowcountry its dramatic, cohesive, sense of place, a sense that is felt especially (if it is not immediately seen) in the rural Sea Islands.

BEAUFORT

Beaufort has been a small town for a long time. Spanish and French explorers came to the area 100 years before the Pilgrims landed at Plymouth Rock, and they were followed, in due course, by English and Scottish settlers. The city of Beaufort is itself on Port Royal Island, one of the 65 islands that make up Beaufort County. It is the county seat. Other islands include St. Helena, Lady's, Fripp, Hilton Head, Daufuskie, Cat, Harbor, Hunting, Coosaw, Dataw, Polowana, Parris, Cane, Bray's, Lemon, and Pinckney.

Formally founded in 1711, it was a frontier settlement and trading center, attacked at times by Yemassee Indians, beset with illness, and populated by the scrupulous and unscrupulous who made the best of the resources they had. The resources, in fact, were plentiful: Beaufort's outlying lands sustained dense forests, which gave up shipbuilding timber and naval stores; vast tracts of land, suitable for raising cattle and raising crops like corn, potatoes, indigo, rice, and cotton; and rich marshes to feed fowl and game. The maze of waterways provided fish and shellfish in abundance.

Over time, investors spotted Beaufort for what it was and staked their

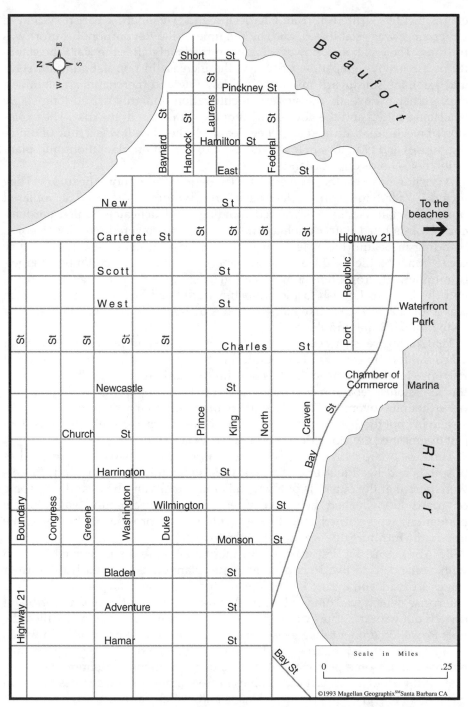

Courtesy of The Greater Beaufort Chamber of Commerce (used by permission)

BEAUFORT

claims. Settlers drifted in from Charleston and Savannah, a parish system of governance was established, and, by the time of the Revolution, Beaufort was bustling. The real boom, however, came immediately after the war. The stability of the newly-independent country, the increase in population (both slave and free), the southward migration of New England merchants and families, and, perhaps above all, the successful cultivation of highly prized long-staple Sea Island cotton and the development of the cotton gin lit the fuse. The explosion of wealth that resulted launched Beaufort's heyday. It was a time of building houses and churches in town and developing cotton plantations and plantation households on the islands.

A visitor can see the legacies of this period throughout Beaufort. They include Palladian-inspired doorways and windows, and huge, pillared porches; ornate Adam-style carved moldings and delicately scaled gardens; churchyards filled with camellias and azaleas, and towered over by steeples. Standing in Beaufort's Waterfront Park, it is easy to imagine a 19th-century scene come to life as dozens of schooners, bateaux, and cottonbox barges, brimming with crops, timber, mail, cotton bales, animals, passengers, produce, and the latest in English fashion and furniture, load or unload goods. There was a lot of activity, for like many societies made newly rich, Beaufort's had a taste for luxury and indulged it.

That, of course, changed abruptly. In another time and place, the shelling of a Federal fort (in this case Fort Sumter) not all that far away, and the Federal response to it, might have produced a shred of hesitation as to the wisdom of the Secessionist rebellion. Not so in Beaufort: it was apparently with great surprise that on November 7, 1861, white Southerners found themselves in flight — leaving hot food on the table, the story goes — from Yankee troops who had just demolished the Confederate port defenses at Bay Point.

Thus the occupation began. Soon the grand old houses were being used as hospitals and headquarters. The area was under military command. Pickets were posted at the outskirts of town and along creeks and boat landings: some on guard duty watched the smoke of rebel campfires across the water. Whole plantations were turned over to regiments who appropriated the cows, the liquor, the furniture, the wagons, and the food crops.

By April 1862, the first wave of Northern abolitionists had arrived in town with a mandate to live in and manage the plantations and teach the former slaves to read and write; essentially to "prepare them for freedom." Their enterprise, which was funded by private missionary societies in the North and carried out with the approval of the federal government, came to be called the Port Royal Experiment. In a sense this was an old-time Peace Corps, in which idealistic, mostly young, men and women volunteered to assist a cause they believed in, at some personal risk and under conditions of definite hardship. Their efforts had an impact on the lives of freedmen which resonates today, in particular at Penn Center on St. Helena Island, which has remained a center for teaching native islanders.

There is something very sad about these fine deserted houses. Ours has Egyptian marble mantels, gilt cornice and centre-piece in parlor, and bath-room, with several wash-bowls set in different rooms. The force-pump is broken and all the bowls and their marble slabs smashed to get out the plated cocks.... Bureaus, commodes, and wardrobes are smashed in, as well as door panels, to get out the contents of the drawers and lockers, which I suppose contained some wine and ale, judging by the broken bottles lying about. The officers saved a good many pianos and other furniture and stored it in the jail for safe-keeping. But we kindle our fires with chips of polished mahogany, and I am writing on my knee with a piece of flower-stand across them for a table, sitting on my camp bedstead.

—Edward S. Philbrick to his wife in Brookline, MA,
from Beaufort, March 9, 1862

From the end of the Civil War right up until World War II, farmers brought their cotton to market in ox-drawn carts.

Courtesy of The Charleston Museum, Charleston, South Carolina

In the years following the Civil War, promises made were often promises broken. Some former slaves were given land; some bought tracts communally; some worked the old fields under a new owner. A nascent phosphate mining industry provided jobs for a while, but it eventually collapsed. The terrible hurricane of 1893, in which some 5,000 islanders died, soured Sea Island soil for fine cotton plants. The scourge of boll weevil in the 1920s dimmed the last hope of large-scale cotton production. For most people, living returned to subsistence level farming and fishing. Photographs from the early 1900s and those taken even as late as 1936 by employees of the Farm Security Administration — Walker Evans and Marion Post Wolcott among them — showed islanders dressed in rags and living in shacks with matted palmetto fronds for a roof. In 1969, Beaufort County was still one of the poorest counties in the United States, the focus of a Hunger Tour by several U.S. Senators. In town, these were the years of unpaved roads and bare feet, when white people were "too poor to paint, too proud to whitewash."

As in many other parts of the South, it took the American entry into World War II to improve the economy. The United States Marines had been a presence in Beaufort since the turn of the century, and at this point their role was expanded. While not exactly prosperous, Beaufort benefited from slow, steady growth. Commercial farming of tomatoes and other vegetables, and seafood processing, became healthy industries. By the mid-1960s, with the development of resort islands like Hilton Head and Fripp, and with the first wave of retirees flocking to its shores, Beaufort's economic future was assured.

It is hard to believe that the downtown Beaufort of today ever suffered reverses. The paint doesn't dare peel. It has become a destination for tourists, a second home to people from the north and west, and a first home for young families who are looking for an ideal, charming, "small town" in which to raise their children. It has been turning up on "Best Small Town" lists for several years. It has even become a character in Hollywood movies: two of native son Pat Conroy's novels have been filmed here, *The Great Santini* and *The Prince of Tides*, as well as *The Big Chill* and *Daughters of the Dust*. Parts of *Forrest Gump, Something To Talk About*, and *The Jungle Book* were shot here, too. Ron and Natalie Daise's acclaimed television series for children, "Gullah Gullah Island," was set in Beaufort and its environs, and featured many local residents in its cast.

It will take a lot more than Hollywood to turn Beaufort's head. The problems associated with regional planning and zoning, improved education, traffic and water service, land preservation, and economic development seem pressing here, as they do on the other Sea Islands. Having spent the better part of this century becoming what it is today, Beaufort, it turns out, is still a work in progress.

LODGING

The WPA Guide, *South Carolina, A Guide to the Palmetto State*, first published in 1941, indicates the presence of three hotels in Beaufort, and a number of "tourist homes" where guests could stay. Then as now, the preferred season was spring, although beginning in the 1920s, there was an informal "winter colony" of artists, playwrights, and others who found the laid-back town to their liking. Many returned every year for an extended stay in rooms at "Tidalholm," an elegant antebellum house in the neighborhood known as "The Point."

In those days, the comings and goings of visitors were duly reported in the local paper — perhaps an indication of what made news in this sleepy town. Other seasonal arrivals included sportsmen from the north who hunted and fished in several vast private preserves which, by the 1940s, claimed up to one-third of the acreage in Beaufort County.

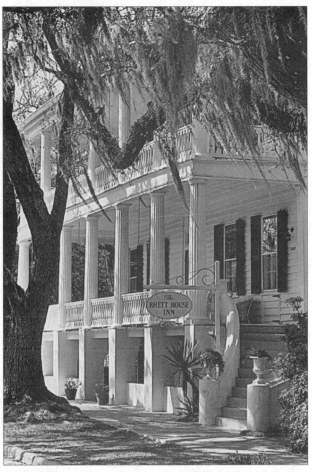

Beaufort's 19th-century prosperity is revived in its grand old homes now open for guests. The typical Lowcountry style of architecture includes high foundations — to catch the breezes off the bay — and multi-tiered porches.

Wade Spees

Today, the visitor in the next room might be a painter or a fly-fisherman, a movie director scouting locations, or a honeymooning couple. It's unlikely the newspaper will pay any attention at all. There are several luxury inns to chose from — quite a selection for a small town — but do ask ahead about their policies regarding children as guests. Smoking is generally permittted on outside porches.

Rates

Inexpensive	Up to $60
Moderate	$60 to $120
Expensive	$120 to $200
Very Expensive	$200 and up

These rates do not include room taxes or special service charges that might apply during your stay.

Credit cards

AE — American Express   DC — Diner's Club
CB — Carte Blanche   MC — MasterCard
D — Discover Card   V — Visa

Locals enjoy casually elegant dining in the Grill Room of the Beaufort Inn.

Wade Spees

BEAUFORT INN
Innkeepers: Rusty and
  Debbie Fielden.
843-521-9000.
www.beaufortinn.com.
809 Port Republic St.,
  Beaufort, SC 29901-1257.
Price: Expensive to Very
  Expensive.
Credit Cards: AE, D, MC, V.
Handicap Access: Yes; full
  ramp, some rooms.

Trimmed in vines, and rimmed with trees and flowering shrubbery, this three-story clapboard building with jutting bays and porches owns its busy corner. There's nothing but luxury inside, including an elevator (one of a handful in Beaufort), long hallways covered in plush carpet, chandeliers, and a vivid decorating style characterized by antiques, patterned wallpapers, draperies and soft curtains, and carefully hidden modern amenities. Its restaurant and cozy bar are equally deluxe. A back cottage with two bedrooms, two baths, and a fireplace is ideal for a family.

CRAVEN STREET INN
Innkeepers: David and
  Paige Solomon.
843-522-1668 or
  888-522-0250.

Located right downtown, this inn offers seven rooms, some with working fireplaces, in the main house, a carriage house wing, and a cottage (two of the rooms share a private porch overlook-

Fax: 843-522-9975.
www.cravenstreetinn.com.
1103 Craven St., Beaufort,
SC 29902.
Price: Expensive.
Credit Cards: AE, MC, V.

CUTHBERT HOUSE INN
Innkeepers: Gary and
Sharon Groves.
843-521-1315 or
800-327-9275.
Fax: 843-521-1314.
www.cuthberthouseinn.com.
1203 Bay St., Beaufort, SC
29902.
Price: Expensive.
Credit Cards: AE, D, MC,
V.
Handicap Access: One
room.

OLD POINT INN
Innkeepers: Joe and Joan
Carpentiere.
843-524-3177.
Fax: 843-525-6544.
www.oldpointinn.com.
212 New St., Beaufort, SC
29902.
Price: Moderate.
Credit Cards: AE, MC, V.

PORT REPUBLIC INN
Innkeepers: Off-site.
843-770-0600 or
888-305-7499.
www.port-republic-
inn.com.
915 Port Republic Street,
Beaufort, SC 29902.
Price: Expensive to Very
Expensive.
Credit Cards: AE, D, DC,
MC, V.

ing a garden). The style is simple, the colors are pale and pastel, and whether you're in the main house or not, there are private entrances for each room. The cottage has a living room, kitchen, and queen-size bed, and is a good choice for a couple taking a long weekend off or travelling with one or two small children.

The Cuthbert House has seen its share of excitement over the last 185 years, and its architecture tells the tale. Moved from its original site in 1810, embellished with fine Federal-period woodcarving, and enlarged with Victorian additions (sun porches and bays), it is renovated for modern comfort. It was the headquarters of Union General Rufus Saxton during the Federal blockade. Accommodations include two one-bedroom suites on the ground level (one is wheelchair accessible) and parlor suites. Its great site on the Beaufort River bluff makes the full Southern breakfast, afternoon tea, evening coffee, or simply lounging, a pleasure.

There are five guest rooms (named for 19th-century authors and characters) tucked away in this little turn-of-the-century Victorian, and the coziest of them are up under the eaves, lit by dormers and skylights. If you sit on the upstairs porch, you will feel embowered, lofted in the treetops, and very much a resident of Beaufort's "Point," one of its Historic District neighborhoods. There's also a nice back patio. Each room has a private bath; full breakfast is included.

Suite accommodations in a historic setting (a frame house circa 1820, bordered by a delicate iron fence that caught photographer Walker Evans' eye) but without the bed-and-breakfast common areas and on-site host. There are two suites on each floor, flanking a central staircase, and an additional single room. All have efficiency kitchens (one suite has a larger kitchen) with a small refrigerator and coffee-maker; complimentary continental breakfast is available at another location.

RHETT HOUSE INN
Innkeepers: Steve and
    Marianne Harrison.
843-524-9030 or
    888-480-9530.
Fax: 843-524-1310.
www.rhetthouseinn.com.
1009 Craven St., Beaufort,
    SC 29902.
Price: Expensive to Very
    Expensive.
Credit Cards: AE, MC, V.
Handicap Access: Two
    rooms.

The Harrisons left their careers in New York's fashion business for good when they came to Beaufort, but they brought along their taste and a meticulous attention to detail. They've lavished it on their ten-room inn and seven-room annex just a stone's throw away. The inn is simply beautiful, circa 1820, full of sunlight and breezes (only steps from the waterfront), furnished with antiques and comfortable chairs, prints, and vases of fresh flowers, flanked in the back by a garden and on the side by a courtyard fountain. Many of the rooms have fireplaces or Jacuzzi tubs; all have private baths and color televisions with cable service. The porches, upstairs and downstairs, are dreamy places to have afternoon cookies and tea, or read and rest — there's even a hammock. The rooms in the annex have private porches and entrances, mini-bars, and six have gas fireplaces. Full breakfast, including homemade breads and muffins, is included and picnic baskets can be made up.

TWOSUNS INN
Innkeepers: Carrol and Ron
    Kay.
843-522-1122 or
    800-532-4244.
www.twosunsinn.com.
1705 Bay St., Beaufort, SC
    29902.
Price: Moderate to
    Expensive.
Credit Cards: AE, D, DC,
    MC, V.
Handicap Access: One
    room.

Facing the Beaufort River at one of its prettiest points, just as it turns the bend and heads away from town, this former residence — now a six-room inn — dates from 1917. Many days, Carrol Kay works at her loom in the front room, or guests gather for tea in the late afternoon. The room's decor reflects Victorian, Oriental, and country themes. Rates include a full breakfast.

SEA ISLAND INN
(Best Western).
843-522-2090 or
    800-528-1234.
www.sea-island-inn.com.
1015 Bay St., Beaufort, SC
    29902.
Price: Moderate.
Credit Cards: AE, CB, D,
    DC, MC, V.

Conveniently located on Beaufort's main street, the locally owned and operated 43-unit motel has a pool, exercise room, and outdoor patio tables. Continental breakfast is served in the lobby. An excellent budget choice.

Further Afield in the Beaufort Area

COOSAW PLANTATION BED AND BREAKFAST (843-883-5088; www.

coosawfarm.com. Coosaw Plantation, Dale, SC 29940) Two cottages located on the grounds of a private home and hunting retreat about 20 minutes from Beaufort (on the way to Charleston) offer privacy and a true sense of the rural countryside — the sounds and smells and stars at night. One has three bedrooms, three baths, a kitchen, billiard room, and living room; the other has two bedrooms. They are on the river; there's a pool, tennis court and dock; hiking, kayaking. A wonderful spot to be left alone. Rates from $105 per night.

DATAW ISLAND (843-838-3838 or 800-848-3838; www.discoverdataw.com; One Club Rd., Dataw Island, SC 29920) Dataw is a private, 870-acre residential community with all the resort amenities, about 20 minutes from Beaufort on the way to the beaches. It has limited accommodations, but if you are interested in viewing sales property (homesites or homes) you may call to make arrangements for an overnight or weekend stay.

FRIPP ISLAND RESORT (843-838-3535 or 800-845-4100; One Tarpon Blvd., Fripp Island, SC 29920) Fripp is a private, 3,000-acre island bordered by an ocean beach about 35 minutes by car from downtown Beaufort. It's a residential community with three golf courses, tennis facilities, miles of biking trails, resort shops, pools, a beach club, and marina. Activity programs in the summer keep children busy. You can stay in homes accommodating 20 or in one-bedroom villas: there are more than 300 listings. In 2001, a weekly home rental in summer (sleeps six) cost from $1,050 to $2,300.

HARBOR ISLAND RENTALS (843-838-4800 or 800-553-0251; www.harborisland-sc.com; 2123 B Sea Island Pkwy., Harbor Island, SC 29920) Some 70 units, including villas and homes for rent on Harbor Island, a small private community with pool, tennis courts, and 2.5 mile beach. Oceanfront/ocean-view two-bedroom homes and villas start at $750 for a week in high season.

PALM KEY (843-726-6468 or 800-228-8420. www.palmkey.com; 26 Coosaw Way, Knowles Island, Ridgeland, SC 29936). The idea at Palm Key is to enjoy the outdoor life of the Lowcountry — crabbing, fishing, kayaking, hiking, fossil-hunting, birdwatching — by slowing down and taking notice, either with a guide or on your own. No television or telephones; you stay in single rooms, suites or attractive, fully equipped cottages. Rooms from $80; cottages from $140. Families welcome; pets a possibility.

ROYAL FROGMORE INN (843-838-5400; 863 Sea Island Pkwy., St. Helena Island, SC, 29920) A modest 50-room inn located midway between Beaufort and the beaches. The Ultimate Eating Restaurant next door is open all day.

National chain motels are also well represented in Beaufort. A list of some of them follows. It's a good idea to make reservations in advance, for they are often booked by family members of the graduating classes (many each year) of "boot camp" recruits from the Parris Island Marine Corps Recruit Depot. Most of these motels are located on Hwy. 21 (Boundary St.) between the Marine Corps Air Station and the National Cemetery.

BATTERY CREEK MARINA VILLAGE (843-521-1441; Hwy. 802 near the main gate of Parris Island).

BEST INN (843-524-3322; 2448 Boundary St., Beaufort).

COMFORT INN (843-525-9366; 2227 Boundary St., Beaufort).

DAYS INN (843-524-1551; 1660 Ribaut Rd., Beaufort).

HAMPTON INN (843-986-0600; 2342 Boundary St., Beaufort).

HOLIDAY INN (843-524-2144; 2001 Boundary St., Beaufort).

DINING

A s Beaufort and the Sea Islands have become popular destinations, restaurants have become more adventurous in tweaking the favorite dishes of a small town for a new audience. Thus, there will be grits and tiny creek shrimp fixed in many ways — with a spicy tasso sauce, with cheese, in soufflés, or served beside fried eggs. The same goes for greens (mustard, collard, kale, and dandelion), crops which are available fresh nearly all year long, and crab, which appears in soft or hard shell, in soups and salads, as a stuffing or a sauce. Tomatoes are a prominent cash crop in late spring and early summer, and are widely featured at that time. (The Sea Islands have a "window" for selling tomatoes on the national market for about three weeks in May, when migrant workers and local people harvest the fields and work in the packing houses well into the night.)

Many other local dishes flourish from late March through May, before the relentless summer heat warms up the creeks and dries out the soil. These include shad roe from the Edisto River, soft shell crabs, strawberries and blueberries, kiwi fruit, and oysters. Game birds, such as dove and marsh hen, and venison, are cooler weather treats.

If you find something you especially like, look for the recipe in *Sea Island Seasons*, a cookbook published by the Beaufort County Open Land Trust, a local non-profit land preservation group. It is available in stores, or by contacting the Trust (P.O. Box 75, Beaufort, SC 29902). Within its covers you'll find out how to make such Lowcountry specialties as Frogmore Stew (sausage, corn-on-the-cob, potatoes, and shrimp in broth); shrimp paste (a spread that retains the delicate, sweet flavor of fresh shrimp); bread-and-butter pickles; and lemon chess pie (the secret ingredient is cornmeal).

The following selections are among the better-known Beaufort restaurants; but don't neglect the smaller spots (listed under **Food Purveyors**) where a modest job can be done extremely well.

Dining Price Code

Inexpensive	Up to $10
Moderate	$10 to $20
Expensive	$20 to $30
Very Expensive	$30 or more

Credit Cards

AE — American Express	DC — Diner's Club
CB — Carte Blanche	MC — MasterCard
D — Discover Card	V — Visa

BEAUFORT INN AND RESTAURANT
843-521-9000.
809 Port Republic St.
Open daily.
Price: Expensive.
Cuisine: American and Continental.
Serving: D; Sunday brunch.
Credit Cards: AE, D, MC, V.

Quiet, white-linen tablecloths, very good-looking, low-key. The menu includes the classics (like sirloin steak and delicate veal dishes) and the presentation is routinely beautiful, with drizzled sauces and crisp vegetables arranged on the edge of oversized dinner plates. There's an extensive wine list for dinner and after-dinner drinks. The cozy Grill Room is a little less of a showcase, has a small bar, and attracts a mix of longtime local people with newly arrived young professionals. Reservations recommended.

DAD'S PLACE
843-522-3237.
2127 Boundary St.
Closed Sun.
Price: Inexpensive to Moderate.
Cuisine: Italian.
Serving: L, D.
Credit Cards: MC, V.

In an unprepossessing location, next to the K-Mart in Jean Ribaut Square, Dad's is a friendly, family-oriented place to go for a big bowl of spaghetti, an antipasto platter, or specialty lasagna. Grandparents take their grandchildren here. Sports memorabilia is tacked to the walls, the service is good and quick if it needs to be, leisurely if not. Great after a hot day at the beach.

11TH STREET DOCKSIDE
843-524-7433.
1699 11th St., Port Royal.
Open daily.
Price: Moderate.
Cuisine: American; Seafood.
Serving: D.
Credit Cards: AE, D, MC, V.

A casual restaurant, excellent for families, right on Battery Creek, where shrimp boats tie up and the sunsets pour color in the sky. The menu offers fried and broiled seafood specialties, as well as steak and pasta. Before dinner, work up your appetite by a visit to the town of Port Royal's marsh boardwalk and observation tower located at "The Sands," a beach to the east of the port terminal at the foot of Paris Avenue. Sharp eyes can find lots of fossilized sharks' teeth here.

Gathering and Corn-Shelling, St. Helena Island

When they go into the field to work, the women tie a bit of string or some vine round their skirts just below the hips, to shorten them, often raising them nearly to the knees; then they walk off with their heavy hoes on their shoulders, as free, strong, and graceful as possible. The prettiest sight is the corn-shelling on Mondays, when the week's allowance, a peck a hand, is given out at the corn-house by the driver. They all assemble with their baskets, which are shallow and without handles, made by themselves of the palmetto and holding from a half a peck to a bushel. The corn is given out in the ear, and they sit about or kneel on the ground, shelling it with cleared corn-cobs. Here there are four enormous logs hollowed at one end, which serve as mortars, at which two can stand with their rude pestles, which they strike up and down alternately....They separate the coarse and fine parts after it is ground by shaking the grits in their baskets: the finest they call corn-flour and make hoe-cake of, but their usual food is the grits, the large portion, boiled as hominy and eaten with clabber.

— Harriet Ware (a young abolitionist and teacher from Boston,
who lived and taught at Coffin Point Plantation,
St. Helena Island) to her parents, May 22, 1862.

EMILY'S RESTAURANT AND TAPAS BAR
843-522-1866.
906 Port Republic St.
Closed Sun.
Price: Moderate to Expensive.
Cuisine: Continental.
Serving: D.
Credit Cards: AE, D, MC, V.

At Emily's you can put together a meal from "tapas" items — small dishes of hot and cold appetizers, which may have light sauces or seafood stuffing. The small restaurant is dark and cozy, attracting local business people, new downtown residents, and boaters cruising through on the Intracoastal Waterway. A good place for a light, late meal: tapas served to 11 p.m.

PLUMS
843-525-1946.
904 1/2 Bay St.
Open daily.
Price: Moderate to Expensive.
Cuisine: American.
Serving: L, D.
Credit Cards: D, MC, V.

Plums, with its checkerboard floor, pale wood banquettes, and narrow, covered, outdoor porch, is a favorite with locals and visitors alike. It could use a facelift, but it's so popular you wonder where the owners would find the time. Hot sandwiches like grilled turkey or reubens, multi-layered clubs, and homemade soups are lunchtime stars; there's peanut butter and jelly for kids. The dinner menu features more elaborate contemporary American food with an eclectic twist: fire-grilled steaks and nightly seafood specials, some traditional Southern fare, and a mix of internationally influenced dishes. Dessert offerings include homemade ice creams prepared at Plums Ice Cream Factory in Port Royal. A full bar serves the lively nighttime crowd.

The porch of Plum's restaurant overlooks the Waterfront Park and is one of Beaufort's prime people-watching spots.

Wade Spees

SHRIMP SHACK
843-838-2962.
1929 Sea Island Parkway, St. Helena Island (about 11 miles south of Beaufort toward the beach).
Closed Sun.
Price: Inexpensive.
Cuisine: Seafood.
Serving: L, D.
Credit Cards: None.

THE STEAMER
843-522-0210.
168 Sea Island Parkway, Lady's Island.
Closed Sunday.
Price: Expensive.
Cuisine: Lowcountry.
Serving: L, D.
Credit Cards: AE, D, MC, V.
No Reservations.

Fresh seafood from the family dock — you can see the shrimp boats from the porch — accompanied by slaw, red rice, hush puppies, and beans. Deviled crab and shrimp burgers (ground, seasoned shrimp on a bun) are specialties. You can eat upstairs on the screened-in porch or in an adjacent gazebo. It's laid back and local, and the hard work of the Upton family keeps the standards high.

A curious though congenial clientele, a mix of transplanted northerners and locals. (The Beaufort bumper sticker "I Don't Give A Damn How You Did It Up North" is often seen on pickup trucks parked here.) There's usually a line for dinner, so be prepared to wait. Broiled and grilled local seafood and shellfish platters are the main dishes. It's noisy, crowded, and informal. If you're curious about Frogmore Stew, a spicy local dish that features sausage, corn on the cob, shrimp, and potatoes, this is the place to try it.

Frogmore Stew at The Steamer features the best of land and sea: sausage, corn, potatoes, and firm, pink shrimp.

ULTIMATE EATING
843-838-1314.
859 Sea Island Pkwy., St.
	Helena Island.
Open daily.
Price: Inexpensive to
	Moderate.
Cuisine: American;
	Southern.
Serving: B, L, D.
Credit Cards: MC, V.

Located between Beaufort and the beach, just minutes from Penn Center, a friendly, modest restaurant with reliable, not-too-fancy food: steak sandwiches, fried fish, local shrimp and crab, full breakfasts. Music on weekend nights.

WHITEHALL PLANTA-
	TION RESTAURANT
843-521-1700.
27 Whitehall Dr., Lady's
	Island.
Closed Sun. and Mon.
Price: Expensive.
Cuisine: Continental.
Serving: L, D.
Credit Cards: MC, V.
Reservations recom-
	mended.

A wonderful setting under a canopy of live oaks by the river, and a dining room that has windows on three sides, makes eating here relaxing and enjoyable. It's the place local people bring their out-of-town guests. It has a nicely settled-in feeling. No one seems to be in a big hurry. The menu offers some surprises: roast lamb, lightly sauced sliced veal, and broiled fish are worth trying.

FOOD PURVEYORS

BAKERIES/COFFEE BARS

Common Ground (843-524-2326; 102 West St. Ext.) An offbeat place (for Beaufort) where people in the local arts world hang out. Smoothies, bagels, coffee, magazines, newspapers, comfortable chairs, a view to the water.

Firehouse Books & Espresso Bar (843-522-2665; 706 Craven St.) Coffees, fancy lattes, juices, muffins, and sweets, set amidst a friendly two-story bookshop next to the Library.

Magnolia Bakery Cafe (843-524-1961; 703 Congress St.) Adjacent to the Visitor's Center, a small restaurant with outdoor dining specializing in homemade bread and desserts, snacks, lunch served all day. Beer and wine available.

CANDY AND ICE CREAM

Chocolate Tree (843-524-7980; 507 Carteret St.) A family-owned shop selling many different kinds of chocolates, truffles, and dipped fruits made right on the premises, plus candy-making accessories, gift boxes, jelly beans, cards, and gifts.

Plums Ice Cream Factory (843-524-7003; 709 E. Paris Ave., Port Royal) Ice cream made right there, simple lunches and snacks. A good place to stop if you've been at the beach at the Sands or the Port Royal Boardwalk.

DELIS AND FAST FOOD

Bay Towne Grill (843-522-3880; 310 West St.) If you see a crowd at the edge of a parking lot, you're here: a tiny building with outdoor tables and stools marks the spot. Burgers, vegetarian sandwiches, salads, subs, and soups. Good food, low prices, lots of character.

Blackstone's Deli & Cafe (843-524-4330; 915 Bay St.) Best breakfast in town, and nice to sit here engrossed in the morning paper. Lunch is also served. Wines and specialty foods for sale, as well as locally produced paintings and furniture.

Fuji (843-524-2662; 81 Sea Island Pkwy., Lady's Island) Seafood, chicken, steak, and vegetables, tossed on the hot griddle, served with rice and salad with ginger dressing. A good bargain choice.

Maryland Fried Chicken (843-524-8766; 1100 Ribaut Rd.) The real thing, by the piece, box, or bucket, as well as side orders like fried okra, mashed potatoes, slaw, and catfish. Drive-thru window.

Upper Crust (843-521-1999; 81 Sea Island Pkwy., Lady's Island) Pizza, salads, subs, beer, and wine. A slice of the super-deluxe house pie and sweet tea before a movie (the theater is located across the street) or after a day at the beach, goes a long way.

CULTURE

As Beaufort has grown, so have its cultural activities, both indigenous and imported. The museums and the annual house tours have gained a professional thoroughness; bookstores sponsor author's signings; the University of South Carolina at Beaufort has an active exhibition space and chamber music series; late night music prospers; there are art galleries and venues for live theatre and dramatic readings. It may be enough to sit and watch the tide go out on a Friday night, but you don't have to in Beaufort anymore.

For information about cultural organizations in town, a walking tour of artists' studios and galleries, or upcoming events, contact: *The Arts Council of Beaufort County*, 843-521-4144; 801 Carteret St., Beaufort, SC, 29902. For events focused on African-American heritage there's a web site at: http://users.aol.com/queen mut/GullGeeCo.html. The local newspapers of Hilton Head and Beaufort sponsor an informative website, including cultural listings and events at www.my lowcountry.com

FILM

Lady's Island Cinema (843-986-5806; Sea Island Parkway, Lady's Island).
Plaza Theaters (843-524-9468; Beaufort Plaza, Hwy. 170).
Plaza 21 Drive-In Theatre (843-846-4500; Hwy. 21).

HISTORIC HOMES, GARDENS & RELIGIOUS SITES

BAPTIST CHURCH OF BEAUFORT
843-524-3197.
601 Charles St.

This is an 1844 Greek Revival beauty. The ceiling plasterwork and ornamented cornices seem to match — in their absolute, solid mass of decoration — the abundant self-confidence of the prosperous little town of Beaufort in its heyday.

CHAPEL OF EASE
Land's End Rd., St. Helena Island.

The ruins of this planters' church, built in the 1740s to serve worshippers far from town, are of brick and tabby, a construction material that blends oyster shells with lime, sand, and water. The site is a wonderful place for photographs — spooky in the fog or at dawn, mellow and ageless at dusk.

JOHN MARK VERDIER HOUSE
843-524-6334.
801 Bay St.
Mon.–Sat. 11–4; last tour at 3:30.
Admission: Adults $4; children $2.

Built circa 1790 for a local merchant according to the plan and Adam-influenced decoration of the day, this house includes a formal parlor and ballroom, ornamental fireplace friezes, carved moldings, and antiques that are original both to the family and to the period of the house. Headquarters of the Historic Beaufort Foundation.

OLD SHELDON CHURCH RUINS
Secondary Rd. 21, 1.7 miles north of the intersection of Hwy. 17 and Hwy. 21.

Beautiful brick columns, fragile arches, and sill slabs remain from a church that was burned twice, first by the British in 1779 and then by the Union Army in 1865. A little temple in the woods. There's a small shaded picnic area on site.

PENN CENTER
843-838-2432.
P.O. Box 126, Martin Luther King, Jr. Drive, St. Helena Island, 29920.
York W. Bailey Museum
Mon.– Fri. 11–4.
Admission: Adults $4; children $2.
Weekend hours by appointment.

Founded in 1862 by two Pennsylvania women as a school for the newly freed slaves, Penn has remained a vital institution to promote education, self-sufficiency, and cultural expression among native islanders. In the days of segregation, it was one place where blacks and whites could meet together, as they did when the Rev. Dr. Martin Luther King planned his march on Washington. The York W. Bailey Museum (843-838-8562) holds a collection of cultural artifacts, African objects, and paintings. Community sings featuring gospel choirs and spirituals, an island tradition to which visitors are welcome, take place in Frissell Hall on the third Sunday of each month from September to May at 7:30 p.m. The entire campus is a National Historic Landmark.

The 18th-century interior of St. Helena's Episcopal Church offers 21st-century worshippers serenity and a sense of history.

Wade Spees

**ST. HELENA'S
    EPISCOPAL CHURCH**
843-522-1712.
507 Newcastle St.
Mon.–Sat. 10–4.

This church, built of brick from England in 1724, is adorned inside with graceful columns, upstairs galleries, and tall, multi-paned windows on the deep sills of which rest buckets of blossoming magnolia, daffodils, or narcissi in season. Its shaded, walled churchyard makes for a lovely stroll.

**TABERNACLE BAPTIST
    CHURCH**
843-524-0376.
907 Craven St.

A lovely, white clapboard building with bell tower; in its churchyard lies the grave — and stands a fine bust — of Robert Smalls, who was born a slave, engineered a daring ship capture during the Civil War, and was later a congressman and significant figure in Beaufort's Reconstruction period.

MILITARY SITES

NATIONAL CEMETERY
1601 Boundary St.,
    Beaufort.

Created by President Lincoln in 1863 for victims of Southern battles, this 29-acre cemetery is the final resting place of some 9,000 Union soldiers and more than 100 Confederates. It is still in service.

**PARRIS ISLAND
    MUSEUM**
843-525-2951.
War Memorial Building,
    Marine Corps Recruit
    Depot.
MCRD ERR, P.O. Box
    190001, Parris Island, SC
    29905.
Daily 10–4:30; except on
    Thursdays to 7 p.m. and
    Friday mornings at 8 a.m.
Admission: Free.

The museum showcases the history and development of the area on which the famous "boot camp" stands, from its earliest settlement through contemporary recruit training. (Artifacts have been recovered from the Spanish village of Santa Elena, circa 1566; from Charlesfort, a French outpost established by Jean Ribaut in 1562; and from Fort San Marcos, circa 1576. Excavation continues at these sites, located near the depot golf course.) Exhibits of uniforms, personal items, weapons, drawings, and documents trace the history of the Marine Corps in its worldwide engagements. You can also consult Platoon Books for listings of Marines. Self-guided driving tour maps are available. If you're interested in observing morning colors or a graduation (held on Fridays), contact the Visitor Center (843-525-3650). You may also picnic in designated areas or have an inexpensive meal at a base restaurant, including the Officer's Club.

MUSEUMS

BEAUFORT MUSEUM
843-525-7077.
713 Craven St.

Located in the old Beaufort Arsenal, rebuilt in 1852, an ochre-colored bastion with a courtyard, the museum is redefining itself from what

Robert Smalls, born a slave on Lady's Island, became a Civil War hero for stealing a Confederate steamer, The Planter, *in Charleston and delivering it to the Union fleet blockading the port. He later served as Congressman during Reconstruction and as Customs Collector.*

Wade Spees

10–5; closed Wed. and Sun. Admission: Adults, $2; children $0.50.

might once have been called Beaufort's "attic" to a center of local history and culture.

NORTH ST. AQUARIUM
843-524-1559.
608 North St.
Thurs.–Sat. 10–6.
Admission: Adults $2; children $1.
Call ahead for group rates.

The aquarium features a collection of sea creatures, some in "touch tanks" — and a knowledgeable host in Bob Bender, who introduces visitors to Lowcountry marine life in a relaxed and interesting way. He can arrange guided walks in the marsh, too.

MUSIC

Hallelujah Singers (843-525-6129; 806 Elizabeth Lane, Beaufort, SC 29901). The group of singers under the direction of Marlena McGhee Smalls, a talented vocalist who has earned a national reputation for her singing and her acting (she was Bubba's mother in the movie Forrest Gump) performs throughout the year, often in a downtown church at the time of annual house tours; weekly during the summer at various sites. Call or write for specific schedules.

Penn Center Community Sings (843-838-2432; P.O. Box 126, St. Helena Island, SC 29920). Community groups, quartets of senior citizens, gospel choirs, spur-of-the-moment vocalists, and soloists who deacon out lines of spirituals to the audience perform at 7:30 p.m. on the third Sunday of every month, from September to May, in Frissell Hall on the historic Penn Center campus.

Community sings held monthly at Penn Center keep the heritage of spirituals and gospel music alive on St. Helena Island.

Wade Spees

The popularity of the sings and the feelings of dignity and fellowship that characterize them are a moving testament to the pride of Sea Islanders in their culture and heritage. Contributions are welcome.

NIGHTLIFE

Banana's (843-522-0910; 910 Bay St.) Jazz combos on the weekends.

Johnson Creek Tavern (843-838-4166; 2141 Sea Island Pkwy., Harbor Island.). A no-frills beach bar about 25 minutes from town, where you'll find campers from Hunting Island State Park, young couples, and "after-party" groups who come for the last set. Anything from bluegrass to rock on the weekends.

Ultimate Eating (843-838-1314; 859 Sea Island Pkwy., St. Helena Island) Live jazz and blues performances Fri.–Sun. evenings.

THEATER

Beaufort Little Theater (843-522-2000; P.O. Box 1422, Beaufort, SC 29901). Beaufort's popular community theater performs well-known works — musicals, comedy, and drama — several times each year.

The Shed Center for the Arts (843-525-0968; 809 Paris Avenue, Port Royal) A large space in Port Royal dedicated to theatre education and performances, both local and regional, and home to the Lowcountry Repertory Theatre.

The "Spirit of Old Beaufort" (843-525-0459; 828-B Bay St.) Costumed guides present the story of Beaufort's history. Call for tickets.

RECREATION

For at least 200 years, Lowcountry people have depended on the reliable bounty of land and sea. They became so accustomed to gathering and returning home with full baskets that the work of it, and the pleasure to be had in it, were easily interchanged. These days the sportsman, the naturalist, and the Sunday painter take to the outdoors in equal numbers — and often with equal results: going in seriousness, returning with, at the very least, a day of pleasure to their name. Such is the natural abundance of the Lowcountry, and the dozens of opportunities to explore it — by power boat, kayak, windsurfer; with fishing pole, crab net, paintbrush, or pup tent — that visitors still have this experience today.

Beaufort, in particular, claims the advantage over Charleston and Savannah of having its rural recreational opportunities close at hand. Informally, residents and visitors can fish or throw cast nets for shrimp at bridges off Hwy. 21 at *Cowan Creek* and *Village Creek*, from the *Waterfront Park*, and at the *Broad River Bridge Fishing Pier*, among other spots. *Hunting Island State Park* is located off Hwy. 21, about a 30-minute drive from town. At the north end of Hunting Island is *Paradise Pier* (843-838-7437), at 1,120 feet, the state's longest. There are dozens of public boat landings within easy reach. Launching is free, and so is parking, but you're on your own — no attendants, telephones, or rest rooms. For locations, inquire at marinas or sporting goods stores or write: *Lowcountry Resort Islands and Tourism Commission* (800-528-6870; P.O. Box 615, Yemassee, SC 29945).

Lowcountry barrier islands are dynamic ecosystems, regularly altered by erosion of the beach in one section and accretion of sand and dunes in others.

Wade Spees

In addition, the development of Beaufort's downtown and nearby coastal resorts has created opportunities for recreation of a more studied sort. There are fine golf courses, tennis complexes, marinas, boat tours, and fishing expeditions of all kinds.

Perhaps the most significant resource for those who love the outdoors and savor its hidden beauty is the *ACE Basin Preserve* — a consolidation of some 350,000 acres of marsh, creek, sound, and forest to the north, east, and west of Beaufort (ACE Basin Preserve, National Wildlife Refuge Office, P.O. Box 848, Hollywood, SC 29449; 843-889-3084). This crescent of landscape encompasses the forested, inland shore of the Ashepoo, Combahee, and Edisto Rivers and their small tributaries. And not all the activity is on the water, either: from points on dry land, birders have identified more than 250 species of resident and migratory birds. *ACE Basin Tours* (843-521-3099 or 888-814-3129; www.acebasin tours.com.) will take you on a 3-hour pontoon boat trip in the ACE. The boat leaves from Coosaw Island at 10 a.m. Weds. and Sats. (Adults, $30; Children 6–12, $15.00; under 6 free when accompanied by a parent.) Call for reservations and directions. Tours may be scheduled on other days, with a minimum 8 passengers.

So here are some options. If your recreational pursuits require clothing or equipment you didn't bring with you, see the shops listed in the **Shopping** section under "Sporting Goods and Clothing."

BEACH ACCESS

Hunting Island State Park (See entry under Camping.) Sunrise–sunset; $3 per
    car.

BICYCLING

Bicycling is a year-round family pastime.

Low Country Bicycles (843-524-9585; 904 Port Republic St.) A shop filled with the latest mountain, cruising, high performance, and kid's bikes, maps, and accessories. Owner John Feeser has good touring suggestions, local and longer distance. Bikes for rent by the hour ($5 adults; $3 children) and day ($20 adults; $12 kids), as well as racks for the car ($10), and helmets, locks, etc. Repairs on-site.

BOWLING

Ribaut Lanes (843-524-3111; 1140 S. Ribaut Rd.).

CAMPING

Camping at Hunting Island State Park.

Wade Spees

Hunting Island State Park (843-838-2011; www.southcarolinaparks.com; 2555 Sea Island Pkwy., Hunting Island, SC 29920) on Hwy. 21, about 30 minutes from Beaufort. 200 sites, 14 cabins, nature trails, picnic sites, showers and dressing rooms, a store, water, and electrical hookups. Some sites can be reserved; some are first come, first served. Some cabins are handicapped-accessible. Campsites from about $19 per night; cabins from $73–$116. The 19th-century Hunting Island lighthouse offers an expansive view of the confluence of the Atlantic Ocean and St. Helena Sound.

Kobuch's (843-525-0653; 246 Savannah Hwy., Burton, SC, 29906; near Parris Island gate). 15 sites, full hookups.

Point South KOA (843-726-5733 or 800-562-2948; I-95 at Exit 33).

Tuc In De Wood Campground (843-838-2267; 22 Tuc In De Wood Lane, St. Helena Island, SC 29920) 74 sites with city water, electricity, and cable television connections; 30 sites with full hookups.

CANOEING AND KAYAKING

Colleton State Park and Edisto River Canoe and Kayak Trail (843-538-8206, between 11 a.m. and 12 p.m.; www.southcarolinaparks.com. The Park is located 11 miles north of Walterboro on U.S. 15, at Exit 68 off I-95). This 56-mile trail winds its way along black-water Edisto River. For more information about the Edisto River Canoe and Kayak Commission, call 843-549-5591.

The Kayak Farm (843-838-2008; 1289 Sea Island Pkwy., St. Helena Island). Accompanied tours either full or half day or instruction; tours to Hunting Island and nearby creeks; longer trips to ACE Basin sites. Naturalists on staff. Custom expeditions and overnight tours by arrangement. Rates from $25 per day per kayak to $75 and up for a full day outing including lunch.

Tullifinny Joe's Outpost (843-726-4545; Hwy. 462 (off I-95) Coosawatchie, SC 29912). A sea-kayaking, saltwater fly fishing, and touring company, located about 35 minutes from Beaufort, offering numerous guided expeditions, instruction, and equipment rental.

FISHING

Fishing guide David Murray starts a trip early in the morning to catch the tide for inshore casting.

Wade Spees

Fishing was and is such a common pastime in the Lowcountry, so thickly woven into the fabric of local life, that in describing it one is likely to end up talking about the entire culture: the way its residents cook, the stories they choose to tell, the skills they wish to pass on, where they live, what they do on weekends, what kinds of politicians they elect, how they judge character, what their values are for their children. Like the Myth of the Old South and Old Families, the lore of fishing confers a kind of lineage by which people know themselves. And where the Old Families might have Old Houses, people who fish have Old Cars, "fishing cars" as they are widely known — dinged-up rust-buckets that make it to the boat landing (not much further) with the faithfulness of a hunting hound.

In fact, the opportunities for fishing are so numerous, the catches still plentiful, the waterways still generally pristine, the tradition so revered, that a book written in 1856, *Carolina Sport By Land and Water* by William Elliott, can be read as a nearly modern account.

Today's enthusiast can choose freshwater or saltwater sites; fish from piers, bridges, boats, banks, or the beach; or troll an artificial offshore reef. Saltwater fly fishing is a new and popular specialty. *Paradise Pier* (843-838-7437) is located on Hunting Island near Beaufort and open 24 hours. The fishing fee is $4. The catch can range from small bream, porgy, and spot — of the family commonly known as "sailor's choice" — to flounder, to big game fish like wahoo, drum, shark, and cobia. In general, the best part of the season extends from April through November, but small panfish remain active beyond those dates.

Licenses are required for freshwater fishing and for saltwater fishing under certain conditions. Most visitors interested in recreational fishing will not need one; they're not necessary for recreational shrimping and crabbing. Licenses are sold in many hardware and hunting stores, K-Marts, and tackle shops. For further information on licenses, and size and catch limits, contact the *South Carolina Wildlife and Marine Resources Dept.* (843-795-6350; P.O. Box 12559, Charleston, SC 29412).

For a comprehensive map indicating recreational fishing facilities in the Lowcountry, including marinas, boat landings, bridges and catwalks, shellfish grounds, and offshore reefs, write the *Lowcountry Resort Islands and Tourism Commission* (800-528-6870; P.O. Box 615, Yemassee, SC 29945).

There's good recreational fishing about 35 minutes north of Beaufort off Hwy. 17 (between Beaufort and Edisto) at the *Bear Island Wildlife Management Area* (843-844-2952 for the Game Warden).

SPORT-FISHING CHARTERS

A sport-fishing charter can take you to the Gulf Stream or to any of the dozen or so artificial reefs offshore. Over 150 years ago, the first artificial reefs used in this area were approximately 6 feet high, log, hut-like structures that were sunk to attract sheepshead; today's reefs are far more elaborate affairs that attract dozens of species. Given that much of the sea floor off the coast is sandy, these reefs provide the hard substrate necessary to create a "live bottom" of invertebrates, small fish, coral, crabs, and sponges. They are active feeding stations for the big fish, and experienced guides know them well. Trips of this sort generally take a full day. Trips closer to shore, in smaller boats, can be easily enjoyed by the half-day.

A listing of some of the many *charter boat services* available follows. Others may be available at marinas listed in the Chapter Two, *Transportation*. Rods, reels, bait, and tackle are provided; lunch or snacks are usually available, but you should check in advance; boats are equipped with safety equipment and licenses; all but the smallest have heads. It is wise to bring sunscreen, windbreakers, and a towel.

Many charters will design a trip to suit your particular interest or prepare a boat for a fishing tournament. If stormy weather is forecast, call ahead to confirm that the trip is on. Also check the reservation, deposit, and cancellation policies of each charter. You'll have to plan your trip around the tides, too. The 2001 prices for half-day trips started at about $100 per person, but varied considerably depending on the type of fishing and distance travelled.

Bay Street Outfitters (843-524-5250; www.baystoutfitr@islc.net. 815 Bay St.) Visitors who are experienced in the art of fly fishing, as well as those who are rank beginners, can find experienced guides, instruction (including fly fishing and casting, one-day and two-day seminars, from $150 per person), and a full line of Orvis outfits, accessories, and specialty rods here. In 2001, guided charters (for two–three anglers), including lunch, cost in the range of $250 to $400 depending on how many hours were spent on the water. Licenses are not required on the charters; drinks and equipment are provided. Call ahead and see what the season has to offer.

Capt. David Murray (843-525-6820; 100 Grayson St., Beaufort). David Murray is an experienced fisherman in many types of water, a guide, an Orvis flyfishing instructor, and an advocate of Lefty Kreh's modern method of flycasting. For one or two persons, his fees are $400 for a full day; $250 for a half-day, including lunch and beverages, aboard a 16-foot Hewes Bonefisher.

Capt. Eddie Netherland (843-838-5661; Fripp Island Marina). Offshore and inshore trips by the day and half-day on a 25-foot Grady-White Sailfisher. King mackerel a specialty.

Low Country Fishing (843-522-8066; 2309 Palm Dr., Beaufort). Captain Doug Gertis. Light tackle inshore fishing for jack crevalle, trout, tarpon, and other species on a 19-foot Maverick Master Angler. Tag and release fishermen get a discount.

Sea Wolf V (843-525-1174; www.scfishnet.com; 5003 Luella St., Beaufort). Major Wally Phinney, Jr. USA, Ret. is your guide. Deep sea fishing, diving, cruising, by day or half-day aboard 32-foot boat. Half-day excursions start at $320; full day and Gulf trips from $600–$1100.

FITNESS FACILITIES

Ray's Gym (843-524-8351; Hwy. 170) Complete gym, fitness training, body-sculpting, Nautilus, weights, fitness machines.

YMCA of Beaufort County (843-522-9622; 1700 Paris Ave., Port Royal). Pool, gym, classes and more in a new facility.

GOLF

The Lowcountry probably has more golf courses per person than any other region in the country, and more with holes offering expansive ocean or marsh views, or such scenic diversions as deer, heron, and the occasional alligator. Many are consistently ranked among the top 100 in the country: visitors can and do spend every day for a week playing a different one.

Whether you're a duffer or scratch golfer, there's pleasure in being on the links, either early in the morning as the heavy dew dries and the temperature rises, or late in the day as the chuck will's widows commence their plaintive call. Lowcountry weather allows for year-round play and (in the summer) late-afternoon starting times. The high-season months are in fall and spring, so it is wise to schedule your playing time well in advance.

On some courses carts are required at peak playing times. Special prices are often posted for midday tee-times in the height of summer. For resort play, it is usually necessary to be an overnight guest. Golf packages that include lodging are numerous, so ask about them. One service, *Golf Beaufort* (800-972-2003 or 843-521-2003; 920 Bay St., Beaufort SC 29902) provides accommodations and tee-times at 10 area courses. Club rentals and instruction are available at all courses. Greens fees/cart rentals reflect 2001 prices.

Public and Semi-Private Courses

Country Club of Beaufort (843-522-1605 or 800-869-1617; 8 Barnwell Dr., Lady's Island) Russell Breedon design, 18 holes, par 72. Three sets of tees: 4,880 yards, 6,089 yards, and 6,489 yards. Pro: Craig Fischer. Greens fees including cart $40–$60.

Fripp Island (843-838-1576 or 800-933-0050; Fripp Island) Set on the rim of the Atlantic and Fripp Inlet, **Ocean Point Golf Links**, par 72, is a George Cobb course, from 4,951 yards to 6,590 yards. The **Ocean Creek Course**, the first designed by Davis Love III, is a par 71, winding through the marshes and interior wetlands. Yardage from 4,884 to 6,629. Walking is an option at both courses. Since they lie within a gated community, you must call ahead to reserve tee times and a visitor's pass. Fees are $50–$80 per person.

Lady's Island Country Club (843-524-3635; 139 Francis Marion Circle, Lady's Island) Pines Course, par 72, 5,421 yards to 6,811 yards; Marsh Course, par 72, 5,192 yards to 5,929 yards. Pro: Dick Tremblay. Greens fees including cart $31 to $80.

South Carolina National Golf Club (843-524-0300 or 800-221-9582; 8 Waveland Ave., Beaufort) George Cobb's last design, par 71. Four sets of tees: 4,970 yards to 6,625 yards. Pro: Charlie Bohmert. Greens fees including cart $49 to $80.

HORSEBACK RIDING

Beaufort Equestrian Center (843-846-4765), *Broomfield Stables* (843-521-1212), *D&L Quarterhorses* (843-521-0467) and *Shalimar Horse Center* (843-521-0419) welcome inquiries from visitors seeking instruction within the ring.

TENNIS

Public courts, some of which are lit for night play, are located on *Boundary Street* across from the National Cemetery; on the corner of *Battery Creek Rd. and Southside Blvd.*, and in the *Port Royal Park* on Paris Ave. in the village of Port Royal. Free. No reservations required.

SHOPPING

ANTIQUES

Bellavista Antiques & Interiors (843-521-0687; 206 Carteret St.) Large-scale furniture and vases, stone ornaments, English pine furniture.

Canup Antiques (843-524-8914; 809 Bay St.) American country furniture, tinware, white ironstone.

Der Teufelhund (843-521-9017; 13B Marina Blvd., near Parris Island) Military books, antique gear, insignias, trunks, and other ephemera of 20th century warfare.

Part of "the showroom floor" at Legacy & Whimsy in downtown Beaufort.

Wade Spees

Legacy & Whimsey (843-524-2685; 812 Port Republic St.) Original architectural elements, linens, and accessories.

Michael Rainey Antiques (843-521-4532; 702 Craven St.) A collection of antiques, frequently refreshed with new purchases, largely from New England, Pennsylvania, and the south. Baskets, boxes, benches, and paintings.

Nest (843-521-4965; 314 Charles St.) French and American antiques, fine fabric, small decorative pieces for the garden or mantle.

BOOKS / RECORDINGS

Bay St. Trading Co. (843-524-2000; 808 Bay St.) Best-sellers, books-on-tape, excellent children's section, comprehensive local and regional history, and many fine photography books. The staff is very knowledgeable, which makes this store the best place to browse downtown.

Beaufort Bookstore (843-525-1066; Jean Ribaut Sq.) A large selection and wide variety of books from best-selling fiction and non-fiction to military and Lowcountry favorites.

Firehouse Books and Espresso Bar (843-522-2665; 706 Craven St.) A charming bookstore with an excellent magazine selection and a coffee bar.

Lady's Island Bookstore (843-524-0444; 136 Sea Island Pkwy.) Paperback classics, good non-fiction, history, and biography.

Low Tide Records and Musical Sundries (843-524-9500; 917 Bay St., in the Old Bay Market Place.) Beaufort native and musician David Dowling's new store reflects a deep knowledge of musical styles and history, and his pleasure in finding unusual instruments and songbooks.

The information revolution links a local newsstand — and local customers — with the World Wide Web.

Wade Spees

Marketplace News (843-470-0188; 917 Bay St., in the Old Bay Market Place.) A bright, well-stocked newsstand with terminals for Internet access.

McIntosh Book Shoppe (843-524-1119; 919 Bay St.) New and used books on South Carolina you'll find no where else. Civil War albums, rare and antique volumes, as well as local writers and local history.

CLOTHING

Deal's (843-524-4993; 724 Bay St.) Cotton sweaters, khakis, shirts in natural fibers, and imported Irish apparel, all at discounted prices.

Elizabeth's (843-524-2734; 1001 Charles St.) Young local women have an exact eye for Beaufort casual and warm-climate dressy. Classics with a twist.

Jasmine (843-524-6660; 919 Bay St.) A women's boutique with dresses, separates, and colorful accessories.

Lipsitz Department Store (843-524-2330; 825 Bay St.) A family-owned and family-run business for 100 years. Everyday wear and shoes in all sizes, superior friendly service.

Plumage (843-522-8807; 104 West St.) Evening clothes with glittering accessories and distinctive casual outfits, including a fine small selection for kids.

CRAFTS

Carolina Stamper (843-522-9966; 203 Carteret St.) Rubber stamps and supplies and lots of ideas for making stationery and artwork.

The Craftseller (843-525-6104; 818 Bay St.) Local and regional artists' work, including jewelry, benches made of recycled wood from local buildings, fabric art, handmade paper, wind-chimes.

Ibile Indigo House (843-838-3884; 869 Sea Island Parkway.) The unique studio and shop of Adrienne King Comer, a fabric and batik artist whose work is based on West African techniques, including dyeing from the indigo plants she cultivates. Hangings, wearable art, yardage, and smaller art pieces are for sale; custom indigo dyeing by appointment.

Ms. Natalie's Workshop (843-838-4446; www.ronandnatalie.com.802 Sea Island Pkwy., St Helena Island). Natalie Daise's shop is animated by the same joyous spirit and creative imagination that made *Gullah Gullah Island* — the award-winning television show for children she created with her husband Ron (and filmed locally) — such a success. There's a craft room for all ages to enjoy, and a selection of baby items, multicultural books and recordings, hand-painted furniture, and crafts for sale.

Sweetgrass Baskets made by local artists can be found on St. Helena Island on Hwy. 21, at a roadside stand by the Red Piano Too Gallery, and at two additional stands further along, between the Gallery and the turn for Coffin Point at Seaside Road. The baskets, which incorporate palmetto frond, pine needle, and rush with the pale grass, come in many shapes and sizes, with individual variations inspired by the utilitarian shapes used in the past. They require enormous amounts of labor and skill and are useful as well as beautiful.

GALLERIES

Art &Soul (843-524-9710; 919-B Bay St., in the Old Bay Market Place.) A new gallery of paintings, prints, ceramics, and textiles with a contemporary feel. Art and craft supplies, too.

Bay Street Gallery (843-522-9210; 719 Bay St.) Original works by Lana Hefner (impressionistic pastels of marsh and woodland scenes) and Sandra Baggette (bright watercolors). A fine collection of Sea Island baskets and tiny ornaments.

Charles Street Gallery (843-521-9054; 914 Charles St.) Original work including bronze sculpture, raku pottery, paintings, and etchings. Full-service framing.

Gloria Dalvini Watercolors (843-521-0221; 101 Scott's St.) A wonderful, tiny building by the Waterfront Park houses dozens of watercolors of Lowcountry houses, gardens, and landscapes.

Indigo Gallery (843-524-1036; 809 Bay St.) Limited and open editions of many of the best-known Lowcountry artists, as well as serigraphs, original art, and framing.

Juxtaposition (843-521-1415; 812 Bay St.) A talented artist who grew up in Beaufort has brought her eye, and her commitment to beautifully made things, to bear in an eclectic gallery of paintings, ceramics, glass, jewelry, and painted furniture.

Longo Gallery (843-522-8933; 407 Carteret St. and 103 Charles St.) Suzanne and Eric Longo, husband and wife, are proficient and playful artists. Her ideas find expression in clay and concrete sculpture; his, in brightly colored, whimsical paintings (sometimes on old roof tin, or boards) and found-object constructions.

The Red Piano Too (843-838-2241; 780 Sea Island Parkway, St. Helena Island) Located just 15 minutes from Beaufort, this gallery has a superior collection of folk art and outsider art by many practicioners — including St. Helena native Sam Doyle — as well as sea grass baskets, quilts, books, furniture, beads, African objects, and prints. It also serves as something of a community center, in the sense that the owners and patrons are particularly interested in the preservation of St. Helena Island as a special rural place, not just a suburb of Beaufort. Fine framing is available. Definitely not to be missed — the gallery represents the best of the Lowcountry.

Rhett Gallery (843-524-3339; 901 Bay St.) Prints and watercolors of the Lowcountry by Nancy Ricker Rhett as well as antique first-edition prints and maps, Civil War and nautical materials, and hand-colored engravings. Custom framing and shipping available.

Shipman Art Gallery (843-524-7722; 904 Bay St.) Watercolor artist Barbara Shipman offers some 100 of her paintings in collectible print editions, as well as originals. She captures the Lowcountry in both intimate and grand ways — from one crab or one blossom to an entire coastline scene.

University of South Carolina at Beaufort (843-521-4144; 801 Carteret St.) The University and Northen Beaufort County Arts Council sponsor numerous shows throughout the year, from scholarly looks at the history of magazine covers to the best works of local artists.

GIFTS

Beaufort Butterfly Company (843-986-0555; 928½ Bay St.) Everything you'll need to attract, observe, identify, catch, and collect butterflies, as well as books about natural history and tee shirts with nature themes.

Boombears (843-524-2525; 501 Carteret St.) Fancy toy stores may be common in cities and upscale malls, but this one, founded and run by a local family, is probably the very best you've ever seen. It is ingenious, unpretentious, and filled with items of the highest quality: toys, books, dolls, games, tin soldiers, stuffed animals, racing cars, and kits of all kinds.

Fordham Hardware (843-524-3161; 701 Bay St.) Everything from hammocks to waste baskets, fireplace tools to floor wax. A Beaufort institution and, like some others, an endangered species in small town America.

Rossignol's (843-524-2175; 817 Bay St.) Fine china patterns, silver and gold jewelry, stationery, and expensive stemware — all suitable for wedding gifts — as well as platters, picture frames, and tea towels that would make good house presents.

Thorndike Williams Antiques and Collectibles (843-524-7688; 308 Scotts St.) Located in a little green and white cottage that looks nearly tropical, you'll find items decidedly un-cottagelike: fine reproduction furniture, prints, lamps, china, brass, fabrics, and antiques.

Verdier House Gift Shop (843-524-6335; 202 Scott's St.) Located beside the historic house museum, it features a collection of books, ornaments, prints, toys and notecards with sketches of Beaufort's old homes.

Waterside Place (843-524-0201; 308 Charles St.) Linens, specialty food items, and special little things for interiors.

GOURMET AND HEALTH FOOD

Local beekeepers and cooks provide home made honey and jellies, as Lowcountry residents have for generations.

Wade Spees

Blackstone's (843-524-4330; 915 Bay St.) A small gourmet grocery and an informal "chandlery" for boaters travelling the Intracoastal Waterway. (See Deli listing, too.)

Cravings By the Bay (843-522-3000 or 800-735-3215; cravingsbythebay.com; 928 Bay St.). Savor Lowcountry flavors as well as memories by ordering soups, condiments, sauces, and specialty books by mail. Shrimp, oysters, clams, scallops, and soft-shell crab can be delivered overnight. Drop by for more information.

Vita Villa Ltd. (843-522-0583; Hwy. 21, Lady's Island Square) Herbs, grains, candies, books, vitamins, local honey, and sugar-free and preservative-free health foods.

W.H. Gay Seafood (843-521-5090; 2242 Boundary St.) Fresh fish, shellfish, and shrimp from local waters, packed in ice to last on the road. Utensils, shirts, and "shrimp boots," in the classic white, low-cut style.

HOME FURNISHINGS/KITCHENWARE

The Cook's House and Linen Loft (843-524-6198; 706 Carteret St.) If there's something you need for the kitchen, from an ergonomic can opener to a baguette pan, you'll find it here, in rooms that are stocked floor to ceiling. A stationery store for anyone who loves the tools of the trade.

Lulu Burgess (843-524-5858; 917 Bay St.) An engaging blend of fashion-forward furniture and decorative items that would look good in pared-down loft, and bird baths that would never leave your side yard. Opened by a young Beaufort native who has brought her good taste back home.

Out of Hand (843-522-9955; 915 Greene St.) A tiny storefront imaginatively decorated and stocked with very special treats for the home: glassware, painted benches, candles, and linens.

SPORTING GOODS AND CLOTHING

Barefoot Bubba's (843-838-5431; 2135 Sea Island Pkwy, St. Helena Island). The latest in surf wear and boards, skim boards, rafts, and toys for the beach.

Bay Street Outfitters (843-524-5250; 815 Bay St.) A full line of high-end sportswear from Orvis and Barbour, as well as fishing gear, reels, binoculars, and books.

High Tide Surf Shop (843-524-2334; 905 Bay St.) Comfortable clothes like corduroys, clogs, Doc Marten's, cool sneakers, and pullovers, as well as swimwear and wet suits, boards, and surfing accessories.

Island Outfitters (843-522-9900; 189 Sea Island Pkwy.) Headquarters for serious gun and bow hunters, campers, and fishermen. Rods, coolers, bait, hooks, ammunition, and a big selection of rugged outdoor camouflage and boots. The expert advice is free.

EDISTO ISLAND

Like the Sea Islands around Charleston and Beaufort, Edisto's history starts with early Native American settlements. Soon after came rice, indigo, and cotton cultivation, slavery, the occupation of Federal troops, and from the end of the Civil War, isolation. Small farming and fishing operations have remained constant over time. However, unlike the other Sea Islands, Edisto while lively in the summer season, due to the scads of modest rentals on Edisto Beach and Edisto Beach State Park, remains quiet the rest of the time. Development is accelerating, but with planning and cooperation, it may reflect the Edisto that has survived thus far. (A preservation land trust seeks to protect and enhance vistas and procure land and easements.) If you're looking for a few days of peace and quiet, enlivened by beachcombing, a good meal, and perhaps a kayak or boat tour, your choice should be Edisto.

Po Pigs Bo-B-Q on Edisto Island serves up Lowcountry specials with a special twist of flavor. As always, they come with sweet tea.

Wade Spees

The island lies about 45 miles south of Charleston by road, and about 80 miles from Beaufort — of course far less by water. From Hwy. 17, take Hwy. 174 (signs alert you to Edisto) the island's main travel route. A variety of creeks and rivers irregularly indent Edisto, so that today, as in the past, there are roads that cross the marsh or wind through the woods in what seems to be the long way around. Original sections of the King's Highway, laid out in the early 18th century, remain in use today. The main road dead ends at the Atlantic Ocean.

For a visitor, Edisto is the least immediately knowable of the Sea Islands. What remains of its "Golden Age," the period between the Revolutionary and Civil Wars, is mostly hidden, tucked away along secondary roads that wind through fields and patches of scrub oak, and meander by the North and South

Edisto Rivers and their tributaries. Historic sites that are listed on the National Register of Historic Places (27 so far) do include churches, but consist primarily of private plantation homes and gardens. A good source of information is the **Edisto Chamber of Commerce** (843-869-3867 or 888-333-2781; www.edistochamber.com; P.O. Box 206, Edisto, SC 29438).

For an overview of the island's history, visit the **Edisto Island Historic Preservation Society's Museum** (843-869-1954; Hwy. 174 at Chisolm Plantation Rd. Hours are 1–4 Tues., Thurs., and Sat. Admission $2; free to children 10 and under.) Island artifacts such as baskets, clothing, farm tools, letters and documents, uniforms, and furniture are displayed in several small rooms. There are old photographs and explanatory remarks. The little gift shop sells a nice variety of natural history items for kids — good to use to explore and collect on their own — as well as a series of excellent reprints of booklets you're not likely to find anywhere else on your travels. They include *"Edisto Island in 1808," "Indigo in America," "Gullah,"* and *"She Came To the Island,"* the Edisto diary of Mary Ames, a Northern abolitionist whose account of teaching and living among the newly freed slaves during the Civil War is among the most poignant of the genre.

Alligators at the Edisto Serpentarium are up close and personal.

Wade Spees

The **Annual Tours of Edisto** generally take place on the second Saturday in October. Contact the **Edisto Island Historic Preservation Society** (843-869-1954; P.O. Box 393, Edisto Island, SC 29438) for information. In 2001, tour prices were $20 for adults; $5 ages 6–16. For an education on the subject of the region's reptile life, visit the new **Edisto Island Serpentarium** (843-869-1171; 1374 Hwy. 174) where more than 500 reptiles are on display in natural habitats.

Across Store Creek from the Serpentarium is one of Edisto's best places to eat. It is the **Old Post Office Restaurant** (843-869-2339; 1442 Hwy. 174) a cozy, moderate-to-expensive place that serves dinner Tuesday–Saturday. Entrees include grilled and sautéed entrees that represent a change from the fried food familiar at beach eateries. Another is *Po Pigs Barbecue and Catering* (843-869-9003; 2410 Hwy. 174) a family-run dining room and business with a cheerful atmosphere and really imaginative food — southern with a twist — like curried rice with sun-dried fruit and pureed country ham salad. The price is inexpensive to moderate.

Continuing across Edisto Island brings you to Edisto Beach, the curve of land that faces the Atlantic then turns to embrace the inner marsh. It has been for years the summer destination of South Carolina families — both as day trippers to the state park or as vacationers who stay for one or more weeks. Families take up residence in the plain, two-story houses that line the boulevards for about three dozen blocks and spill across adjacent avenues. There's nothing fancy about Edisto Beach: it's informal, full of kids riding bikes and loaded minivans parked in the sand. A high point of the day is watching the shrimp boats come in.

Many of these houses rent by the week, and several rental agencies list them. The summer prices range from $630 for a house on a golf course for 6 people to $1200 per week for a house that sleeps nine. For information contact:

The Atwood Agency (843-869-2151 or 800-476-0126; www.atwoodagency.com).
Edisto Realty (843-869-2527 or 800-868-5398; www.edistorealty.com).
The Lyons Co. (843-869-2516 or 800-945-9667).

A small resort, *Fairfield Ocean Ridge* (843-869-4527 or 800-251-8736; 1 King Cotton Rd., Edisto Island, SC 29438) also offers rentals (877-296-6335; www.fairfieldvacations.com) and its 300-acre layout includes amenities such as tennis, golf, swimming, a restaurant, and a kid's summer program. The accommodations are more rustic at *Edisto Beach State Park* (843-869-2756; www.southcarolinaparks.com; 8377 State Cabin Rd., Edisto Island, SC 29438). Sites include 97 spots for tents and RVs (two are designated for handicapped visitors) and five two-bedroom cabins. Some sites may be available by advance reservation. There's a boat ramp and general store, trails, showers, water and electrical hookups, and interpretive programs. The beach is a wonderful place to hunt for fossils and shark's teeth.

Because of its location at the confluence of the North and South Edisto Rivers, the Atlantic, and St. Helena Sound, Edisto Beach offers probably the easiest access to the ACE Basin and all sorts of fishing, boating, and watersports. For maps and information about sightseeing and bird-watching, contact the *ACE Basin National Wildlife Refuge Headquarters* (843-889-3084; 8675 Willtown Rd., Hollywood, SC 29449) or write the *South Carolina Department of Natural Resources* (843-844-8957; 585 Donnelly Drive, Green Pond, SC 29446.) If you want to tour the ACE Basin by water, contact the guide services below or stop by the *Edisto Beach Welcome Center* (843-869-4528; 101 Jungle

In a campground clearing at Edisto Island State Park, your "bed" will be soft sand and your bedtime music the rustle of the wind in the palmetto fronds and the swish of breaking waves.

Wade Spees

Rd., Edisto Beach, SC 29438) or the *Edisto Marina* (843-869-3504; 3702 Dock Site Rd., Edisto Beach, SC 29438) for other ideas. *Pon Pon Guides Unlimited* (843-869-7929; www.ponponguides.com; P.O. Box 441, Edisto Island, SC 29438) specializes in boat tours on the Edisto River, including birding expeditions and nocturnal outings (from $35 per person).

The following stores and services also offer beachcombing tours on uninhabited islands, inshore and offshore fishing charters, parasailing, and boat, kayak, or waverunner rentals.

Edisto Essentials (843-869-0951; 495 Hwy. 174).
Edisto Watersports and Tackle (843-869-0663; 3731 Dock Site Rd.).
Hat Cat Blue Charters, Inc. (843-869-4152).
Mudslinger Charters (843-869-3320).

BLUFFTON

A most common mistake of visitors to Bluffton is that they make too much of the place, fret that they've missed something that was "there." In fact, an hour spent in walking along its quiet streets, looking through the bramble and old fences at some of its 19th-century frame houses, visiting the church on the bluff, browsing in a few shops, and doubling back to your parked car about does it for Bluffton.

Why bother? For one thing, Bluffton is one of the Lowcountry's last, true cul-de-sacs. It's not moving, and it's not bothered by your coming or going, either. There are a couple of "Historic" this-and-that signs nailed up, it is true, but what you thought it ought to have been and whether or not it ever becomes that scrubbed-up, idealized version of itself is of no concern. Tiny Bluffton has all the charm of a wonderful, barefoot kid who is not going to live up to some schoolmarm's idea of "potential."

However, it should be noted that Bluffton in the last 18 months has annexed so much adjacent land (in an effort to manage development) that the difference between the old, insouciant, square-mile village and the vast sprawl it now controls is dizzying. Like other parts of the Lowcountry, it's faced with the prospect being overrun by generic subdivision/big box store development or becoming a museum of itself. Hopefully it will resist the extremes.

VISITING BLUFFTON

Bluffton Center is a tiny place where festivals and street fairs bring residents and visitors together.

Wade Spees

From Beaufort (about 35 minutes) follow Hwy. 21 to Hwy. 170 and continue as if you were going to Hilton Head, across the Broad River Bridge until the intersection with Hwy. 278. Turn left on Hwy. 278 and about four miles ahead, exit right at the Hilton Head sign and loop around. After a couple of miles, you will see Hwy. 46 marked as a right turn. Take it into Bluffton.
From Hilton Head, cross the bridge on Hwy. 278. Turn left on Hwy. 46 and follow it to Boundary Street.

Bluffton was a summer community of island planters, and in 1863 it was nearly burned to the ground by Union troops. Ten antebellum buildings remain; another 16 or so houses were built after the Civil War. Taken together, they give a view of classic Lowcountry village life. Far from extravagant, they are nonetheless suffused with a sense of form appropriate to the landscape and to their function as seasonal dwellings belonging to families who had most likely seen better days. It is worth the trip alone to see the *Church of the Cross* on Calhoun St., an unpainted wooden church (circa 1857) with beautiful interior detailing, original pews, and Gothic-style windows.

A complete, self-guided walking tour takes about two hours — houses are marked by plaques, but not all are visible from the street. One book will help you appreciate them. It is: *No. II A Longer Short History of Bluffton, South Carolina and its Environs* produced by the Bluffton Historical Preservation Society (843-757-3650; P.O. Box 742, Bluffton, SC 29910). The price is $9.95. It includes historic essays and descriptions of homes, a map, and wonderful photographs. The town's Historic Center is at the *Heyward House* (843-757-6293; www.heywardhouse.org. 52 Boundary St.), an 1840s Carolina farmhouse. It's open Wed.–Sat. from 10 a.m.–3 p.m.; admission $3 adults, $2 students. The biggest day of the year is the Saturday before Mother's Day: Bluffton's Village Festival, a loose gathering of vendors of all sorts and fine local artists.

Some sites of interest in Bluffton are the working studio of potter **Jacob Preston** (843-757-3084; Church St. between Boundary St. and Calhoun St.; Tues.–Sat. 1–6 or by appointment) and the large gallery at *Crossroads Fine Art & Framing* (843-757-5551; 107 Towne Center) which features work in many media by local and regional artists. *Eggs 'n Tricities* (843-757-3446; 71 Calhoun St.), which is located in an old filling station, has funky furniture outside and inside, and sells everything from 1940's era lamps and linens, to contemporary tableware. *The Store* (843-757-3855; 56 Calhoun St.) covers some of the same ground with similar esprit. *Stock Farm Antiques* (843-757-8046; 1263-B May River Rd.) offers prints, porcelain, silver, rugs, and furniture — some American, some English — chosen with a sense of what fits in the big new houses at the resorts as well as the real old ones. Or you could try your luck for treasures at *Early Attic/Late Garage* (843-815-5255; 46 Kitty's Crossing) or *Another Man's Treasure* (843-757-8498; 142-B Burnt Church Rd.), consignment / antique shops that carry a little bit of everything.

Locals eat breakfast at the *Copper Kettle* (843-815-4557; Hwy. 46) for homestyle meals and at a new, little Mexican restaurant *Mi Tierra*. (843-757-7200; 101 Mellenchamp Rd.) For a gourmet sandwich, blue-plate special, or snack, visit *Vino & Vitto* (843-815-7777; vinoandvitto.com; Hwy. 278 in Home Depot Center) an outstanding fine food, wine and cheese shop, bakery and deli. Also off Hwy. 278 (the highway to Hilton Head) are two fine upscale restaurants: *Cafe at Belfair* (843-815-7818; 1G Sherington Dr.) where lunch and dinner entrees include fancy pastas, duck confit, and grilled seafood; and *Sigler's Rotisserie and Seafood* (843-342-5030; 12 Sheridan Cir.) where roast chicken and seared meats are dinner favorites.

CHAPTER SIX
Courts, Courses, Sails, and Sand
HILTON HEAD

The Hilton Head Island that a visitor sees today is a far different place from what it was 30 years ago. It represents a startling change to residents who, in the past, were accustomed to seeing growth in their region come slowly, if it came at all. It is the Lowcountry's boom town, envied for its tax base, business opportunities, and recreational resources, scrutinized as an example of the conflict between planned growth and overdevelopment. Its sometimes unenviable popularity

Wade Spees

The Harbour Town lighthouse and marina at Sea Pines on the southern tip of the island are well-known symbols of the resort-plantation lifestyle that was invented here in the early 1960s.

caused the mayor to remark: "We're just trying to keep from getting run over."

Unlike the rest of the Lowcountry, Hilton Head is a place of condensed pleasure: in one day, a visitor can enjoy a range of activities that might have taken a week's vacation to savor in the past, had even the possibilities existed. The island is twelve miles long and five miles wide, shaped like a boot. It's on the Intracoastal Waterway, so there's river, ocean, and marsh access, with a mild year-round climate. Shops, tennis courts, golf courses, marinas, and restaurants prosper and proliferate. The commercial districts are discreetly screened from view and even the busiest thoroughfare, Highway 278 (William Hilton Parkway), lacks neon signs. It's easy to understand why more than 1.8 million visitors come every year. Summer is the busiest time.

Until about 1960, soon after a bridge linked Hilton Head to the mainland, the island's history resembled that of its Sea Island neighbors. First settled by planters with slaves who raised rice, indigo, and cotton on about 16 plantations, later occupied during the Civil War by Federal troops, and faced with hard times and isolation after that, the island remained as rural and self-suffi-

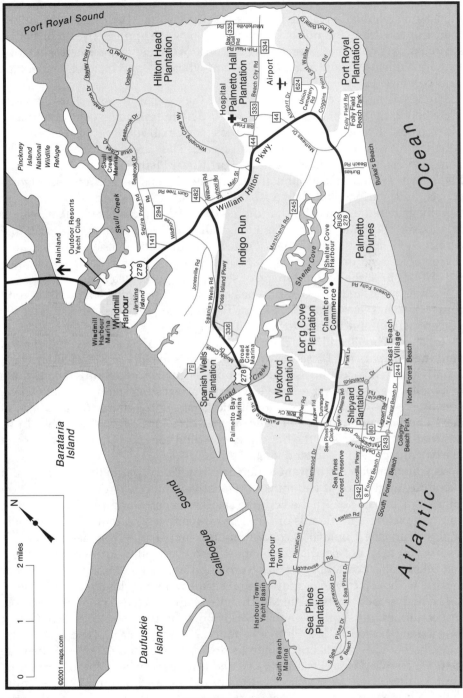

HILTON HEAD

cient as any place was. The African-American families who made up most of the island's population farmed and fished; the visitors who came were gentleman hunters from the north. Transportation was supplied by small packet steamers, sailboats, and barges. (For the best overview of the island's history, stop by *The Museum of Hilton Head Island* where a 4-part historical videotape runs continuously.)

The resort and residential development that began in earnest in the early 1960s led to the "plantation" layout that orders the island's geography today. Most resort activities are based in those original subdivisions, which are accessed by security gates and called private. They are: Sea Pines Plantation, Shipyard Plantation, Palmetto Dunes, Port Royal Plantation, and Hilton Head Plantation. Within and around them are the dozens of golf courses, tennis courts, and marinas that define island recreation. Stores and restaurants are usually gathered in a mall cluster (there's one enclosed mall at Shelter Cove) or in modest shopping "strips"; many smaller residential areas lie scattered across the island, some of them "gated" communities, others not. Because place names tend to sound alike — "cove" this and "water" that — and town regulations limit the size and shape of signs, it's a good idea to carry a map.

Even as the island's topography has changed (much of it sculpted into golf courses), so has its population. Census figures categorize residents by race (90 percent white) and by age (nearly 30 percent over 60 years old). There are established schools and churches that didn't exist 35 years ago, and a good daily newspaper, *The Island Packet*. Continuing development on Hilton Head Island, and in adjacent areas that might be called "resort suburbs," contribute to a feeling of newness, if not novelty. For a contrasting sense of timelessness, you must seek out the island's authentic Lowcountry character: its vistas of marsh and ocean, the flocks of pelicans that dive for fish, the loggerhead turtles that lay their eggs in the dark, the whistling songbirds, and the groves of live oak and pine that shelter deer and dove.

As you plan, you might want to decide what, if any, particular quality you'd like your trip to have. If you think you mostly want to play golf or tennis, you might look into options in the **Lodging** section for "stay-and-play" packages. If you're traveling with friends or family, you may want to rent a house or villa (a fully furnished unit in a condominium complex). If you decide upon a resort, you may not need a car — most resort amenities are within walking and biking distance, and you will be provided with airport transportation. For touring without a car, an island-wide bike trail system is close to completion.

The high season starts in late March, when families come on spring vacation, and continues into April, with the WorldCom Classic—The Heritage of Golf, a tournament hosted at Sea Pines Plantation. May and early June tend to be quiet, before the crowds of summer, as do September and October. When the island is crowded expect traffic tie-ups and lines everywhere. Inter-island trips can take three times as long, and getting off-island during morning or evening rush-hour is a war of nerves. Some of the congestion has been alleviated by the

Cross Island Expressway, a new toll road. Get a commercial overview at *www.hiltonheadisland.com*.

Oceanfront hotels dominate some sections of the beach, but their presence is diminished by dunes and nearby private residences.

Wade Spees

There are more than 3,000 hotel and motel rooms and 6,000 rental units, including cottages, houses, and villas scattered across the island, from sites on or near the beach to those around golf courses, marinas, lagoons, in residential subdivisions or low-rise housing complexes, even on the main highway. Another 1,000 units are dedicated to "timeshare" arrangements and may be available for rent, too. Some "vacation ownership" properties offer weekend packages to attract potential purchasers: *Disney's Hilton Head Island Resort* (843-341-4080 or 800-341-2636) and Marriott's *Vacation Club International Grande Ocean Resort* (843-686-7394 or 800-473-6674) are among the newest.

Your accommodations may be elegant or simple; offer as much or as little privacy as you wish; come with or without kitchens; lie within walking distance, or not, from the beach and recreational amenities.

Rates vary from as little as $60 per night (off-season) for an economy motel room to $6,000 per week for a luxurious oceanfront home with a swimming pool. The range reflects differences in size and location — oceanfront is premium; resort privileges add to the price — and also the time of year: summer is the most expensive season, followed by April. The fall brings ideal golfing conditions, so prices can stay high through mid-October. In the winter months, rates can be half what they are in the high season. Like many resort areas, Hilton Head adds an accommodations tax to lodging bills, and some establishments place a surcharge on credit-card payments. Ask for an estimate of your total bill when you are booking.

Whatever accommodation you choose, inquire about special rate packages or coupons offered for restaurants, health clubs, or shops. Many hotels have discounts for golf and tennis; some have family plans, including activities for kids. In larger hotels, children often stay for free. Lodgings that are not located in private resorts often have arrangements to allow you access to some of their recreational facilities.

The easiest way to make reservations in a hotel or motel (listed directly below) is direct contact. To inquire about home and villa rentals, call a property management company (listed under "Vacation Property Rentals"). Central reservation agencies can give you a sense of the whole picture, and they may be especially helpful in designing a package tailored to your specific interests. The *Hilton Head Chamber of Commerce* (www.hiltonheadchamber. org) is a good place to start. If you're interested in camping, look into the two recreational vehicle parks listed under **Recreation**, later in this chapter. If you're staying on a boat, see the section on Marinas, also in the **Recreation** listings.

The following rates are for one night's stay, per person, double occupancy. They do not include taxes, surcharges, or any special recreation/entertainment discounts. Prices quoted are for high season accommodations. Note that the rates for Luxury Accommodations are at least in the "Very Expensive" category: they can easily run to $260 per night.

Rates

Inexpensive	Up to $60
Moderate	$60 to $120
Expensive	$120 to $200
Very Expensive	$200 and up

Credit Cards

AE — American Express	DC — Diner's Card
CB — Carte Blanche	MC — MasterCard
D — Discover Card	V — Visa

LUXURY HOTELS AND INNS

CROWNE PLAZA RESORT
843-842-2400 or
800-334-1881.
www.crowneplazaresort.
com.
130 Shipyard Dr., Shipyard
Plantation.
Price: Very Expensive.
Credit Cards: All major cards.
Handicap Access: Yes.

A 340-room oceanfront luxury hotel with full concierge service, two restaurants, and a popular lounge for evening entertainment. Pools, 27 holes of golf and a putting green, tennis courts, a 24-hour health center, sailing, and water sports all on site.

DAUFUSKIE ISLAND CLUB AND RESORT
843-842-2000 or
800-648-6778.
www.daufuskieresort.com.
On Daufuskie Island.
Price: Very Expensive.
Credit Cards: All major cards.
Handicap Access: Yes.

Though not on Hilton Head, the Daufuskie Island resort is modeled on its neighbor's plan: a well-groomed private plantation (two golf courses, a tennis complex, beach and water sports, etc.) with access, in this case, by ferry: the embarkation point is near the bridge to Hilton Head, off Hwy. 278, on the north end of the island. Accommodations are in a main inn and in several cottages of two and four bedrooms. It's not spoiled by overdevelopment (no traffic, no crowds) and offers a chance to be in a more rural world (the island is 5 miles long by 2.5 miles wide), which you can see on horseback or on an island tour. If you need the commercial buzz, it's just a short ferry ride away.

HILTON OCEANFRONT RESORT
843-842-8000 or
800-845-8001.
23 Ocean Lane, Palmetto Dunes.
Price: Very Expensive.
Credit Cards: All major cards.
Handicap Access: Yes.

A luxury, 295-room hotel that claims the largest rooms on the island — 560 sq. ft. each — with private balconies and kitchenettes. At the oceanfront setting there's an adults-only pool and a family pool, whirlpools, and a fitness center. Activities for kids (4–16) can be arranged for an additional charge — even at night. Restaurants and nightclubs within the complex.

HYATT REGENCY OCEANFRONT
843-785-1234 or
800-233-1234.
1 Hyatt Circle, Palmetto Dunes.
Price: Very Expensive.
Credit Cards: All major cards.
Handicap Access: Yes.

The largest hotel on the island, with 505 rooms, indoor pool, Olympic-sized outdoor pool, and children's pool. Health club available to guests, as are tennis and golf privileges (3 courses), sailboat and bicycle rental, and lots of beachfront. Several restaurants and a piano bar offer both formal and casual poolside dining. Children's program (additional fee) available weekends year-round; daily in summer.

INN AT HARBOUR TOWN
843-785-3333 or
888-807-6873.
www. innatharbourtown. com.
1 Lighthouse Lane, Sea Pines Plantation.
Price: Very Expensive.
Credit Cards: All major.
Handicap Access: Yes.

This 60-room inn is the newest addition to the Harbour Town complex, at its core a Mediterranean-style marina village whose lighthouse is probably the best-recognized symbol of Hilton Head. The Inn is situated just off the water, in a quieter location by the golf courses. It's more thoughtfully designed than the functional fun-and-sun architecture, or the low-slung Tahiti-roof look of Sea Pines, and its provision of service (butlers on each floor, glorious bathrooms) and serenity (a quiet library and elegant-but-casual furniture and decorations) seem to suggest another way to enjoy the resort experience: to be in it, perhaps, but not of it.

MAIN STREET INN
843-681-3001 or
  800-471-3008.
www.mainstreetinn.com.
2200 Main St.
Price: Very Expensive.
Credit Cards: All major
  cards.
Handicap Access: Yes.

The rare place on Hilton Head that offers the privacy of a lovely home and the service (and superior website) of a resort. There are 33 luxury rooms, an outdoor lap-pool and hot tub, and lounge areas with fireplaces where, depending on the time of day, breakfast, tea, dessert, and coffee are laid out. The European spa offers skin-care treatments and many types of massage; the Charleston-style, vest-pocket urban garden enhances the feeling of an oasis.

WESTIN RESORT
843-681-4000 or
  800-937-8461.
www.westin.com.
2 Grasslawn Ave., Port
  Royal Plantation.
Price: Very Expensive.
Credit Cards: All major
  cards.
Handicapped Access: Yes.

Often considered the most luxurious of the island's oceanfront resort hotels, with 412 rooms and 30 suites, Westin Resort is praised for its Sunday brunch, the elegant decorations hung for the annual "Twelve Days of Christmas" celebration, the rooms with balconies, and a good childrens' program. By day, there are all the standard excellent amenities; by night, light entertainment and dancing.

SMALLER HOTELS

**FOUR POINTS
SHERATON**
843-842-3100 or
  800-528-1234.
38 S. Forest Beach Dr.
Price: Expensive.
Credit Cards: All major
  cards.
Handicapped Access: Yes.

A 140-room hotel featuring rooms with kitchenettes, mini-refrigerators, and cable television. Complimentary Continental breakfast, two pools, and beach access directly across the street.

HAMPTON INN
843-681-7900 or
  800-752-3673.
1 Dillon Rd.
Price: Moderate.
Credit Cards: All major
  cards.
Handicapped Access: Yes.

Most convenient motel to the airport; 124 rooms; shopping nearby at Port Royal Plaza. Swimming pool, complimentary breakfast, and fitness room.

**HOLIDAY INN
  OCEANFRONT**
843-785-5126 or
  800-423-9897.
1 S. Forest Beach Dr.
Price: Expensive.
Credit Cards: All major
  cards.
Handicapped Facilities: Yes.

The island's most popular public-access beach is at your doorstep, and there's plenty of people-watching at the beachside snack bar. Outdoor pool and rock music during the summer months.

**MARRIOTT RESIDENCE
  INN**
877-247-3431.
www.residenceinnhhi.com.
12 Park Lane, in Central
  Park.
Price: Expensive to Very
  Expensive.
Credit Cards: All major
  cards.
Handicapped Facilities: Yes.

Each of the 156 studios and bi-level suites features a fully equipped kitchen; some suites have wood-burning fireplaces. A recreation area includes basketball, volleyball and tennis courts, pool, Jacuzzi hot tub, jogging trails, and a playground. Free shuttle to the beach.

**SOUTH BEACH MARINA
  INN**
843-671-6498 or
  800-367-3909.
In Sea Pines Plantation.
Price: Expensive to Very
  Expensive.
Credit Cards: AE, D, MC, V.

Located in a New England-style marina village in Sea Pines Plantation, this 17-room inn sits above waterfront shops and restaurants. The rooms are condominium suites with living and dining rooms and kitchenettes, overlooking the courtyard or marina. The inn has a Cape Cod feeling: throw rugs, brass beds, hardwood floors. Tennis, water sports, restaurants, and the beach close by.

BUDGET CHOICES

Each of these national chain motels of approximately 100 rooms has a swimming pool and is close to inexpensive restaurants or shopping areas.

COMFORT INN (843-842-6662 or 800-228-5150; 2 Tanglewood Dr.).

HOLIDAY INN EXPRESS (843-842-8888 or 800-465-4329; 40 Waterside Dr.).

RED ROOF INN (843-686-6808 or 800-843-7663; 5 Regency Parkway).

SHONEY'S INN (843-681-3655 or 800-367-3909; Hwy. 278 at Main Street Village).

VACATION PROPERTY RENTALS

Most vacation rental properties are concentrated on the south end of the island in Sea Pines Plantation, Shipyard Plantation, South Forest Beach, and Palmetto Dunes Resort. Several villa rental complexes are located mid-island on or near Folly Field Beach. The northern half of the island is geared mainly to permanent residents; the island's other private communities do not generally permit short-term rental programs.

Villas and homes usually rent by the week, but nightly rates are available. The least expensive summer rates are about $675 per week, which can buy you a small villa outside a plantation more than one-half mile from the beach. In 2001, about $3,500 per week in the summer would secure an oceanfront home with pool. From November to March, rates drop substantially.

Most rental companies manage properties in a variety of sizes, shapes, and locations. A desirable vacation rental would offer free swimming, free or discounted tennis, discounts on golf, and should be within walking distance of the beach. Some offer dining and shopping discounts, too. Before you make your final decision, you might consider where you want to be and what it is you wish to do. You need not pay premium oceanfront prices if you're going to be on the links all day.

Before you sign a rental agreement, make sure you understand policies regarding deposits, refunds in the event of cancellation, times of arrival and departure, and charges, if any, for cleaning services. If you have special needs — handicap-accessible rooms, cots or cribs for children — alert the agent from the start. The agencies listed below are just some of many.

Harbour Town Rentals (843-671-1400 or 800-541-7375; harbourtownresorts.com) Villa and condo rental in the marina village at Sea Pines.

Hilton Head Island Beach and Tennis Resort (843-842-4402 or 800-475-2631) Located at Folly Field, a 180-unit oceanfront villa complex with 10 tennis courts, two pools, restaurant, and pool bar.

Island Getaway Rentals (843-842-4664 or 800-608-8364; www.islandgetaway .com.) Beachfront and ocean-oriented homes and villas, mostly in Palmetto Dunes. Golf packages for more than 20 courses.

Palmetto Dunes Resort (843-785-1161 or 800-845-6130; www.palmettodunes-resort.com) Manages more than 400 villas and homes throughout Palmetto Dunes, including Shelter Cove Marina condominiums.

Properties in Paradise (843-681-6900 or 800-662-7061; www.hhivacations.com) More than 300 properties in Sea Pines and South Forest Beach.

Sea Pines Resort (888-807-6873; www.seapines.com) One- to six-bedroom accommodations in private homes and villas in the island's most exclusive and well-known resort.

Shoreline Rental Co. (843-842-3006 or 800-334-5012; www.shoreline rentals. com) More than 200 villas and homes, mostly ocean-oriented except for those at Sea Pines' Harbour Town.

Worthy Rentals (843-785-5577 or 800-476-9674) Longtime family-owned property management company with about 350 homes and villas listed in Sea Pines Plantation. Golf discounts on 23 island courses.

RESERVATION SERVICES

The following services can assist you with making reservations in advance of your trip:

Hilton Head Accommodations and Golf Hotline (843-686-6662 or 800-444-4772; www.hiltonheadusa.com).

Hilton Head Central Reservation (843-785-9050 or 800-845-7018; www. hilton-headcentral.com).

Vacation Company (843-686-6100 or 800-545-3303; www.vacationcompany.com).

RECREATIONAL VEHICLE PARKS

Outdoor Resorts Motor Coach Resort (843-785-7699 or 800-722-2365; 19 Arrow Rd.) Full hookups, 401 sites, six tennis courts, pool, man-made lake, shuffleboard, horseshoes, basketball, playground, laundry, bathrooms with tubs and saunas.

Outdoor Resorts RV Resort, Marina, and Yacht Club (843-681-3256 or 800-845-9560; Jenkins Island, north end of Hilton Head) Full hookups, 200 RV sites, bath houses, two pools, three tennis courts, laundry, exercise room, sauna, and whirlpool.

DINING AND NIGHTLIFE

Many Hilton Head restaurants capitalize on sublime ocean or marsh views — still plentiful despite the island's rapid development.

Wade Spees

The restaurants included in the listing below are just some of the hundreds of places to eat or relax and listen to music. There are selections in every price category. Where you go may depend on whether you're traveling with children or not (if you're at a resort, ask the concierge about baby-sitting services), whether you like rock bands, acoustic guitar, jazz or dance music, where on the island you're staying, and your budget. Fast food and moderately priced national-chain restaurants are well represented on Hilton Head, too.

The nightspots following the restaurant listings are, also, some of many. They deserve special mention at Hilton Head because they are so numerous and so much a part of its resort culture. Of course, what is popular one year may be B-list the next, but the descriptions are an attempt at an overview. Very few have cover charges; most serve at least finger food.

The price categories are the same described elsewhere in the guide, and represent per person expenses estimated without tax, tip, or bar beverages. In general, dining out is more expensive on Hilton Head than in similar restaurants elsewhere, although there are savings to be found in eating before the crowd (early-bird specials) or on a particular evening when the restaurant has an advertised special.

Inexpensive	Up to $10
Moderate	$10 to $20
Expensive	$20 to $30
Very Expensive	Over $30

BRIAN'S
843-681-6001.
1301 Main Street Village.
Open daily.
Price: Expensive to Very Expensive (less-expensive Early Bird menu 5 p.m.–6 p.m.).
Cuisine: Continental.
Serving: D.
Credit Cards: All major.

Located in a quiet "village" setting at Hilton Head Plantation and, perhaps mercifully for some, off the beaten track, Brian's manages to be casual but not island-informal. There are reliable heavy-hitters on the menu, like steak and lobster, but you could be surprised by the contemporary, gourmet twist on such appetizers as fried green tomatoes or grilled shrimp.

CAFE AT WEXFORD
843-686-5969.
Village at Wexford.
Open daily.
Price: Expensive to Very Expensive.
Cuisine: Country French.
Serving: L, D. Sat. and Sun. brunch.
Credit Cards: All major.

A charming place that feels like Provence: interior brick walls, open kitchen, windows with real "cafe-curtains," accents of dried herbs and flowers. French specialties include veal and duck. There's a small alcove for al fresco dining. Brunch replaces lunch on the weekends.

CHARLESTON'S
843-785-5008.
8 New Orleans Rd.
Open daily.
Price: Expensive to Very
Expensive.
Cuisine: Southern.
Serving: D, Sun. brunch.
Credit Cards: All major.

The new Southern cuisine that got its Lowcountry launch in Charleston is showcased here. The idea was to take local staples, define them to their essence (this was tricky — the essence of grits) and then pair them with more exotic fruits and treat them with spices so that the resulting dish offered not just a tweak but a new taste. You can also find pasta and steaks, and a selection of rotisserie entrees. The upbeat feeling, the modern decor, the well-groomed, casual look of the place and its patrons completes the picture. Reservations recommended.

Wade Spees

Fresh seafood, caught and delivered daily, is on every menu.

CHARLIE'S L'ETOILE VERTE
843-785-9277.
1000 Plantation Center.
Open Tues.–Sat.
Price: Expensive to Very
Expensive.
Cuisine: Continental.
Serving: L, D.
Credit Cards: All major.

Charlie Golson, a Savannah native, never went to cooking school and spent vacations in quiet Bluffton, but his years abroad amidst friends (who were mostly French chefs) seem to have fed his talent. His restaurant is often called the best on Hilton Head. Dinner features a dozen fish dishes like sauteed flounder or poached scallops with ginger. Soup stocks are made up from scratch; the country bread is baked on bricks every day in the open kitchen; most of the wine list is French. The two connecting dining rooms can be noisy when full. You might share a gorgeous salad at lunch; you'll probably have to share a homemade dessert. Reservations highly recommended.

HILTON HEAD DINER
843-686-2400.
Open daily, 24 hours.
Price: Inexpensive.
Cuisine: American.
Serving: B, L, D.
Credit Cards: All major.

An update on the classic American roadside eatery. Breakfast is served all the time — but there are big sandwiches, dinner entrees (with potato, salad, and vegetable) and beer and wine available, too. Coffee, of course, and desserts from the cold case.

HUDSON'S SEAFOOD
843-681-2772.
Squire Pope Rd.
Open daily.
Price: Moderate.
Cuisine: Seafood.
Serving: L, D.
Credit Cards: AE, DC, MC, V.

Large, informal family restaurant, one of the first on the island, in a rustic setting overlooking the Intracoastal Waterway on the docks at Skull Creek. Lunch is served in the Oyster Bar. Entrees include fresh local seafood like crab or shrimp (fried, sautéed, boiled) and blackened or stuffed specials. No reservations — it can get crowded on summer nights.

JULEP'S
843-842-5857.
14 Greenwood Dr.
Open: daily.
Price: Expensive to Very Expensive.
Cuisine: Upscale Southern.
Serving: D.
Credit Cards: AE, MC, V.

A kind of restaurant made popular by the young professional class of the New South, where basic foodstuffs are tweaked and glorified, but not to an unrecognizable (or unpronounceable) state. There's always a light pasta, sauced veal, beef or fish. Formal setting with white tablecloths and fresh flowers. Reservations recommended.

MARKET STREET
843-686-4976.
1 N. Forest Beach Dr.
Open daily.
Price: Inexpensive.
Cuisine: Mediterranean.
Serving: B, L, D.
Credit Cards: AE, MC, V.

If on a starry summer night you've decided to walk the beach near the Coligny Beach access point and hear Greek music, you must be nearby. Come back after your walk to enjoy informal grill food — gyros, pita wraps — or Greek specialties like moussaka, dolmati, and spanakopita.

MI TIERRA
843-342-3409.
Fairfield Sq.
Open daily.
Price: Inexpensive to Moderate.
Cuisine: Mexican.
Serving: D.
Credit Cards: AE, MC, V.

It's not that easy to find Mi Tierra (on Hwy. 278 at the north end of the island, near the Cross Island Parkway exit) but that hasn't slowed the crowds (local retired people, chefs from Beaufort, native islanders, newly arrived Central American workers). The dirt parking lot can be full by 5 p.m. It's as unassuming as can be: tile floor, wooden booths and tables, linens and walls in festive colors, and mostly Spanish-speaking wait staff. The food is very good, the atmosphere welcoming, the portions enormous.

OLD OYSTER FACTORY
843-681-6040.
Marshland Rd.
Open daily.
Price: Moderate to
    Expensive.
Cuisine: Seafood.
Serving: D.
Credit Cards: All major.

**SIGNE'S HEAVEN
    BOUND BAKERY &
    CAFE**
843-785-9118.
Closed Sunday.
Price: Inexpensive.
Cuisine: American.
Serving: B, L.
Credit Cards: MC, V.

SPARTINA GRILL
843-689-2433.
70 Marshland Rd.
Open daily.
Price: Moderate to
    Expensive.
Cuisine: American.
Serving: D.
Credit Cards: AE, MC, V.

TRUFFLES CAFE
843-671-6136.
www.trufflescafe.com.
Sea Pines Center.
Open daily.
Price: Inexpensive to
    Moderate.
Cuisine: American;
    Continental.
Serving: L, D.
Credit Cards: All major.

VIENNESE CAFE
843-842-7670.
24 Palmetto Bay Rd.
Closed Sunday.
Price: Moderate to
    Expensive.
Cuisine: American;
    Continental.

Situated on Broad Creek, this relaxed, down home, bar and restaurant overlooks extensive marshes, and on Tuesday nights in the summer from the back porch, offers a good view of the fireworks at Shelter Cove. If you go for the happy hour (5 p.m. to 7 p.m.) specials on oysters and crab legs you'll miss the stunning sunset — but you may avoid the crowds. It's very popular.

Founded in 1972 by an enterprising cook, nationally recognized many times since, and a regular stop for returning visitors and for residents who appreciate fresh, healthy, food. Here are salads and soups, many kinds of homemade bread and muffins, fabulous pastry, and desserts. The French toast is probably an inch thick; the brownies and blondies even thicker. The cafe itself is very modest — it's the bakery display cases that aren't.

Locals like it here because the menu offers a reassuring blend of the familiar and the exotic — and the exotic can come in small servings ("tapas") for tasting and sharing. The grilled fish and steaks are among the best around, served in a comfortable setting, indoors or out, with a view of Broad Creek.

Casual atmosphere, homemade soups, huge salads, French bread sandwiches, quiche, fresh vegetables, and grilled entrees. Light meals like black bean cakes or smoked salmon are inexpensive, and you can order them at any time. A couple of dozen wines by the glass. The market is full of gourmet items and take-out. It's a cross between a fern bar and a wine bar, with a bistro menu.

This charming, imaginative cafe of a dozen tables looks like a small farmhouse kitchen in Europe, with textured walls washed by light and colored in muted blues and mustards. The lunch menu offered by Teresa and Eric Ulph, the owner/chefs, is hearty and simple: soup served in a big mug, a couple of salads, sandwiches on focca-

Serving: L; D (Wed.–Sat.)
Credit Cards: AE, MC, V.

cia or a croissant. At dinner there's still a sense of modesty and simple presentation but the entrees are superb choices, classically prepared: rack of lamb, pan-seared salmon, tenderloin.

NIGHTLIFE

The beat goes on and on at Hilton Head, and especially in summer, the crowds jam the dance floor or find piano bar music in the resort lounges or in some of the places listed below. Check ahead for cover charges or drink minimums. The legal drinking age is 21; bars close at midnight Saturday unless special liquor licenses are in hand.

Cheryl's Le Cabaret Piano Bar (843-842-7227; 13 Heritage Plaza) A cafe/cabaret featuring local talent. Nice place to dance for an over-30 crowd. The music starts at 8:45 p.m. and on the last Sunday of the month there's Dixieland jazz in the afternoon.

Jazz Corner (843-842-8620; www.thejazzcorner.com. Village at Wexford) National and regional jazz artists of all types perform here Tuesdays–Saturdays. Shows start at 7:30 p.m.

Kingfisher (843-785-4442; Shelter Cove Harbour) Dinner and music nightly until 10 p.m., including Big Bands, jazz combos, soft rock. Dance if you wish; bar menu or full meals (steak, pasta seafood) served.

Monkey Business (843-686-3545; 25 Park Plaza) Big, upscale dance club with a band or a deejay depending on the night, and music from rock to beach to house.

Quarterdeck (843-671-2222; Harbour Town) Laid-back waterfront lounge, island classic since 1970. Peak periods include late afternoon, suppertime (kids welcome), and late night. Outdoor rocking chairs make sunset viewing a treat. Upstairs and downstairs bars; beach music, folk/rock, steel drums.

Reilly's (843-842-4414; Hilton Head Plaza) Irish pub in feel, sports-talk in the air. Popular Friday happy hour for weary locals. Friendly, neighborhood-bar atmosphere.

Two Eleven Park Wine Bar & Bistro (843-686-5212; 211 Park Plaza) Close to the movies, so it's a great place for a late meal, including eggs and grits. Dozens and dozens of wines by the glass.

CULTURE

As Hilton Head has grown, so has its arts community. It is infused with energy from new, young residents and cultivated by the many retired people hoping to recreate in their adopted home the range of cultural activities that interested them in the cities and towns they left behind. Check the Arts & Entertainment section of *The Island Packet* for weekly listings.

A new addition to the cultural landscape is the *Self Family Arts Center* (William Hilton Pkwy., Shelter Cove; 843-842-2787; www.artscenter-hhi.org), a top-notch visual and performing arts facility. Residents and visitors alike benefit from its 350-seat theater, gallery space, classrooms for continuing education, and offices, which gather diverse elements of the arts community under one roof. Several times each year, it showcases the *Hallelujah Singers*, a group of men and women who, in story, song and dance, celebrate Gullah heritage in the Sea Islands. It also is a venue for events that are part of February's month-long *Native Islander Gullah Celebration* (888-856-4982) which offers visitors a glimpse of African-American heritage by way of tours, art exhibitions, performances, and lectures.

ART

Hilton Head Art League (843-671-9009; Sea Pines Center) A gallery with regularly scheduled shows of work by members and others.

Self Family Arts Center–Walter Greer Gallery (843-686-3945; www.artscenter -hhi.org.14 Shelter Cove Lane).

CINEMA

Island Theatre (843-785-5001; Coligny Plaza) One screen.

Main Street Cinemas (843-785-5001; Park Plaza) Five screen complex.

Northridge Ten Cinemas (843-342-3800; 435 Wm. Hilton Pky.) Ten screens.

DANCE

Hilton Head Dance Theater (843-842-3262; 24 Palmetto Business Park Rd.) Talented students from local schools and visiting companies perform at the Self Family Arts Center.

HISTORIC SITES

Several sites dating as far back as the time of Native American settlements and covering the period of the Civil War are accessible to visitors. For more information and location maps, contact *Coastal Discovery Museum on Hilton Head Island* (see address and hours below).

Baynard Ruins (Sea Pines Plantation) The remains of a plantation house and outbuildings first constructed circa 1800 can be seen on a short, self-guided walk. A well-written brochure introduces its history and construction, and cotton cultivation. The ruins are made of tabby, a popular homemade Lowcountry building material that resulted from the burning of oyster shells (to make lime), which were then mixed with whole shells, sand, and water. This is one of few sites where you can still see it.

Coastal Discovery Museum on Hilton Head Island (843-689-6767; 100 William Hilton Parkway, Hilton Head Island, SC 29925) Located at the north end of the island, near the bridge, **Coastal Discovery** is an enormous addition to a place where so much is new. Archaeological digs have yielded a collection of more than 75,000 artifacts relating to the island's history and culture, some of which are on display in a small exhibition space. Efforts to record island life through oral history interviews are ongoing; solid scholarship produced a fine four-part videotape (which is shown at the museum) documenting early habitation, the years of slavery, Reconstruction and the decades of small farming, and the fishing, oystering, and timbering industries. The gift shop offers the widest and best selection of books on the Lowcountry of any place on Hilton Head Island. Call for reservations for any number of excellent off-site programs, including walking tours of the marsh, the beach, and other natural areas including historic sites; marine study cruises; bird-watching; and science and nature study for children. Museum hours are Mon.–Sat. 10–5, Sun. 12–5. Museum admission is a $2 donation. For the outdoor programs, a fee is charged, depending on the event. Call to reserve places.

Fish Haul Plantation (off Beach City Rd., near the county baseball complex) Only the chimneys of slave dwellings remain of what was once a thriving Sea Island cotton plantation. Federal troops camped here from the time of Union occupation in November, 1861.

Fort Howell (Beach City Rd.) A large earthwork built by the Union troops in 1864 to strengthen the defense of Mitchelville.

Fort Mitchel (Hilton Head Plantation) An earthwork fortification circa 1862, constructed as part of the island's defense system.

Indian Shell Ring (Sea Pines Forest Preserve) Native Americans occupied Hilton Head and other Sea Islands some 4,000 years ago, and left their mark in huge rings and shell middens. It is thought that this site represents the refuse of oyster shells piled behind each of many huts that stood in a small circle.

Zion Chapel of Ease (William Hilton Pkwy. at Mathews Dr.) A small chapel, built circa 1786 for the convenience of worshippers who lived too far from the Episcopal church at Beaufort, once occupied this site. The Baynard Mausoleum, circa 1846, within its cemetery is the largest antebellum structure extant on the island.

MUSIC

Hilton Head Jazz Society (843-842-4457) The group sponsors formal and informal performances at various island sites on the first Sunday of each month.

Hilton Head Orchestra (843-842-2055; 10 Office Park Rd.) Performances of symphonic and popular music throughout the year, held in the First Presbyterian Church, 540 William Hilton Pkwy.

THEATER

Dunnagan's Alley Theatre (843-785-4897; Dunnagan's Alley at Arrow Rd.) Originally a community theater, now administered under the umbrella of the Self Family Arts Center which brings local, regional, and national productions to Hilton Head.

RECREATION

In the last 20 years, Hilton Head has come into its own as a town that services full-time residents, but its identity still rests on its reputation as a place where visitors come to pursue golf, tennis, fishing, and water sports, and to enjoy the beach. The following listings offer some sense of the amazing range of activities the island has to offer.

BEACH ACCESS

Twelve miles of gently sloping beaches define the island's ocean edge. They can be as wide as 600 feet at low tide, providing a hard surface for fat-tired bicycles. (For tidal information, tune into island cable television or check *The Island Packet*.) Although many entry points to the beach are restricted — behind private resort plantation gates — there are four public beach access points. The most popular are *Coligny Beach Park* (located at the end of Pope Ave.), *Folly Field Beach Park* (off Folly Field Rd.), *Dreissen Beach Park* (off Bradley Beach Rd.) and Alder Lane (off S. Forest Beach Dr.) All offer metered parking spaces ($.50 to $1 per hour) and Coligny and Dreissen have long-term lots where you can park for $4 a day. Within the plantation resorts, the beaches are accessible by marked footpaths.

Hilton Head's wide, flat beaches are popular destinations for bike riding and strolling.

Wade Spees

On some nights (May through October), it is possible to watch the amazing loggerhead turtle, an endangered species, crawl ashore and lay its eggs in nests it digs on the beach; or to see hundreds of loggerhead hatchlings make their way back to the ocean. Volunteer groups monitor the beach and sometimes move the eggs to higher ground or protected sites, away from tides and hungry raccoons. The turtles are slow-moving and docile, but chary: do not disturb them with light, or touch the nests. Just seeing these huge creatures is magical.

Dogs are not permitted on the beach from 10 a.m. to 5 p.m. from the beginning of Memorial Day weekend through Labor Day weekend. Motor vehicles, alcohol, glass containers, and nudity are not allowed. Fishing, boating, surfing, ball-playing etc. is prohibited in designated swimming areas. The beaches are patrolled by sheriff's deputies.

BEACH ACTIVITIES: DOING THE DUNES

If you haven't brought your beach equipment with you, you can stock up at the *Coligny Banner and Kite Company* (843-785-5483; Coligny Plaza) or rent larger items such as boogie boards, chairs and umbrellas, floats, Hobie Cat boats, and aqua cycles from *Shore Beach Service* (843-785-3494; 116 Arrow Rd., outlets on the beach).

Coastal Discovery, a series of educational programs sponsored by *The Museum on Hilton Head Island* (843-689-6767), offers guided walks several days per week on the island's beaches, and, on some evenings, a turtle tour to see the loggerheads nesting or hatching. Each tour lasts about 90 minutes and explains the island's ecology, flora, and fauna. Children will like learning about shells and hunting hermit crabs. Call in advance to purchase tickets — they range from $5 to $10.

BICYCLING

You can rent bikes of all varieties — including the newest electric bikes and scooters — in many locations, and expect island-wide pick-up and delivery. If you're traveling with youngsters, you'll be able to get baby-carriers, helmets, bikes with training wheels, baby "trailers" that hook on the back of bikes, and jogging strollers.

Public bike paths extend from the tip of North Forest Beach to the end of South Forest Beach, along Pope Ave., and up William Hilton Pky. to Squire Pope Rd. and beyond. Bike paths also thread through the plantations. If it's not too windy, riding on a hard-packed beach is an exceptional pleasure.

Rental charges for bicycles start at about $12 per day and between $20–$30 per week. A Zappy electric bike is $20 for two hours. Check the following outlets:

Taking a break at the beach.

Wade Spees

All American Bikes (843-842-4386).
Bicycle Club of Hilton Head (843-842-2453).
Harbour Town Bicycle (843-671-3006).
Hilton Head Bicycle Company (843-686-6888 or 800-995-4319).
Pedals (843-842-5522).
Peddling Pelican (800-424-8048; www.pelicancruiser.com).
Zapworld (843-842-9271).

BIRD WATCHING

Hilton Head still has some very quiet places for birds to nest and feed. According to the island's Audubon Society chapter, some 200 species of birds regularly visit, and in the last 10 years, more than 350 species have been sighted. Among the most distinctive "frequent flyers" are the snowy egret, great blue heron, white ibis, and osprey. Catch a glimpse of them for yourself during daylight hours at the following sites:

Coastal Discovery (843-689-6767) offers guided walks in the Forest Preserve and has a birding exhibit on display at its headquarters in the Museum on Hilton Head Island (100 William Hilton Parkway). For nearby, off-island sites, see the **Nature Preserves** heading in the Savannah and Beaufort Chapters.

Newhall Audubon Preserve (Palmetto Bay Rd.).

Sea Pines Forest Preserve (843-842-1449; entrances at Greenwood Dr. and Lawton Dr. in Sea Pines Plantation; $5 admission per car to enter Sea Pines Plantation). This 400-acre site offers a self-guided walking tour, which takes 1–2 hours. There are also picnic areas with grills.

Whooping Crane Conservancy (Hilton Head Plantation) features a boardwalk and self-guided nature trail.

BOATING AND WATER SPORTS

For sailboat charters and bare-boat rentals, contact the companies listed below and also check the **Marina** section in this chapter. If you want to nurture a wilder streak, look into waterskiing or kneeboarding, floating with a parasail, riding a wave-runner, or "sledding" on a rubber tube. Some companies have special lessons/day programs for kids, so ask. Parasailing costs between $45 and $85 per person; waterskiing (5 people maximum) is about $175 for 2 hours; hourly waverunner rental costs $69 for a single, $79 for double. Make reservations in advance.

Action Watersports (843-785-7368; www.nvo.com/actionws; Palmetto Bay Marina) Waverunners, motor boats (17 feet to 19 feet) and pontoon boats for rent.

Breakwater Adventures (843-689-6800; Hudson's Landing, Squire Pope Rd.) Runabouts, pontoon boats, and cruisers equipped with appropriate fishing gear, charts, and safety equipment. Licensed guides available. Also waterskiing, kayak tours, and dolphin-watch expeditions.

Commander Zodiac (843-671-3344; South Beach Marina) Sunfish, Hobie Cat, and Prindle sailboats for rent, private lessons, and rides. Sailing school for youngsters to age 16. Visit the dolphins or Daufuskie Island in engine-powered rubber rafts.

H2O Sports Center (843-671-4386; www.H2osportsonline.com. 149 Lighthouse Rd., Sea Pines) Rentals for, and instruction in, parasailing, waverunning, kneeboarding, hydrosliding, waterskiing.

Island Parasail (843-686-2359; Shelter Cove Marina) Soar up to 1500 feet. It looks safer than bungee jumping.

Island Watersports (843-671-7007; South Beach Marina) Power and sail boats for as many as 14 passengers, by the hour, half-day, or day. Guided private cruises, sailing lessons, sunset sails. Wave-runners and skis for rent.

Jarvis Creek Water Sports (843-681-9260; 104A Wm. Hilton Pkwy.) The hydrobikes look like sleek bicycle assemblies mounted on even sleeker rowing shells, pedal-powered by one or two people. Or you could rent a canoe.

The Intracoastal Waterway beside Hilton Head Island is a main passage for transportation and recreation.

Wade Spees

Waterski & Wake Club of Hilton Head (843-290-2802; Shelter Cove Harbour)
A good family option, maximum six passengers: learn to water ski, or ride the wake on a kneeboard or waveboard, or just get pulled along on a rubber tube. Three hours. Bring a picnic.

CANOEING AND KAYAKING

It's ironic that Hilton Head, with perhaps more constructed, managed, and expensive recreational sites per square mile than any place in the United States (golf courses, tennis courts, pools, health clubs, bike trails, marinas) has literally in its own back yard, superior low-tech, low-impact recreational options that are just now being fully appreciated. They are found in the creek.

Today you can explore miles of Lowcountry waterways in a canoe or kayak, on your own or with a guided tour, by the half-day, the day, at sunset, on an overnight expedition. No experience is necessary; all safety equipment and basic instruction is provided; kids are welcome. You may end up paddling out to a sandbar, fishing, taking a birding tour, or threading through the web of coastal marshlands, pristine rivers, and nature preserves. Some outfitters offer extended programs for teens.

In 2001, a two-hour rental and basic kayaking lesson cost about $35; rentals by the half-day about $55. Two-hour guided tours of local waters like Broad Creek, where you are likely to see lots of birds and fish in action, start at about $35 per person; $17.50 for kids 12 and under; from $48 for half-day tours; $60 for full-day. Longer tours run about $80–$125 per person, depending on the arrangements.

To get simple and leave the world behind, contact: *Adventure Kayak Tours* (843-342-3699); *Awesome Expeditions* (843-842-9763); *Outside Hilton Head* (843-686-6996 or 800-686-6996; www.outsidehiltonhead.com); *Southern Exposure Adventures* (843-683-6900).

CRUISES

Adventure Cruises (843-785-4558; Shelter Cove Harbour) has several sightseeing outings, including trips to Daufuskie Island (land tour of historic sites costs extra), 90-minute dolphin watch cruises, evening shark trips, and sunset dinner cruises. Daufuskie cruise: Adults $18, children $8; Dolphin watch: Adults $17; children $7.

Dolphin Adventure & Nature Cruise (843-681-2522; www.hiltonheadisland. com/dolphintour.htm. Broad Creek Marina) Narrated environmental tours (90 minutes) aboard the 21-passenger S.S. Pelican. Adults $15, kids $9.

Flying Circus and Pau Hana (843-686-2582; Palmetto Bay Marina) is a fast-moving catamaran offering 2-hour daylight and sunset cruises for a maximum of six passengers. Tickets are $25. Pau Hana, a larger catamaran, can carry 49 passengers. Prices are $13–$15 for kids under 12; $18–$20 for adults.

Schooner Welcome (843-785-5566; www.schooner.net. Shelter Cover Harbour) Three-hour tours aboard a 62-foot wooden Concordia yacht rigged with a unusual gaff and topsail combination. From $25 for adults.

Spirit of Harbour Town (843-842-7179; Harbour Town) Narrated cruises, an enclosed dining room, air conditioning — a deluxe way to spend a sunset dinner, a commute to Savannah or evening fireworks. Reservations required. Adults: $39–$55; kids $20–$30.

Sport Crabbing (843-785-4298; Shelter Cove Harbour) Take a two-hour trip on the comfortable, covered, Crabber J II and cast for crabs in the calm waters of Broad Creek. Adults $19; kids $14.

Stars & Stripes (843-842-7933; Harbour Town) This is the 12-meter America's Cup yacht, 65 feet long and powered by the wind in 2,000 square feet of sail. Call for reservations and sailing times; prices vary according to trip.

FAMILY AMUSEMENTS

On the beach: it doesn't get any better than this.

Wade Spees

If you're coming with your children to Hilton Head, there are simple pleasures at hand: beachcombing, bike-riding, flying a kite, sunset concerts,
weekly fireworks displays. *Island playgrounds* are located at *Harbour Town*
(in Sea Pines; $5 admission), *Shelter Cove Harbour*, and the *Island Recreation
Center* (20 Wilborn Rd. at the north end of the island). *Bristol Sports Arena
Skate Park* is located off Arrow Rd., on the island's south end. The Rec Center
features a handicapped-accessible area with a swing for wheelchairs. Check
newspaper listings to confirm schedules or find special family-oriented events.
Some of the following listings may be of help on a rainy day, or for older kids
who might prefer arcades.

Adventure Cove Family Fun Center (843-842-9990; www.adventurecove.com.
Folly Field Rd. and Hwy. 278) Mini-golf, batting cage, arcade, laser tag, driving range, bumper cars, and more.

Coastal Zone Education Center (843-837-4848; Sawmill Creek Rd., Bluffton)
Call ahead for information about scheduled beach and marsh walks, and
mini-classes in nature and ecology studies.

Island Recreation Center (843-681-7273; 20 Wilborn Rd.) A year round activity
center with camps, clinics, and sports programs organized by the day, week,
and month for children, teens, and adults. Check to see if events like bike
races, fishing tournaments, rollerblading races, water carnivals or craft
classes (among others) might coincide with your visit. Call ahead: registra-
tion may be required.

Summer Concerts: In the evening, family entertainers gather large audiences
for free concerts and shows. Check the local paper for listings, and plan to
arrive early to secure parking. In Sea Pines Plantation (under the Liberty

Oak at Harbour Town; Sea Pines gate pass $5) singers and guitarists perform nightly from 8 to 10 except Saturday. The audience sits on benches and kids are encouraged to participate. Family sing-alongs also take place Tuesday through Saturday at Shelter Cove Harbour, and once a week, usually Tuesday, there are fireworks. Various musicians, puppeteers, and clowns also turn up at Coligny Plaza (off Pope Ave.) each night to entertain families. At South Beach Marina (Sea Pines Plantation) you can enjoy music while the sun sets over the docks.

Waterfun Park (843-842-8108; 6 Tanglewood Dr.) Putt-putt golf course, three waterslides, arcade games, and a toddler's pool.

FISHING

If you want to go fishing, it's easy to do, but have in mind the kind of experience you're looking for. There are many options: size of the boat, length of the day, level of challenge, location, number of anglers, type of catch, and, of course, the probability of success. (All but the last can be provided.) Fly fishing is also available. Boats are fully equipped with tackle, etc., and depart from several marinas for inshore waters, flats, artificial reefs, and the Gulf Stream. Potential catches include tarpon, marlin, and sailfish in the Gulf Stream; amberjack, shark, king mackerel, and bluefish closer to shore; and flounder, red drum, sea trout, and sheepshead in the coastal flats. In 2001, prices for four to six passengers for a half-day of fishing ran from about $275 to $380. Here are some suggestions.

A Fishin' Mission (843-785-9177; 43 Jenkins Island Rd.) Flat-water and off-shore fishing from a custom 35-foot craft. Maximum six passengers.

Atlantic Fishing Charters (843-671-4534; Harbour Town Yacht Basin) Four boats (23 feet to 40 feet long) rigged with fish-finding equipment; fish at night for shark.

Blue Water Charters (843-671-3577; 232 S. Sea Pines Dr., South Beach Marina) Trophy fishing and taxidermy services.

Bonanza Sportfishing (843-689-5873; 405 Squire Pope Rd.) A well-known island fisherman and angling authority takes you on inshore charters on a 20-foot, 4 passenger boat.

Capt. Hook (843-785-4558; Shelter Cove Harbour) A good family choice for fishing: large boat with enclosed cabin and restrooms, food on board. The Tuesday night shark-fishing tip includes the fireworks show; at $40 for adults, a relative bargain.

Lowcountry Outfitters (843-837-6100; 1533 Fording Island Rd. at Moss Creek Village, just off-island) Serious hunters and fisherman often gather and trade stories here. Guided fly-fishing and light tackle expeditions for one or two passengers on an open 18-foot boat are available. Equipment provided (or you can bring your own). Late-October through late-April you're looking for redfish and speckled trout; other times, ladyfish, spanish mackerel, jack crevalle, and bluefish. Prices for a half-day started at $250; $400 for a full day.

Palmetto Bay Marina's Fishing Fleet (843-785-7131 or 800-448-3875; Palmetto Bay Marina) Five boats and five captains can take you offshore fishing, to the Gulf Stream, or inshore to the flats.

FITNESS CENTERS

Breakthrough Fitness Center (843-341-2166; 130 Arrow Rd.)

Hilton Head Health Institute (843-785-7292 or 800-292-2440; 14 Valencia Rd.) A full-service spa where you can also go for extended visits to embark on a personalized program of fitness, diet, and healthier lifestyle.

Hilton Vacation Station (843-341-8056; Hilton Oceanfront Resort)

GOLF

The world's pro golfers play the course at Sea Pines every spring (following The Masters on the tour) during the MCI Heritage of Golf Tournament.

Wade Spees

There are more than 30 courses in the Hilton Head area; of these 22 are on the island itself. The oldest course was built in Sea Pines Plantation in 1961. Most of the area's courses are open to the public and resort guests, though some are for members (and their guests) only. Even so, except for a handful of courses off the island, they are not public in the traditional sense of the word. They are located within private communities like Sea Pines and Shipyard Plantations, Palmetto Dunes Resort, and Port Royal Plantation, and may have dress codes and time limits. For courses in and around Beaufort — all of them less than an hour's drive from Hilton Head — check that chapter.

Reservations to secure tee times are important — some courses accept reservations from non-resort guests up to 90 days in advance, others just 30 to 60 days in advance. (It gets crowded — 800,000 rounds of golf are played annually at Hilton Head.) Unless noted, all courses are 18 holes. Appropriate dress calls for shirts with collars for men and no blue jeans, gym shorts, or jogging shorts.

Price Codes

Prices include greens and cart fee unless mentioned otherwise. Walking is permitted on several courses — check ahead for caddy help. Reduced rates available for resort guests. The rates listed, and range of price if there is one, are the two-tiered high-season rates — spring and fall. Summer fees are slightly less. By the low season — winter months — prices can drop by 40 percent. Rates are lower for afternoon or twilight play. Rates are lower for some combination-course or two-day golf packages. For an island golf guide, call 1-888-GOLF-ISLAND; www.golfisland.com.

Inexpensive	Up to $50
Moderate	$50 to $65
Expensive	$65 to $80
Very Expensive	Over $80

Hilton Head Plantation

Country Club of Hilton Head (843-681-4653) Par 72. Range: 5,373-yard ladies course to 6,919-yard champion course. Pro: Tim Eckstein. Price: Expensive.

Oyster Reef Golf Club (843-681-7177 or 800-728-6662) Rees Jones course. Par: 72. Range: 5,288 ladies course to 7,027 champion course. Pro: Mike Bartholomew. Price: Expensive to Very Expensive.

Indigo Run

Golden Bear Golf Course (843-689-2200) Par 72. Range: 6,184-yard course to 7,014-yard championship course. Pro: Bob Thomas. Price: Moderate to Expensive.

Palmetto Dunes Resort

Arthur Hills Course (843-785-1138) Par 72. Range: 4,999-yard ladies course to 6,651-yard champion course. Pro: Clark Sinclair. Price: Very Expensive.

George Fazio Course (843-785-1130) Named one of Golf Digest's 100 top American courses. Par 70. Range: 5,273-yard ladies course to 6,873-yard champion course. Pro: Bobby Downs. Price: Expensive.

Robert Trent Jones (843-785-1136) The lagoon system is a factor in 11 holes here. Par 72. Range: 5,425-yard ladies course to 6,710-yard champion course. Pro: Ken Conroy. Price: Expensive.

Palmetto Hall Plantation

Arthur Hills Course (843-689-4138) Par 72. Range: 4,956-yard ladies course to 6,918 champion course. Pro: Bob Faulkner. Price: Expensive.

Robert Cupp Course (843-689-4100) Par 72. Range: 5,220-yard forward course to 7,079-yard tour course. Pro: Bob Faulkner. Price: Expensive.

Port Royal Plantation

Barony Course (843-689-4653 or 800-234-6318) Par 72. Range: 5,253-yard ladies course to 6,530-yard champion course. Pro: Mike Beverly. Price: Moderate to Expensive.

Planter's Row Course (843-689-4653 or 800-234-6318) Par 72. Range: 5,126-yard ladies course to 6,520-yard champion course. Pro: Mike Beverly. Price: Moderate to Expensive.

Robber's Row Course (843-689-4653 or 800-234-6318) A Pete Dye renovation of a George Cobb course near what was Fort Walker, a Civil War camp. Par 72. Range: 5,000-yard ladies course to 6,642-yard champion course. Pro: Mike Beverly. Price: Moderate to Expensive.

Sea Pines Plantation

Harbour Town Golf Links (843-363-4485 or 800-955-8337) The Heritage Golf Classic is played on this course, designed by Jack Nicklaus and Pete Dye, rated among the top 25 in the world. Par 71. Range: 5,019-yard ladies course to 6,912-yard "Heritage" course. Pro: John Farrell. Price: Very Expensive.

Ocean Course (843-363-4485 or 800-955-8337) First course on the island, redesigned in 1995 by Mark McCumber. Par 72. Range: 5,325-yard ladies course to 6,906-yard champion course. Pro: John Richardson. Price: Expensive to Very Expensive.

Sea Marsh Course (843-363-4475 or 800-955-8337) Par 72. Range: 6,619-yard ladies course to 6,515-yard champion course. Pro: John Richardson. Price: Expensive.

Shipyard Plantation

Shipyard Golf Club (843-689-4653 or 800-234-6318) Par 72, 27 holes. A favorite of the senior PGA Tour. Range: 5,391-yard ladies course to 6,830 champion course. Manager: Ted Ketchum. Price: Expensive.

Off-Island

Executive Golf Club (843-837-6400; www.brigadoongolf.com. Hwy. 278, Bluffton, at entrance to Hilton Head National) Nine holes, par 30, lit for night play. Range: 1,452-yard "grey" course and 1,656-yard "maroon" course. Price: Inexpensive.

Hilton Head National (843-842-5900 or 888-955-1234Hwy. 278, Bluffton) Par 72, Gary Player-designed course. Range: 4,649-yard course to 6,779-yard champion course. Pro: Jeff Osler. Price: Moderate.

Island West Golf Club (843-689-6660; Hwy. 278, Bluffton) Par 72. Range: 4,948-yard ladies course to 6,803-yard champion course. Dir. of Golf: Arthur Jeffords. Price: Inexpensive to Moderate.

Old South Golf Links (843-785-5353 or 800-257-8997; Hwy. 278, Bluffton) Par 71/72. Range: 4,776-yard ladies course to 6,772-yard champion course. Pro: Brady Boyd. Price: Inexpensive to Moderate.

Rose Hill Country Club (843-842-3740; Rose Hill Plantation, Hwy. 278, Bluffton) Par 72. Range: 5,099-yard ladies course to 6,808-yard champion course. Pro: Matt Minasi. Price: Inexpensive to Moderate.

Sun City/Okatie Creek Golf Club (843-705-4653 or 800-978-9783; Sun City Hilton Head, Hwy. 170). The first of three planned courses at this new resort, designed for the over-55 crowd. Five sets of tees per hole accommodate the skilled and less-skilled golfer. Par 72. Range: 4,763-yard forward course to 6,734-yard Okatie course. Director of Golf: Jeff Seman. Price: Inexpensive to Expensive.

HORSEBACK RIDING

Call ahead for reservations. Small groups and families are welcome; all equipment is provided.

Happy Trails Stables (843-842-7433; Bluffton — behind Old South Golf Links) Rides in and around the golf course and forest preserve start at $25 for adults; $20 for ages 12 and under. Reservations suggested.

Lawton Stables (843-671-2586; 190 Greenwood Dr., Sea Pines) Seventy-minute walking trail rides for adults and kids over eight years old (unless they've had riding experience) through the 600-acre Sea Pines Forest Preserve start at $30 per person; pony rides for the younger set are $5. Lessons (all levels) start at $35 per half-hour and include preparation of the horse.

Sandy Creek Stables (843-342-2771; 102 Jonesville Rd.) Boarding, lessons, and trail rides along the edge of the marsh and in the woods.

Sea Horse Farms (843-681-7746; 34 Mitchelville Rd.) Unique, one-hour beach rides leave four times per day except Sunday. Riders must be 7 years old or older. $35 per person.

IN-LINE SKATE RENTALS

Outside Hilton Head (843-686-6996; Shelter Cove or 843-671-2643; South Beach Marina) Individual and group lessons for beginners through advanced skaters from $20 per person; rentals $12–$20.

Player's World (843-842-5100; 32 Q Plaza, Shelter Cove) Rent Bauer skates for recreation, roller hockey, or trick skating, at $9 per hour or $15 per day. Safety equipment included.

MARINAS

The Hilton Head area has 9 marinas that offer numerous boat rental facilities, transient berths, fishing charters, and services, such as dry-dock storage, launching ramps, fuel, showering facilities, ship's stores, and repair shops. The nine that are open to the public are listed below. Cost for berthing ranges from $.50 to $2 per foot; or fees by the month. Charter fishing boats, small powerboats, sailboats, and yachts as long as 150 feet are berthed side by side, offering a striking example of the myriad ways residents and visitors choose to enjoy the water. Renovations and dredging in 2001 may change some of the information listed below; call for information.

Broad Creek Marina (843-681-3625; Marshland Rd.) 33 slips accommodating boats up to 100 feet. Ship's store with boat cleaning supplies and equipment. Charters and sightseeing, sailing instruction, and kayaking available. Low tide draft: 15 feet.

Freeport Marina (843-785-8242 or 800-398-7687; Daufuskie Island) The gateway to Daufuskie for large tour boats and the island touring headquarters. Golf-cart rental for transportation; restaurant, cookouts, gift shop, and marina store. Low tide draft: 15 feet.

Harbour Town Yacht Basin (843-671-2704.www.harbourtown.com; Sea Pines Plantation) 85 slips accommodating boats up to 150 feet. Marina store, various types of boats for rent; tours, instruction, and cruises available. Near shops and restaurants in Harbour Town. Low tide draft: 8 feet.

Outdoor Resorts Yacht Basin (843-681-3256; Jenkins Island at northern tip of Hilton Head) 101 slips, maximum boat length 70 feet. Amenities of Outdoor Resorts RV Park (see **Lodging** listing in this chapter) as well as charters, waterski rentals and instruction, ship's store. Low tide approach depth: 8 feet; 20 feet at dockside.

Palmetto Bay Marina (843-785-7131 or 800-448-3875; 164 Palmetto Bay Rd.) 140 slips, maximum length 85 feet. Marina store, boat repair, fishing and sailing charters, parasailing, and youth sailing program. Low tide draft: No limit.

Schilling Boathouse (843-681-2628; 405 Squire Pope Rd.) Dry stack only; maximum 33 feet. Ship's store; near restaurants.

Shelter Cove Harbour (843-842-7001; Palmetto Dunes Resort) 170 slips, maximum length 155 feet. Fish and tackle store, charters, cruises, rentals; rod and reel rental. In village-like area of shops and restaurants. Low tide draft: 9 feet.

Skull Creek Marina (843-681-4234; Hilton Head Plantation) 180 slips, maximum length 200 feet. Sailing charters and night fishing, restaurant and lounge, courtesy bike and van transportation. Low tide draft: 10 feet.

South Beach Marina (843-671-6699; Sea Pines Plantation) 100 wet slips, 20 dry slips, maximum length 35 feet. Tackle and bait shop, boat and motor repair, rentals, cruises, instruction, and junior sailing school. Restaurants and shops at the marina village. Approach depth at low tide: 3 feet.

MINIATURE GOLF

A half-dozen courses (par 40 to par 65), featuring water-hazards, dog legs, and sand traps laid out in realistic settings. A great way to spend two hours. Most lit for night play. From $5.95 per adult.

Adventure Cove (843-842-9990; William Hilton Parkway at Folly Field Rd.).

Legendary Golf (Two locations: 843-686-3399; 900 William Hilton Pkwy. and 843-785-9214; 80 Pope Ave.).

Pirate's Island Adventure Golf (843-686-4001; William Hilton Parkway and Marina Side Dr.).

Waterfun Park and Mini Golf (843-842-8108; 6 Tanglewood Dr.).

SCUBA DIVING

Island Scuba Dive & Travel (843-689-3245; 130 Mathews Dr.) Scuba gear, rentals, and instruction.

TENNIS

There are more than 300 tennis courts — hard, clay, and even grass surfaces — on Hilton Head, spread through 19 clubs. Seven of them are open for public play: they are listed below. Call ahead for reservations — the staff may even be able to set you up with a game. Pros on site offer lessons, daily stroke clinics, and intensive camps year round; fully stocked shops provide stringing services and sales of equipment, clothing, and accessories. Court rental fees range from $15 to $22 per hour — usually with discounts for resort guests or visitors renting villas within the plantation. Many places offer reduced walk-on rates for midday play (12–4). Free exhibitions take place at 5:30 p.m.

Tennis is a year-round sport at Hilton Head, where resorts feature clinics, national tournaments, top-ranked professionals, and tennis-training camps.

Wade Spees

Mon.–Thurs. and Sunday afternoons, at different clubs, on a rotating basis. Call to confirm.

Hilton Head Island Beach and Tennis Resort (843-785-6613; 40 Folly Field Rd.) 10 hard, lighted courts.

Palmetto Dunes Tennis Center (843-785-1152; Palmetto Dunes Resort) 23 clay, 2 hard courts. Hard courts and six clay courts are lighted for night play.

Port Royal Racquet Club (843-686-8803; Port Royal Resort) 10 clay, 4 hard, 2 natural grass courts. Night play available on six courts.

Sea Pines Racquet Club (843-363-4495; Sea Pines Plantation) 24 clay, 5 hard courts.

South Beach Racquet Club (843-671-2215; Sea Pines Plantation) 11 clay courts, 2 lighted.

Van der Meer Tennis Center (843-785-8388 or 800-845-6138; DeAllyon Rd.) 28 courts: 25 hard, 3 clay. Night play available on 8 courts. The center is internationally known for its rigorous teaching programs and camps for kids and pros, as well as serious players. The island's top youngsters often train here.

Van der Meer Tennis University/Shipyard Racquet Club (843-686-8804 or 800-438-0793; Shipyard Plantation) 20 courts: 11 clay, 9 hard. Night play on 8 courts.

TOURING

If you're interested in exploring more of Hilton Head and the surrounding area, here are some suggestions. The towns of Bluffton and Beaufort are easy day trips. (For detailed information on these destinations, see Chapter Five.

Parts of Daufuskie Island are cherished for representing a simpler style of rural living that prevailed before the resorts.

Wade Spees

Beaufort, Edisto, and Bluffton). Each has a historic area of old houses, as well as shops and restaurants. ***Daufuskie Island*** is served by tour boat operators who offer cookouts and on-shore touring options. ***Savannah*** is about an hour away, and in a day you could tour the historic district, shop, have at least one meal, and be back in time for sunset over the marsh. A trip to ***Charleston*** requires a bit more time and planning, including approximately four hours by car round trip.

Airstream Aviation (843-785-7770; Hilton Head Airport) Private charters and tours of the island, the Lowcountry, or Savannah, from $49.95 per person, two person minimum.

Camelot Limousine and Tours (843-842-7777) On and off-island transportation, personalized tours, maximum of six people per vehicle.

Discover Hilton Head (843-842-9217) Daily tours of the island by car.

Gullah Heritage Trail Tours (843-681-7066) Two-hour tours through 10 neighborhoods and to sites prominent in the island's African-American culture.

Jenna Lee (843-290-5500; Shelter Cove Harbour) Daily cruises aboard a 40-foot luxury sailing yacht. Maximum six passengers. From $250 for half-day.

Low Country Adventures (843-681-8212 or 800-845-5582; lowcountryadventures.com) Island and off-island tours in a 10-passenger tour van or 21-passenger bus, including day trips with a tour guide to the historic area of Charleston ($65 per person). Door-to-door shuttle service to Savannah International is $25 one way, $45 round trip.

Spirit of Harbourtown and Vagabond (843-842-7179 or 843-842-4155; Harbour Town Marina, Sea Pines). Two high-powered vessels take you to Savannah's River Street or Daufuskie Island and pick you up after sightseeing is done. Prices vary, from $25 adults; $17 kids.

SHOPPING

As Hilton Head has grown, it has tried to minimize the visual impact of strip development along its major thoroughfare, Hwy. 278 — the William Hilton Parkway. (You have to look hard to spot the fast-food outlets, for though they exist, their signs are required to be less garish here than elsewhere.) As a result of this wish to maintain some degree of natural landscape, the small shopping centers and larger malls that have sprung up to serve 1.5 million visitors per year are destinations. They have their own plentiful parking, and a mix of tenants that includes restaurants, pizza and ice-cream counters, supermarkets, and boutiques. Here are some highlights.

Harbour Town, in Sea Pines Plantation, remains the only shopping area with a genuine village character — in its case, rather Mediterranean in feel, located around the harbor basin, clustered near the lighthouse. There's a $5 gate fee to enter Sea Pines. You can head toward Harbour Town, or pay your gate fee, park your car inside the Sea Pines Greenwood Gate, and take a free trolley (every 20 minutes) to Harbour Town. *South Beach Marina*, a Cape Cod-style village, is also in Sea Pines Plantation. For info: www.harbourtown.com.

Roadside fruit and vegetable stands provide fresh local melons, grapes, greens, boiled peanuts, and seafood.

Wade Spees

The Mall at Shelter Cove is a more conventional shopping center, anchored by big department stores. National chains like Saks, Williams-Sonoma, Banana Republic, Ann Taylor, and Talbot's are represented. There is a food court and the mall is enclosed, making it a good rainy-day outing.

Main Street Village (north island, just inside the entrance to Hilton Head Plantation — no gate fee) feels like a few downtown blocks in a prosperous suburb with its boutiques, a couple of pubs and restaurants, and "real" stores that sell ordinary things like beer and diapers. *Village at Wexford* has the most interesting collection of stores, restaurants, and more "arty" locales, like a gallery and a jazz club. The *Gullah Flea Market*, located at the traffic-signal intersection of Hwy. 278 and Squire Pope Rd., offers everything from African art to golf balls. Collections of shops around marinas at *Shelter Cove Harbour* and *Palmetto Bay Marina* support the boating and watersport activities located there. *Coligny Plaza* is oriented toward kids and visitors, refreshingly informal, a good to find beach toys, souvenirs and inexpensive resort-wear.

In addition, there are collections of outlet stores: *Shoppes on the Parkway* and *Pineland Station* face William Hilton Parkway (Hwy. 278) Hilton Head; just off the island on Hwy. 278 is the *Hilton Head Factory Stores 1 & 2*. There are bargains in every category: housewares, toys, shoes, eyeglasses, children's clothing, linens, high fashion, and sportswear. Dozens of name-brand manufacturers are represented. Some of the higher-end retailers include Coach, Brooks Brothers, J. Crew, Donna Karan, Dansk, Waterford/Wedgewood and Nike.

As off-island growth continues, small, non-chain shops and restaurants are opening near the "big box" stores (Home Depot, Target). If one is recommended, locate it by reference to its larger neighbor (signage on Hwy. 278 is not particularly good and access often requires crossing lanes of speeding traffic.)

ART AND ANTIQUES

S ome galleries have limited hours but welcome visitors by appointment. If you're interested in more than browsing, call ahead to check.

Altermann & Morris (843-842-4433; 807 Wm. Hilton Pkwy.) A large selection of 19th and 20th century American representational art, including painting and sculpture.

America. Oh Yes ! Folk Art Gallery (843-785-2649; 17 Pope Ave., Executive Park, #4; www.americaohyes.com) More than 250 self-taught and visionary artists have work displayed here, and there are pieces for the beginning or experienced collector of folk art.

Barry Honowitz (843-842-2400, ext. 7655; Crowne Plaza Resort, Shipyard Plantation) This watercolorist has created many lithographs of famous island scenes as well as the annual MCI Classic / Heritage of Golf lithograph. Originals and reproductions for sale.

Decorator's Wholesale Antiques (843-681-7463; 1 Cardinal Rd.) Stripped pine furniture from Europe favored by the "shelter" magazines for beach houses.

Endangered Arts Ltd. (843-785-5075; South Island Square) The featured artist, Wyland, is responsible for murals of whales and dolphins that can be seen on the sides of buildings in cities across the country. His originals and limited editions, in many forms, are available here, as well as work of other artists specializing in natural landscape and wildlife themes.

The Gilded Age Antiques (843-750-7766; 578 Wm. Hilton Pkwy.) High-end antiques and small Georgian and Edwardian era boxes.

Guggenheim's (843-785-9580; 72 Arrow Rd.) Antiques and collectibles, on consignment. A place you could get lucky.

Harbour Art Gallery (843-785-2787; Shelter Cove Harbour) Paintings and limited edition works of Beaufort, Savannah, and island scenes by artist R. Bolton Smith.

Island Ideas (843-842-6261; 800 Plantation Center) Original artwork in various media, framing, reproductions.

Joe Bowler Collection (843-757-6711; 9 Banyard Cove Rd.) Original and limited-edition proofs and reproductions of well-known island scenes and fine portraits, such as children on the beach.

Joe Pinckney Art Enterprises Ltd. (843-681-5661; 15-I Airport Rd.) Original portraits and wildlife art.

John Stobart Gallery (843-671-2739; Harbour Town) Limited edition maritime prints; original oils, and watercolors. Ship models and sculptural sea animals.

Moonshell Art Gallery (843-341-3339; 37 New Orleans Rd.) Varied collection of works and styles, from impressionistic Lowcountry scenes to children's portraiture.

Red Piano Art Gallery (843 785 2318; 220 Cordillo Parkway) Lowcountry landscapes, sculpture, and fine art from the 19th and 20th centuries. A regular stop for collectors.

Swan House Antiques (843-785-7926; 88 Arrow Rd.) Consignments make the collection eclectic and interesting: rugs, china, silver, paintings and prints, furniture.

BOOKS AND MUSIC

Audubon Nature Store (843-785-4311; Village at Wexford) Field guides, children's guides on local flora and fauna.

Author's Cafe & Bookstore (843-686-5020; The Village at Wexford) A place to read and sip.

Barnes & Noble (843-342-6690; 20 Hatton Place) The superstore for books, with many local authors and events featured each week

Book Warehouse (843-689-9419; 45 Pembroke Dr., Festival Center) Remainders and contemporary books discounted in all categories.

Disc Jockey (843-842-2844; Mall at Shelter Cove) Music in all formats; videos and accessories.

Gullah Bookstore (843-342-2002; 148-1 William Hilton Pkwy.) A comprehensive selection of books, tapes and gourmet products relating to the African-American experience.

Heaven Sent Christian Bookstore (843-837-4727; 1540 Fording Island Rd., Bridge Center Shoppes) Inspirational literature, Bibles, children's books.

Island Bookseller (843-671-3773; Sea Pines Center) Adult and children's titles, local authors.

Paperback Exchange (843-842-5614; Village Exchange, 32 Palmetto Bay Rd.) A wide and constantly changing selection of used books. Books on tape for rent here, too.

Waldenbooks (843-785-4301; Mall at Shelter Cove) Books for beach reading, children's section, history, cooking, and coffee-table books.

CLOTHING

Camp Hilton Head (843-842-3666; www.camphiltonhead.com. Shelter Cove) Fun, casual beachwear embossed with unique logo of Camp Hilton Head. Locations at Harbour Town and Coligny Plaza, too.

Island Child (843-686-5437; Village at Wexford) Fancy clothes for kids who live where "dress-up" is usually very casual.

Jamaican Me Crazy (843-785-9006; Coligny Plaza) Wacky resort wear, hip beach accessories.

Knickers (843-671-2291; Harbour Town) Classic outfits in linen, cotton, tweeds, and madras. An institution.

Loose Lucy's (843-785-8093; Coligny Plaza) A little bit of the 60s featuring tie-dye, old jeans, Indian prints, bandannas.

Shopping for bargains at the Hilton Head Factory Outlets.

Wade Spees

Outside Hilton Head (843-686-6996; Plaza at Shelter Cove) Top-of-the-line durable sports clothing (Patagonia, Woolrich, Teva), footwear, and accessories. Also at South Beach Marina.

Penelope Jane's (843-785-5522; 219 Park Plaza) Designer clothes for women, including some with a black, edgy, city feel (to wear to a museum) and some with a dressy-but-sporty feel (to wear to a polo match).

Porcupine (843-785-2779; The Village at Wexford) Designer sportswear for women, lingerie, excellent shoe selection, swimwear. The classiest fashion stop on the island.

Sweet Peas (843-836-3252; 1540 Fording Island Rd., Bridge Center) Designer clothes for kids — the best and latest fashions.

CRAFTS

Art Cafe (843-785-5525; 10 Heritage Plaza) A hands-on pottery studio, where you select an unadorned object (mug, plate, bowl, etc.), choose the glazes and tools, and decorate it until it's unique. A good family project.

Sweetgrass baskets woven by native islanders are for sale at the Gullah Market on William Hilton Parkway.

Wade Spees

The Flying Cow (843-785-3557; Village Exchange, Palmetto Bay Rd.) Large as life animal sculptures (in wild colors), folk art and paintings on boards, silly signs for your beach house or bathroom.

Harbour Town Crafts (843-671-3643; Harbour Town) Quality American handcrafts, large and small, whimsical and functional.

Inspirations, Ltd. (843-842-6606; The Village at Wexford) Home accessories and handpainted furniture; painted glassware; original "portrait" dolls.

Smith Galleries of Fine Crafts (843-842-2280; www.smithgalleries.com. Village at Wexford) More than 300 American artisans are represented in media such as glass, wood, metal, clay, and textiles.

Stamp Heaven Crafts (843-686-3932; 32 Palmetto Bay Rd., Village Exchange) Zillions of rubber stamps and ink pads, cards, stencils, stationery, and paper products on which to create your stamped fantasy.

Unique Lines' Stitchery (843-842-5614; 32 Palmetto Bay Rd.,Village Exchange) Materials and designs for needlework, knitting, and embroidery projects.

GIFTS

Creative Kitchens (843-785-8516; The Village at Wexford) An excellent kitchen and fine houseware supply store. Cooks love it; anyone who needs a bridal gift should, too. Another location at Main St. Village (843-689-9460).

The Goldsmith Shop (843-785-2538; 3 Lagoon Rd.) Gold charms of dolphins, starfish and boats, studded with tiny jewels.

Hammock Company (843-686-3636; Coligny Plaza) Limited edition wildlife and duck stamp prints; Pawley's Island hammocks, porch rockers, garden benches, swings; bird feeders, and wind chimes.

Legends Sports Cards (843-681-4444; Main St. Village) Old and new trading cards, autographed memorabilia, and Ted Williams signature items.

Magic Puppet (843-785-3280; Coligny Plaza) Toys, puppets, magic tricks, Playmobil sets, books.

Mole Hole (843-785-8090; Coligny Plaza) Figurines and china collectibles; cards and oil lamps. Also at the Mall at Shelter Cove.

Seasons South (843-785-6280; 38 New Orleans Rd.) Garden furniture, ceramics, tiles and tools.

Ship's Store (843-842-7001; Shelter Cove Harbour) Everything for the sailor including charts, boat shoes, and nautical accessories.

GOURMET AND FUN FOOD

Chocolate Canopy (843-842-4567; www.chocolatecanopy.com. Crossroads Center, Palmetto Bay Rd.) Homemade chocolates galore.

Cinnamon Bear Country Store (843-661-5558; Main St. Village) Gourmet coffee, candies, and gifts.

Healthy Days Natural Food Store (843-785-7297; Coligny Plaza) Flours, herbal teas, sugar-free items.

Rann & Tiffs (843-341-3441; #2 Coligny Beach Market) Sixty kinds of ice-cream sundaes, banana splits, shakes and sodas. Clown performances nightly.

Signe's Heaven Bound Bakery (843-785-9118; 2 Bow Circle) Fresh baked breads, pastries, cakes, cookies, soups.

Truffles Market (843-671-6136; Sea Pines Center) Sandwiches, pate, salads, breads, pastries and wine.

Vino &Vitto (843-815-7777; www.vinoandvitto.com. Hwy. 278, Bluffton, adjacent to Home Depot). A superior gourmet food store, as good as any in a metropolitan area, with an enormous variety of baked goods, sandwiches, wines, cheeses, salads, and condiments. Daily Blue-Plate Specials. There are simple tables and chairs, or eat in the on-site bistro, Fresco's.

SPORTSWEAR AND SPORTS EQUIPMENT

Hilton Head Surf Shop (843-785-7873, Village at Wexford; 843-363-2170, beach Marina) Bodyboards, skimboards, surfboards, and all the accessories.

Lowcountry Outfitters (843-837-6100 or 800-935-9666; Moss Creek Village) Fly-fishing equipment, fine guns, clothing and hunting-related gifts.

Nevada Bob's Golf Shop (843-686-4653; 1016 Wm. Hilton Pkwy) All you need for the links at discounted prices. Club rentals.

Outside Hilton Head (843-686-6996, Plaza at Shelter Cove or 843-671-2643, South Beach Marina) Equipment for windsurfing, canoeing, kayaking, and camping. Patagonia, North Face clothing lines. The island standard for outdoor activity and experienced staff.

Player's World (843-842-5100; Plaza at Shelter Cove) Island's largest sporting goods store. Another branch (843-785-4653; Shoppes on the Parkway) specializes in golf equipment and accessories.

Sportline (843-686-8855; 890 Wm. Hilton Pkwy.) Tennis racquets and same-day stringing; shoes and accessories for runners and soccer players.

CHAPTER SEVEN

Practical Matters & Seasonal Events

INFORMATION

There's always room, and time, for a pick-up game in the old neighborhoods.

Wade Spees

What follows is information to make your visit to the Lowcountry run more smoothly. It's a modest compendium of essentials — what's here and how it works — intended to make planning your trip easier and enjoying your stay simpler. The chapter covers the following topics:

AMBULANCE, FIRE & POLICE

The general emergency number in the Lowcountry is *911*, whether you're in Charleston, Beaufort, Hilton Head, or Savannah. Outside the cities, most of the counties have basic 911 service. Naturally, in an emergency, you can always dial "0" for the Operator's assistance in reaching the right agency.

A selected roster of other numbers, for emergencies or other business, follows:

First Call For Help (Information and referral service):

Beaufort/Hilton Head	843-524-4357
Savannah	912-651-7730

Poison Control:

South Carolina	800-922-1117
(from within S.C.)	
Georgia	800-282-5846
(from within Ga.)	

Rape Crisis Hotline:

Charleston	843-722-7273
Beaufort/Hilton Head	800-637-7273
or 843-525-6699	
Savannah	912-233-7273

Disaster/Hurricane Emergency Preparedness:

Charleston County	843-740-6400
Beaufort County	843-525-7353
or 800-686-6397	
Colleton County	843-549-5632
Hampton County	843-943-7522
Jasper County	843-726-5583
Chatham County	912-651-3100

State Police:

S.C. Highway Patrol:

Charleston Area	843-740-1660
Beaufort/Hilton Head	843-524-0163
Ridgeland	843-726-8076

Ga. Highway Patrol:

Savannah Area	912-651-3000

Police (non-emergency):

City of Charleston	843-720-3892
Town of Edisto Beach	843-869-2440
City of Beaufort	843-525-7580
Town of Port Royal	843-986-2220
Town of Hilton Head (sheriff)	843-689-4300
Town of Bluffton	843-757-2263
Town of Hardeeville	843-784-2233
City of Savannah	912-232-4141

AREA CODES, TOWN GOVERNMENT & ZIP CODES

AREA CODES

If you live on a boat, the sensible thing to do is lash your mailbox to a piling.

Wade Spees

The area code for the South Carolina Lowcountry is **843**. The area code for Savannah, Georgia and its metropolitan region is **912**.

TOWN HALLS

The cities of Charleston, Beaufort, Hilton Head, and Savannah are governed by a mayor and city/town council; their outlying lands controlled by county government. This form of organization has been in place for some time, except at Hilton Head, where the residents' desire to have some autonomy from Beaufort County — specifically to control the island's tremendous growth — spurred action some 15 years ago ago to form a "limited service" town government. In the last two years, tiny Bluffton found itself similarly beseiged and responded by annexing a wide swath of land along and on either side of the highway to Hilton Head — a move that today makes Bluffton one of the largest (in acreage) towns in the state.

In general, though, the trend in government is toward consolidation of services, whereby the cities or towns and the counties they are part of share in the cost and delivery of these services.

Charleston, Beaufort, Walterboro, Ridgeland, Hampton, and *Savannah* are the region's county seats. For general information call:

Charleston County	843-958-4000
Beaufort County	843-470-2800
Colleton County	843-549-5221
Jasper County	843-726-7703
Hampton County	843-943-7500
Chatham County	912-652-7869

There are also smaller, scattered municipalities governed by smaller councils. For general information, contact the following town/city hall offices:

Town	Address	Telephone
Beaufort	302 Carteret St., 29902	843-525-7000
Bluffton	Hwy. 46, P.O. Box 386, 29910	843-757-2642
Charleston	80 Broad St., P.O. Box 652, 29402	843-577-6970
Edisto Island	2414 Murray St., 29438	843-869-2505
Folly Beach	21 Center St., 29439	843-588-2447
Hampton	304 Lee Ave., 29924	843-943-2951
Hilton Head	1 Town Center Court, 29928	843-341-4600
Isle of Palms	1207 Palm Blvd., 29451	843-886-6428
Port Royal	1406 Paris Ave., 29935	843-986-2200
Ridgeland	108 E. Wilson; P.O. Drawer B, 29936	843-726-3351
Walterboro	242 Hampton St., P.O. Box 709, 29488	843-549-2545
Savannah	Bay St., P.O. Box 1027, 31402	912-651-6790
Thunderbolt	2702 Mechanics Ave., 31404	912-354-5537
Tybee Island	401 Butler Ave., 31328	912-786-4573

BANKS

South Carolina and Georgia banks are linked electronically to banking systems and debit card accounts throughout the United States. Money can be wired from your home bank or funds can be withdrawn from automatic teller machines provided your ATM/credit card corresponds with the regional networks. Many supermarkets and filling stations accept debit cards. The following list provides information on several banks throughout the Lowcountry.

Bank	Phone	Networks
Charleston		
Bank of America	843-724-1500	Honor, Plus, Visa
BB&T	843-720-1500	Honor, Visa
First Federal of Charleston	843-529-9100	Honor, Mastercard/Visa, Cirrus
First Union Bank	800-275-3862	Plus, Honor, AFFN, Cirrus
Beaufort		
Bank of America	843-521-6002	Honor, Plus, Visa
Regions Bank	843-525-8418	Honor, Cirrus
Hilton Head		
The Anchor Bank	843-785-4848	Honor, Avail
First Union	843- 686-5100	Honor, Cirrus, Plus, Visa,Mastercard
Wachovia	843-686-9343	Avail, Cirrus, Honor, Mastercard, Plus, Visa
Savannah		
First Liberty	912-351-2201	Honor, Plus
First Union	912-944-2000	Honor, Plus, Cirrus
The Savannah Bank	912-651-8200	Avail, Honor, Plus, Cirrus

BIBLIOGRAPHY

L owcountry life, past and present, is well documented, and its bookstores have ever-growing "local history" sections to prove it. Many volumes that had been out of print have been reprinted recently in response to new demand. Originals may be still found in second-hand bookstores, although at premium prices. Here is a suggested reading list of some classics, the books you're likely to find in residents' libraries.

These days, there are more "homegrown" histories available, courtesy of laptop publishing. Don't overlook them and the gems of local lore they contain. And, since the best part of a trip is often reliving it at home, check your local bookstore upon returning for further reading. The boxed quotes scattered throughout the text are taken from books included in the list below.

The list is by no means complete: think of it as a mere guide to the shelves.

ART & ARCHITECTURE

Cole, Cynthia, ed. *Historic Resources of the Lowcountry.* Yemassee, SC: Lowcountry Council of Governments, 1979, second ed. 1990. 202 pp., illus., photos, index, $29.95. The definitive four-county survey of historic houses and sites with fine historical and architectural explanation.

Dugan, Ellen, ed. *Picturing the South: 1860 to the Present.* Atlanta, GA: Chronicle Books, the High Museum of Art, 1996. 213 pp., index ,$29.95. Based on a 1996 exhibit at the Photographic Galleries of the High Museum in Atlanta, the selection of pictures (from the Library of Congress Collections, private donors, historical societies, and museums) is honed to perfection and the accompanying essays (by several southern writers of the first rank) is excellent. The book is moving without being sentimental.

Lane, Mills. *Architecture of the Old South: South Carolina.* Savannah, GA: Beehive Press, 1984. 258 pp., photos, $75. Exquisite, large format, black and white photos.

————. *Architecture of the Old South: Georgia.* Savannah, GA: Beehive Press, 1986, 252 pp., photos, $75.

Ravenel, Beatrice St. Julian. *Architects of Charleston.* Columbia, SC: University of South Carolina Press, 1992. 338 pp., photos, index, bibliog., $19.95. First published in 1945, a detailed examination of the lives and works of the city's builders, engineers, and architects.

Rosengarten, Dale. *Row Upon Row: Sea Grass Baskets of the South Carolina Lowcountry.* Columbia, SC: McKissick Museum, 1986. 64 pp., photos, $10. A thorough and lovingly documented catalogue of a vibrant Sea Island art. It is the authoritative text on the shapes, weaving style, and uses of island baskets.

Severens, Kenneth. *Charleston Antebellum Architecture & Civic Destiny.* Knoxville, TN: University of Tennessee Press, 1988. 330 pp., photos, index, $49.95. A specialized topic explained in clear prose for the interested amateur or professional architect.

Severens, Martha R. *Charles Fraser of Charleston.* Charles L. Wyrick, Jr., ed. Charleston, SC: Carolina Art Assoc., 1983. 176 pp., illus., $14.95. The subject was a miniaturist of the 19th century whose portraits of local gentry, in the collection of the Gibbes Art Gallery, are exquisite and incisive.

————.*The Charleston Renaissance.* Charleston, SC: Robert M. Hicklin, Jr., Inc., 1999. 232 pp., illus., $65. A scholarly, beautifully illustrated chronicle of the artists in early 20th-century Charleston who were inspired by the city's heritage and story and expressed themselves in a variety of media.

Talbott, Page. *Classical Savannah: Fine and Decorative Arts 1800–1840.* Savannah: Telfair Museum, 1995. 320 pp., illus., $24.95. An overview of a period during which Savannah was deeply influenced by English Regency and Continental architecture and interior style.

Vlach, John Michael. *Back of the Big House: The Architecture of Plantation Slavery.* Chapel Hill, NC: University of North Carolina Press, 1993. 236 pp., illus., photos, index, $18.95. A serious, well-written, and fundamental study of the relationship of plantation "spaces" — the outbuildings, the quarters, the "Big House", the allées or avenues, fields, docks, and waterways — to the black and white people who lived there and to each other. Numerous plantation plans are cited.

AUTOBIOGRAPHY, BIOGRAPHY, DIARIES & LETTERS

Bartram, William. *Travels through North & South Carolina, Georgia, East & West Florida.* New York: Viking Penguin, 1988. 452 pp., $7.95. The account of an 18th-century trip through the Lowcountry by the famous botanist.

Chesnut, Mary Boykin. *A Diary From Dixie.* Cambridge, MA: Harvard University Press, 1980. 608 pp., $12.95. A classic account, good on Charleston society.

Daise, Ronald. *Reminiscences of a Sea Island Heritage.* Columbia SC: Sandlapper, 1986. 103 pp., photos, $18.95. Archival black-and-white photos accompanied by text and stories of Sea Island Gullah culture. Daise and his wife, Natalie, were the creators and stars of the television series for children, Gullah Gullah Island, and continue to perform nationally.

Egerton, Douglas. *He Shall Go Out Free: The Lives of Denmark Vesey.* Madison, WI: Madison House, 1999. 272 pp., illus., $34.95. A complete, well-researched and well-argued account of the failed slave uprising in Charleston in 1822.

Elliott, William & Theodore Rosengarten. *Carolina Sports by Land and Water, Including Incidents of Devil-Fishing, Wild-Cat, Deer, and Bear-Hunting, Etc.* Columbia, SC: University of South Carolina Press, 1994. Illus., $14.95. A reprint of Elliott's 1850s original, it is still funny, easy to read, and as full of suspense as ever.

Forten, Charlotte L. *The Journal of a Free Negro in the Slave Era.* New York: Norton, 1981. 286 pp., index, $8.95. The vivid impressions of a northern teacher who came to the Sea Islands to educate the newly freed slaves.

Georgia Writers' Project, ed. *Drums and Shadows.* Athens, GA: University of Georgia Press, 1986. $11.95. The collection of oral histories first published under the WPA program in 1940. It allows you to hear the voices of the coast.

Higginson, Thomas Wentworth. *Army Life in a Black Regiment.* New York: Norton, 1984. 279 pp., appendix, index, $6.95. Higginson, a Boston Brahmin, was the white commander of the First South Carolina Volunteers, headquartered in Beaufort, S.C. during the Civil War. Its honest, self-effacing narrative of camp life, countrysides, and skirmishes is invaluable.

Kemble, Frances Anne. *Journal of Residence on a Georgia Plantation in 1838–1839.* Athens, GA: University of Georgia Press, 1984. 488 pp., $11.95. Although the setting is the coastal Georgia plantation of the author's husband, Pierce Butler, her insights into plantation life and the culture of black female slaves make this perhaps the best account of that time.

McTeer, J.E. *High Sheriff of the Lowcountry.* Beaufort, SC: JEM Co., 1995. 101 pp., $19.70. Newly reprinted, it contains the colorful recollections of the author's days as a Lowcountry lawman and his encounters with voodoo and witch doctors, rum runners, and local scoundrels.

Olmsted, F.L. *A Journey in the Seaboard Slave States.* Westport, CT: Negro Universities Press of Greenwood Pub., 1969. Illus., index, $35.00. A reprint of the 1856 edition in which the author acutely observes the coastal region and standards of living there.

Pearson, Elizabeth Ware, ed. *Letters From Port Royal 1862–1868.* New York: Arno Press, 1969. $14.00. In 1862, dozens of Northern abolitionists flocked to the Federally occupied area around Beaufort, S.C. to educate the newly freed slaves and manage the abandoned cotton plantations. This collection of letters by the Boston contingent is as forceful and moving a commentary on race relations and liberal expectations as exists.

Pennington, Patience. *A Woman Rice Planter.* Cambridge, MA: Belknap Press of Harvard University Press, 1961. The author was a Lowcountry native who managed her father's rice plantations after the Civil War and wrote about the experience for New York newspapers. The illustrations are by Alice Ravenel Huger Smith, a lyrical interpreter of the rural Lowcountry.

Pinkney, Roger. *The Beaufort Chronicles.* Beaufort, SC: Pluff Mud. 110 pp., $9.95. A new collection of remembrances and essays on small-town life and its simple pleasures.

Towne, Laura. *Letters and Diary Written from the Sea Islands of South Carolina, 1862–1884.* New York: American Bio. Series, 1991. 310 pp., $79. Another wonderful journal of a teacher; she established Penn School, the first school for freed slaves in the United States.

Verner, Elizabeth O. *Mellowed By Time.* Charleston, SC: Tradd St. Press, 1978. $15.00. Sketches and memories of old Charleston by a distinguished artist who favored etchings, pastel, and pencil drawing.

CULTURAL STUDIES

Bluffton Historical Preservation Society. *No. II A Longer Short History of Bluffton, South Carolina and its Environs.* Bluffton, SC: Bluffton Historical Preservation Society, 1988. 49 pp., photos, $9.95. An excellent local history with photographs of classic Lowcountry cottages.

Carawan, Guy & Candy, eds. *Ain't You Got a Right to the Tree of Life? The People of John's Island, South Carolina — Their Faces, Their Words & Their Songs.* Athens, GA: University of Georgia Press, 1989. 256 pp., photos, $29.95.

Johnson, Guion G. *A Social History of the Sea Islands.* Westport, CT: Greenwood Press, 1969. 185 pp., index, bibliog., $38.50. A reprint of the 1930 edition of a series in which scholars from the University of North Carolina examined the lives, speech, culture, and folkways of Sea Island natives. Others include Folk Culture on St. Helena Island by Guy B. Johnson and Black Yeomanry by T.J. Woofter, which, if you can find it, has stirring documentary photographs.

Jones-Jackson, Patricia. *When Roots Die: Endangered Traditions on the Sea Islands.* Athens, GA: University of Georgia Press, 1987. 189 pp., photos, bibliog., $19.95.

Parrish, Lydia. *Slave Songs of the Georgia Sea Islands.* Athens, GA: University of Georgia Press, 1992. 252 pp., photos, musical notation, $19.95. A reprint of the 1942 original by the wife of artist Maxfield Parrish, documenting the islanders' songs from the praise house to the play yard.

Taylor, John Martin. *Hoppin' John's Lowcountry Cooking.* New York: Bantam, 1990. 345 pp., illus., $24.00.

———. *The New Southern Cook: 200 Recipes.* New York: Bantam, 1995. 287 pp., illus., $27.95. A superb follow-up to Taylor's first book, this one ranges a bit further but maintains the author's discriminating judgments and lack of pretension.

Terry, Elizabeth, with Alexis Terry. *Savannah Seasons: Food and Stories from Elizabeth on 37th.* New York: Doubleday, 1996. 340 pp., $30. Recipes and memories, written by mother and daughter, of the family's nationally acclaimed Savannah restaurant, which opened in 1980. There's a useful "source list" for ingredients available from speciality vendors by mail, too.

Vernon, Amelia Wallace. *African-Americans at Mars Bluff, South Carolina.* Columbia, SC: University of South Carolina Press, 1995. 200 pp., illus., photos, index, bibliog., $16.95. A wonderful documentary account of an African-American community north of Charleston, S.C.

Welty, Eudora. *The Eye of the Story: Selected Essays and Reviews.* New York: Vintage International, 1990. 355 pp., $14.00.

Westmacott, Richard. *African-American Gardens and Yards in the Rural South.* Knoxville, TN: University of Tennessee Press, 1992. 175 pp., illus., photos, index, bibliog., $24.95. One of the most thoughtful and inspired books ever written on African-American rural life (some in the Lowcountry), it focuses on several families and the way they create color, style, whimsy, and usefulness in their immediate landscape. It is part scholarly, part oral history, and the tone is just right.

FICTION

Berendt, John. *Midnight in the Garden of Good and Evil.* New York: Random House, 1994. 388 pp., $22.00. A wild romp in Savannah — and it's all true.

Conroy, Pat. *The Water is Wide.* New York: Bantam, 1972. 320 pp., $4.95. This was the book based on Conroy's experiences as a Beaufort County schoolteacher on isolated Daufuskie Island. His other books include *The Great Santini, The Prince of Tides,* and *Beach Music* and have Beaufort as their setting (even in the movie version).

Griswold, Francis. *Sea Island Lady.* Beaufort, SC: Beaufort Book Co., reprint of the 1939 original. 964 pp., $19.95. A big, fat Southern novel set in Beaufort.

Hewyard, Du Bose. *Porgy.* Charleston, SC: Tradd St. Press, 1985. 130 pp., illus., $20. A reprinting of the great tale, set in and around Charleston.

Humphreys, Josephine. *Rich in Love.* New York: Viking Penguin, 1987. 262 pp., $8.95. Set in Mount Pleasant, near Charleston, this novel (basis of the 1993 movie) captures the world view of a precocious 17-year-old girl. The author's other novels, *Dreams of Sleep* (1984) and *The Fireman's Fair* (1991), also have the Charleston area as their setting.

Naylor, Gloria R. *Mama Day.* New York: Random House, 1989. 312 pp., $9.95. A magical story set in a mythical place that nearly mirrors the Georgia/South Carolina Sea Islands.

Peterkin, Julia. *Scarlet Sister Mary.* Marietta, GA: Cherokee Press, 1991. 352 pp., $18.95. A reprint of the 1928 edition.

Powell, Padgett. *Edisto.* New York: Farrar, Strauss & Giroux, 1984. 192 pp., $11.95. A boy's coming-of-age on a Sea Island.

————. *Edisto Revisited.:* New York: Henry Holt, 1996. 145 pp., $20.

Sayers, Valerie. *Due East.* New York: Doubleday, 1987. 264 pp., $15.95. The first novel in a group that chronicles life in a town like Beaufort, S.C., where the author grew up. Others include *How I Got Him Back* (1989) and *Who Do You Love* (1991).

Worthington, Curtis, ed. *Literary Charleston: A Lowcountry Reader.* Charleston, SC: Wyrick & Co., 1996. 360 pp., $24.95.

HISTORY

Bridenbaugh, Carl. *Myths and Realities: Societies of the Colonial South.* New York: Atheneum, 1963. 208 pp., index, bibliog., $1.25.

Dollard, John. *Caste and Class in a Southern Town.* Madison, WI: University of Wisconsin Press, 1989. 466 pp., index, $14.50. A reissue of the 1937 work which, while not specifically about the Lowcountry, has everything to say about race relations in small towns throughout the region.

Jacoway, Elizabeth. *Yankee Missionaries in the South: The Penn School Experiment.* Baton Rouge, LA: LSU Press, 1980. 301 pp., index, bibliog.

Jones, Katharine M. *Port Royal Under Six Flags.* Indianapolis, IN: Bobbs-Merrill, 1960. 368 pp., illus., bibliog. A good general introduction to the area, with long passages quoting original documents.

Rogers, George. *Charleston in the Age of the Pinckneys.* Columbia, SC: University of South Carolina Press, 1984. 198 pp., index, $9.95. If there is one book you should read about Charleston's heyday, this is it.

Rose, Willie Lee. *Rehearsal For Reconstruction: The Port Royal Experiment.* New York: Oxford University Press, 1976. 450 pp., index, bibliog., $13.95. A beautifully written and meticulously researched account of the Northern abolitionists who went to the Sea Islands of Beaufort at the time of the Civil War. If you have a serious interest in the subject, the bibliography of this book is where you should start.

Rosen, Robert. *A Short History of Charleston.* San Francisco, CA: Lexikos, 1982. 160 pp., illus., photos, bibliog., $8.95. A popular introduction to Charleston by a native son.

Rosengarten, Theodore. *Tombee: Portrait of A Cotton Planter.* New York: McGraw, 1988. 752 pp., index, $15.00. This prize-winning book reproduces the diaries of an antebellum St. Helena Islander, Thomas B. Chaplin, and creates a context of explanation for them. This is the story — not the myth — of life on a cotton plantation, handled in vivid prose by the region's best historian.

Stampp, Kenneth. *The Peculiar Institution: Slavery in the Ante-Bellum South.* New York: Vintage, 1989. Index, $10. A classic study, first published in 1956.

Wise, Stephen R. *Lifeline of the Confederacy: Blockade Running During the Civil War.* Columbia, SC: University of South Carolina Press, 1988. 403 pp., illus., index, $16.95.

———. *Gate Of Hell: Campaign for Charleston Harbor, 1863.* Columbia, SC: University of South Carolina Press, 1994. 218 pp., illus., index, $29.95.

Wood, Peter. *Black Majority: Negroes in Colonial South Carolina from 1670 through the Stono Rebellion.* New York: Norton, 1975. 384 pp., index, $9.95.

PHOTOGRAPHIC STUDIES

Blagden, Tom. *The Lowcountry.* Greensboro, NC: Legacy Publications, 1988. 104 pp., photos, $49.95. Views of the coastal world by an immensely talented photographer. His words of introduction, of praise for the region's natural beauty, resonate with visitors and locals alike.

———. South Carolina's *Wetland Wilderness: The ACE Basin.* Englewood, CO: Westcliffe Publishers, Inc. 1992. 110 pp., $29.95. A sumptuous study of the land and estuarine ecosystem in and around the Ashepoo, Combahee, and

The swans of Middleton Place symbolize the elegant beauty of the Lowcountry.

Wade Spees

Edisto Rivers, much of which is being protected by federal, state, local, and private organizations.

Dabbs, Edith, ed. *Face of An Island.* An album of the early 20th century photographs taken on St. Helena Island by Leigh Richmond Miner and reproduced from the glass plates. A treasure.

Ellis, Ray. *South by Southeast.* Birmingham, AL: Oxmoor House, 1983. 122 pp., $50. Watercolors of the coastal region by noted painter and Hilton Head resident.

Isley, Jane, Agnes Baldwin, and William P. Baldwin. *Plantations of the Lowcountry.* Greensboro, NC: Legacy Pub., 1987. 151 pp., $19.95. Color photographs and histories of historic homes.

McLaren, Lynn, and Gerhard Spieler. *Ebb Tide, Flood Tide.* Columbia, SC: University of South Carolina Press, 1991. 105 pp., $40. Color photographs of favorite Beaufort sites...natural and man-made.

Schultz, Constance, ed. *A South Carolina Album. 1936–1948.* Columbia, SC: University of South Carolina Press, 1992. 143 pp. A collection of the photographs taken under the auspices of the Farm Security Administration, and later under the direction of its chief, Roy Stryker.

RECREATION/TRAVEL

Baldwin, William P. III. *Lowcountry Daytrips: Plantations, Gardens, and a Natural History of the Charleston Region.* Greensboro NC: Legacy Publications, 1993. 283 pp., illus., photos, index, bibliog., $18.95. The best new guide of the area, written by a Lowcountry native. It is a model of organization (with maps and mileage clearly spelled out), good design, practicality, and a writing style that lends itself to reading aloud. The book you'll lend to anyone who takes your advice and visits the Lowcountry.

Ballantine, Todd. *Tideland Treasures.* Columbia, SC: University of South Carolina Press, 1991. 218 pp., $15.95.

Crowley, Rebecca Kaufmann. *Hilton Head Guidebook.* Beaufort, SC: Coastal Villages Press, 1995. 135 pp., $9.95.

Federal Writers' Project Staff. *The WPA Guide to the Palmetto State.* Walter B. Edgar, ed. Columbia, SC: University of South Carolina Press, 1988. 514 pp., photos, index, $16.95. A reprint of the superb guide.

Georgia Conservancy. *A Guide to the Georgia Coast.* Savannah, GA: The Georgia Conservancy, 1989. 199 pp., illus., index.

Moeller, Jan and Bill Moeller. *The Intracoastal Waterway.* Camden, ME: Seven Seas Press, 1979 (updated 1991). 149 pp., $16.95.

Trask, Fred. *A Guide to Historic Beaufort.* Beaufort, SC: Historic Beaufort Foundation, 1970. 125 pp., maps, illus., photos. The definitive guide, especially good in describing walking and driving tours.

Wright, Cantey Holmes. *The Edisto Book.* Columbia, SC: Mac Kohn Printing, 1988. 109 pp., map, illus. Good local history.

Wyrick & Co. *The Charleston Guide.* Charleston, SC: Wyrick & Co., 1987. 30 pp., $3.50.

CLIMATE, WEATHER & WHAT TO WEAR

B efore spring was celebrated with house tours in Charleston and St. Patrick's Day parades in Savannah, there was just the season to rave about. Tourists came to see the blossoms and they weren't disappointed — azaleas bursting into bloom all over downtown, jasmine flowering on fence posts, dogwood and magnolia peeping out from under the shadows of live oaks in the woods.

In fact, there is something in bloom year-round in the Lowcountry, from late-summer mums to camellias to paper-white narcissus which scent the air at Christmas. This comes as a result of the semitropical to subtropical climate and the ever-present breezes that characterize the coastal region. Rarely do days pass in succession without sunshine. The annual rainfall for the region is about 51 inches.

The winters are generally mild — maybe 9 days of frost, and a half-dozen hard freezes. Spring comes early. Farmers generally break ground on February 1. In the old days, the cotton crop was finished by "lay-by time" in late August, when slaves, temporarily released from heavy field work, would tend to their cemeteries and families.

Endless Summer

From this early spring-time onward, there seemed no great difference in atmospheric sensations, and only a succession of bloom. After two months one's notions of the season grew bewildered, just as very early rising bewilders the day. In the army one is perhaps aroused after a bivouac, marches before daybreak, halts, fights, somebody is killed, a long day's life has been lived, and after all it is not seven o'clock, and breakfast is not ready. So when we had lived in summer so long as hardly to remember winter, it suddenly occurred to us that it was not yet June. One escapes at the South that mixture of hunger and avarice which is felt in the Northern summer, counting each hour's joy with the sad consciousness that an hour is gone.

—From *Army Life in a Black Regiment*, 1869
by Thomas Wentworth Higginson

By May 1, it's hot, and that heat will penetrate every living thing through the end of September. They say the mean (and it sure is) summer temperature in the Lowcountry runs between 70 degrees and 88 degrees. Now that we've given a name — the Heat Index — to what it feels like when the 90 percent humidity is factored in, it's really probably near 95 degrees, or so it feels, for several months each year.

If you arrive in summer, be prepared to move slowly, wear a hat, slather on the sunscreen, and drink plenty of liquids. Even on a hazy day the sun will burn you. Take extra precautions if you're planning athletic pursuits: the tennis court is no place to be at midday. The wild cloudbursts that drench the region in summer, and the often-spectacular thunder and lightening shows that accompany them, may cool things off a bit. More likely, they'll just bring mosquitos.

Water and warm air, an unbeatable Lowcountry combination.

Wade Spees

Then there are the gnats. Just when you're enjoying a creamy autumn day in the 70s, they find you. Avon's Skin So Soft has proved an effective repellent, as does staying out of the shade or standing in a breeze.

The seasons each bring their color, their migratory birds, their harvest of fish or shellfish, duck or deer. And twice a year it seems as if a whole new shipment of air is carted in, too — in late October, when the marsh has turned golden and the clouds pull themselves into exquisitely defined cumuli; and again in late February, when the prevailing northeast winds of winter start to shift south and southwest.

But perhaps the best quality of Lowcountry weather is its subtlety and contradiction: the warm day in January that you were not expecting, the roaring fire in October that banishes the dampness and chill in the morning, but by late afternoon seems an inferno.

For clothing, always take more cotton shirts than you think you'll need: flowers should wilt, not people. Take comfortable shoes for touring (high-heeled shoes are often forbidden in House Museums and on tours) and a light sweater or windbreaker. An overcoat or parka may be too much in winter; sweaters and shells work better.

Weather Information

Charleston	843-744-3207
Beaufort	843-524-2999
Savannah	912-964-1700

HANDICAPPED SERVICES

Most of the region's accommodations, museums, restaurants, and touring services provide access and facilities for those with special physical needs — but call ahead to confirm details: problems remain in retrofitting the older historic buildings for complete handicapped access. Your guides, hosts, or the Visitor Center's staff in each city will gladly assist you — several offer handicap-accessibility guides. See the section **Tourist Information** at the end of this chapter for addresses of city or county offices of tourism and travel.

HOSPITALS

Charleston

Bon Secours St. Francis Hospital 2095 Henry Tecklenburg Dr.; 843-402-1000.
Medical University of South Carolina 171 Ashley Ave.; 843-792-2300.

Roper Hospital 316 Calhoun St.; 843-724-2000.
Trident Regional Medical Center 9330 Medical Plaza Dr.; 843-797-7000.
Veteran's Administration Medical Center 109 Bee St.; 843-577-5011.

Beaufort

Beaufort Memorial Hospital 121 S. Ribaut Rd.; 843-522-5200.

Hilton Head

Hilton Head Medical Center and Clinics 25 Hospital Center Blvd.; 843-681-6122.

Savannah

Immediate Med 2014 E. Victory Dr.; 912-927-6832.
Memorial Medical Center 4700 Waters Ave.; 912-350-8000.
St. Joseph's / Candler Health System 11705 Mercy Blvd.; 912-925-4100.

LATE NIGHT FOOD AND FUEL

The metropolitan areas of Charleston and Savannah, and the resort centers of Hilton Head, stay lit and active well after midnight — especially during the spring and summer — so finding gas or even grits should not be a problem. However, if you're traveling at night, remember that the Lowcountry is largely rural, traversed by long stretches of quiet highway. Unless you plan to gig for flounder and fry them up by the side of the road, it's best to travel with snacks.

Charleston

Circle-K Convenience Store (grocery and fuel) 2284 Savannah Highway. Open 24 hours.
International House of Pancakes (food) 1521 Savannah Highway. Open 24 hours Sunday through Thursday, to midnight Friday and Saturday.

Beaufort

Huddle House (food) Sea Island Parkway. Open 24 hours.
Island Plaza (grocery and fuel) Highway 21, St. Helena Island. Open 24 hours.
The Pantry (grocery and fuel) 2231 S. Ribaut Rd. Open 24 hours.
Winn Dixie (food) Island Square, Lady's Island. Open 24 hours.

Hilton Head

Huddle House (food) Northridge Drive. Open 24 hours.
The Pantry (grocery and fuel) Hwy. 278 and Arrow Road. Open 24 hours.
Winn Dixie (food) Northridge Plaza. Open 24 hours.

Savannah

BP Gas 7203 Abercorn (grocery and fuel) Open 24 hours.
International House of Pancakes (food) 110 Mall Blvd. Open 24 hours on weekends.
Kettle Restaurant (food) 6801 Abercorn. Open 24 hours. Wheelchair accessible.

MEDIA

Charleston

NEWSPAPERS AND MAGAZINES

Charleston City Paper (843-577-5304; 689 King St., Charleston 29403) Weekly paper, excellent listings.
Charleston Magazine (843-971-9811; P.O. Box 21770, Charleston 29413-1770) A glossy bi-monthly featuring stories about the city of Charleston, local politics, development, and some art features. Reviews and columns, too.
The Post and Courier (800-648-2223; www.postnandcourier.com. 134 Columbus St., Charleston 29403) The daily paper of Charleston.
Skirt! (843-883-3281; P.O. Box 806, Sullivan's Island 29482) Irreverent, fresh, funny, and good-looking, with a feminist angle. Monthly.

RADIO

WEZL-FM 103.5; Light pop.
WSCI-FM 89.3; S.C. Educational Radio.
WSSP-FM 94.3; Hip-hop.
WTMA-AM 1250; Talk radio.
WWBZ-FM 98.9; Beach, boogie, and blues.
WXLY-FM 102.5; Oldies.
WYBB-FM 98.0; Classic rock.

TELEVISION

WCBD-TV Channel 2, NBC.
WCIV-TV Channel 4, ABC.
WCSC-TV Channel 5, CBS.
WITV-TV Channel 7, PBS.
WTAT-TV Channel 24, Fox.

Beaufort and Hilton Head

NEWSPAPERS AND MAGAZINES

The Beaufort Gazette (843-524-3183; www.beaufortgazette.com. P.O. Box 399, 1556 Salem Rd. 29902) Daily. Local coverage, wire-service features, and columns.

Carolina Morning News (843-524-5448; 818 Bay St., Beaufort 29902) Daily regional coverage.

The Gullah Sentinal (843-982-0500; 1010 Charles St., Beaufort 29902) A weekly with an African-American perspective, local and syndicated columnists, and provocative editorials.

The Hilton Head News (843-785-5255; 1316 Fording Island Rd., Hilton Head 29928) Weekly.

The Island Packet (843-785-4293; www.islandpacket.com. P.O. Box 5727, Hilton Head Island, 29938) A good daily paper that has grown as the island has. Excellent local political coverage, a wide variety of local columnists, and wire stories.

RADIO

WFXH-FM 106.1; Rock.
WGZR-FM 104.9; Country.
WHHR-AM 1130; News/Sports.
WIJY-FM 108; Easy-listening music from the 60s-90s.
WJWJ-FM 89.9; S.C. Educational Radio.
WLOW-FM 107.9; Big Band, nostalgia.
WVGB-AM 1490; African-American culture, news, talk.
WYKZ-FM 98.7; Rock, contemporary hits.

TELEVISION

WJWJ-TV Channel 16, S.C. Educational Television.
WTGS-TV Channel 28, Fox.

Savannah

NEWSPAPERS AND MAGAZINES

The Georgia Guardian (912-238-2434; 528 Indian St., Savannah 31401) Weekly newspaper, published by the Savannah College of Art and Design.

The Herald (912-232-4505; 1803 Barnard St. 31401) Weekly, featuring news of the African-American community.

Savannah Morning News (912-236-9511; www.savannahnews.com. 111 W. Bay St. 31401) Daily and Sunday.

Savannah Tribune (912-233-6128; 916 W. Montgomery St. 31401) Weekly, featuring news of the African-American community.

RADIO

WBMQ-AM 630; Talk Radio, News, Sports.
WIXV-FM 95.5; Rock.
WJCL-FM 96.5; Country.
WLOW-FM 107.9; Big Band, American Music Classics.
WSIS-FM 104; Rythm and Blues Oldies.
WSVH-FM 91.9; Public Radio.

TELEVISION

WJCL-TV Channel 22, ABC.
WSAV-TV Channel 3, NBC.
WTGS-TV Channel 28, Fox.
WTOC-TV Channel 11, CBS.
WUBI-TV Channel 34, WB.
WVAN-TV Channel 9, PBS.

REAL ESTATE

If you came to the Lowcountry and couldn't bear to leave without owning a piece, take your place in line. Practically every new resident who has settled here recently was once in your position. Even the ones who thought the Lowcountry would be their "retirement home" have quit fighting the urge and moved in early. In Beaufort County alone, the rate of building exceeds 500 units each year and the population has increased 40 percent in the last 10 years.

There are hundreds of real estate agents, many independent, some affiliated with national brokerage firms. One of them might be the proprietor of your bed and breakfast; if not, he or she will have a suggestion. For starters, you should pick up the free, widely available, real estate magazines that are published weekly throughout the Lowcountry. These will give you a general idea of what's out there and how much it costs. Gated communities usually have exclusive sales teams, offering houses or lots that come with a variety of conditions attatched. Walk-ins are welcome, but if you can't find what you're looking for, ask for referrals in other towns, too.

ROAD SERVICE

Here is a list of some emergency road services in the Lowcountry.

Charleston

AAA Carolina Motor Club (800-477-4222; 843-766 2394).
Mikell Towing (843-572-9333) 24-hour towing.

Beaufort

Barnard Tire Co. (843-524-4728).
Duke's Muffler and Towing (843-525-0144).

Hilton Head

Coastal Towing (843-689-3869) 24-hour towing.
Driessen's Grocery and Station (843-785-3914) 24-hour towing.

Savannah

Auto Intensive Care Towing and Recovery (912-355-5388) 24-hour towing.
Jackson Bros. Car Care Center (912-236-0631) 24-hour towing.

SEASONAL EVENTS IN THE LOWCOUNTRY

The following list highlights annual events in the Lowcountry that might coincide with the time of your visit. Some of them, like outdoor concerts in a park, offer informal pleasures that you can enjoy on a whim with your family. Others, like house tours, Spoleto performances, or tennis and golf tournaments, require a bit of planning: purchasing your tickets in advance is a good idea, as is securing lodgings, especially in the busy spring tourist season. For specific information regarding dates, schedules, performance times, admission or ticket prices (if applicable), call or write in advance, check on-line ,or in local media. For lodging and dining suggestions, see specific venue chapters.

JANUARY

Charleston

Wade Spees

Hundreds turn out for the annual oyster roasts at Boone Hall Plantation.

Lowcountry Oyster Festival (843-577-4030; www.tgcra.com. Greater Charleston Restaurant Association) A huge oyster feast, held on the grounds of Boone Hall Plantation in Mt. Pleasant. Games, entertainment, and contests for the whole family.

Hilton Head

1st Sunday Jazz (843-842-4457; Hilton Head Jazz Society) An informal jam session held monthly at various island locations.

FEBRUARY

Beaufort

Daffodil Daze Festival (843-524-3163; Beaufort Chamber of Commerce, P.O.

Box 910, Beaufort, SC 29901) A celebration of the annual daffodil harvest on a local farm. Bring your camera — the colors recall Monet.

Charleston

Lowcountry Blues Bash (843-762-9125; P.O. Box 13525, Charleston, SC 29422; e-mail: emusic@mindspring.com; Internet: www2.discovernet.com/blues/index.html) Ten days of performances by top blues players in many venues.

Southeastern Wildlife Exposition (843-723-1748 or 800-221-5273; www.sewe. com. 211 Meeting St., Charleston, SC 29401) A comprehensive, multi-site exhibition of wildlife art in various media, and presentations promoting habitat conservation and wildlife appreciation. A huge, three-day national event that draws collectors, artists, hunters, and bird-watchers.

Savannah

Georgia Heritage Celebration (912-233-7787; Historic Savannah Foundation) A 12-day celebration of the founding of Georgia and the Savannah colony which features tours, re-enactments of colonial life, lectures, art exhibits, music, dance, and crafts. At various city locations.

MARCH

Beaufort

St. Helena's Episcopal Church Spring Tours (843-524-0363; P.O. Box 1043, Beaufort, SC 29901) Tours of historic homes, gardens, and churches in Beaufort and on the Sea Islands.

Charleston

Drayton Hall Candlelight Concert (843-766-0188; 3380 Ashley River Rd., Charleston, SC 29414) When this house is lit only by candles, it seems at its height of serene beauty. The concert continues the century-old tradition of piano music in the plantation house.

Festival of Houses & Gardens (843-722-3405; www.historiccharleston.org.40 E. Bay St. Charleston, SC 29401) The Historic Charleston Foundation's tours of private homes, plantations, gardens, and churches usually start toward the end of the month and last four weeks. A superbly organized event — a tradition for more than 50 years — it will enrich your understanding of the Lowcountry. Although the city may be crowded, it seems warmly accommodating, especially in the narrow streets late at night, where laughter and conversation drift from gardens and homes.

Hilton Head

Native Islander Gullah Celebration (888-856-4982) A month-long look at island culture and its African roots.

SpringFest (Hilton Head Hospitality Assoc.; 843-686-4944 or 800-424-3387) Activities include musical performances; college tennis championships and exhibition play; festivals of food, wine, and chocolate; kayak tours and clinics.

Savannah

First Saturday Arts and Crafts Festival March — November (Savannah Waterfront Association; 912-234-0295) Once a month in the good weather, live bands, pushcarts, open-air theatre performances, and craftspeople bring excitement to River Street.

Fountain in Forsyth Park, Savannah

Wade Spees

Savannah Onstage International Arts Festival (912-236-5745 or 800-868-3378; www.savannahonstage.org) Ten days of jazz, blues, theater, classical music performances held in the Historic District.

Savannah Tour of Homes and Gardens (912-233-7787; 18 Abercorn St., Savannah, GA 31401) For four days, Savannah's historic homes, churches, and gardens are open to visitors.

St. Patrick's Day Parade (912-233-4804; Parade Committee, P.O. Box 9224, Savannah, GA 31412) Savannah claims a substantial Irish heritage and celebrates it with abandon on this holiday. Mobs of people turn out to watch the downtown parade, which starts at 10 a.m. and dominates all other city activity for the day and night.

APRIL

Charleston

Family Circle Magazine Cup Tennis Tournament (800-677-2293; familycirclecup.com. The Tennis Centre at Daniel Island, Daniel Island, SC 29403) A new home and tennis stadium for a top womens' tennis tournament.

Plantation Oyster Roast at Drayton Hall (Historic Charleston Foundation, 843-723-1623).

Hilton Head

WorldCom Classic — The Heritage of Golf (843-671-2448 or 800-234-1107; 71 Lighthouse Rd., Hilton Head, SC 29928) Falling about a week after the Masters at Augusta, this premiere golf tournament brings thousands of people and the top PGA players to Hilton Head.

Savannah

NOGS Garden Tour: The Hidden Gardens of Savannah (912-897-9169).

Walterboro

Colleton County Rice Festival (843-549-9595; P.O. Box 426, Walterboro, SC 29488) Arts and crafts, cooking demonstrations, and rice-husking celebrate the Lowcountry's rice-growing heritage.

MAY

Beaufort

Gullah Festival (843-524-3163; Beaufort Chamber of Commerce, Box 910, Beaufort, SC 29901) Held in late May, the festival features performances, plays, concerts of spiritual and gospel music, films, and lectures related to the West African heritage of the Sea Islands.

Bluffton

Bluffton Village Festival (843-757-3855; Bluffton Town Hall, Bluffton, SC 29910) A very small, old-fashioned street festival featuring artisans, food, and entertainment, usually held the second Saturday of May.

Charleston

Confederate Memorial Day Observance (843-722-8638; Magnolia Cemetery Trust, P.O. Box 6214, Charleston, SC 29405) The United Daughters of the Confederacy and other groups sponsor a program honoring the Confederate War dead. (A similar celebration takes place in Savannah.)

Piccolo Spoleto (843-724-7305; Office of Cultural Affairs, 133 Church St., Charleston, SC 29401). The more informal aspect of Spoleto celebrates art, music, dance, and outdoor events which highlight regional artists.

Spoleto Festival U.S.A. (843-722-2764; P.O. Box 157, Charleston, SC 29402) Beginning in late May and lasting for about 18 days, Spoleto brings the best of international theater, music, art, and dance to Charleston. It's a magical time in the city.

Hilton Head

St. Luke's Tour of Homes and Gardens (843-785-4099; St. Luke's Episcopal Church).

Savannah

Scottish Games and Highland Gathering (912-369-5203; P.O. Box 13435, Savannah, GA 31401) Scottish dancing, pipe bands, and traditional games honoring Scotch heritage, usually held in mid-May.

JUNE

Colleton County

Edisto Riverfest (843-549-9595; Walterboro Chamber of Commerce, P.O. Box 426, Walterboro, SC 29488) Join a guided canoe and kayak flotilla as it winds down the Edisto River. Food, entertainment, and displays of equipment featured at two state parks along the way. Usually held the second weekend of the month.

Hampton

Hampton County Watermelon Festival (843-943-3784; Chamber of Commerce, Box 122, Hampton, SC 29924) The oldest festival in the state celebrating the county's best crop. Held at the end of the month and lasting a week, featuring seed-spitting contests, beauty queens, and a big parade.

Hilton Head

King Mackerel / Cobia Fishing Tournament (843-842-7001; Shelter Cove Marina).

Savannah

Concerts in Johnson Square From June to August, enjoy two-hour lunchtime concerts every Wednesday and Friday, starting at 11:30 a.m., in one of the city's loveliest settings.

JULY

Fourth of July Fireworks take place in several Lowcountry resorts as well as these locations: Brittlebank Park (Charleston), Parris Island (Beaufort), Hilton Head, Bluffton, Savannah's Riverfront, and Tybee Beach.

Beaufort

Beaufort County Water Festival (843-524-0600; Chamber of Commerce, P.O. Box 910, Beaufort, SC 29901) A 10-day festival starting in mid-July that features special events each day and night: croquet, fishing, tennis, Ping-Pong, and golf tournaments, a juried art show, antiques show, kid's day, parade, and several outdoor dances. The air shows and acrobatic water-ski demonstrations are especially fun to watch.

Edisto Island

Edisto Summer Festival (843-869-3867; P.O. Box 206, Edisto Island, SC 29438) A weekend of family-oriented fun on the beach, in the water, on the links. Street dances, local food specialities, and entertainment.

Hilton Head

Banana Open Doubles (843-785-1151; Palmetto Dunes Tennis Center).

AUGUST

Hilton Head

King Mackerel Fishing Tournament (843-785-7001; Shelter Cove).

SEPTEMBER

Charleston

Candlelight Tours of Houses and Gardens (843-722-4630 or 800-968-8175; www.preservationsociety.org. The Preservation Society, 147 King St., Charleston, SC 29402) More than one dozen different candlelight walking tours of private homes and gardens are offered over a period of about four weeks by the city's oldest preservation organization. Lectures and small concerts are also scheduled.

MOJA Arts Festival (843-724-7305; Office of Cultural Affairs, 133 Church St., Charleston, SC 29401) A celebration of the African-American and Caribbean heritage in the Charleston area. The influence on southern culture is traced through music, dance, art, food, stage performances, and more.

Scottish Games and Highland Gathering (843-884-4371; P.O. Box 21109, Charleston, SC 29413) Competitions in dancing and athletics held in a fair-like atmosphere at Boone Hall Plantation.

Hardeeville

Catfish Festival (843-784-2231; Chamber of Commerce, P.O. Box 307, Hardeeville, SC 29927) Family entertainment, boat races on the Savannah River, and of course, catfish, are the focus of this festival, which takes place the third weekend in September.

Hilton Head

Celebrity Golf Tournament (843-842-7711; Chamber of Commerce, P.O. Box 5647, Hilton Head Island, SC 29938) Held Labor Day weekend, at several island courses, the tournament draws lots of celebrities who play for fun and charity.

Savannah

Savannah Jazz Festival (912-356-2381; Coastal Jazz Assoc., P.O. Box 8004, Savannah, GA 31412) All styles of jazz played in spots throughout the city.

OCTOBER

Beaufort

Historic Beaufort Foundation Fall Tour of Homes (843-524-6334; P.O. Box 11, Beaufort, SC 29901) A weekend of candlelight and daytime tours of homes and gardens in and around Beaufort; the final day often features tours of outlying plantations, such as the rarely seen Auldbrass designed by Frank Lloyd Wright and meticulously restored inside and out.

Edisto Island

Edisto Historic Preservation Society Tour of Homes (843-869-1954; P.O. 206, Edisto Island, SC 29438) Day-long tour of homes.

Hilton Head Island

An Evening of the Arts (843-785-3673; Chamber of Commerce, P.O. Box 5647, Hilton Head Island, SC 29938) A festive charity auction featuring work by local artists.

Head of the Broad Regatta, Palmetto Rowing Club (843-681-4207; Broad Creek Marina).

Ridgeland

Gopher Hill Festival (843-726-8126; P.O. Box 1267, Ridgeland, SC 29936) A one-day celebration with arts and crafts, music, and food. The Ridgeland area was long known as Gopher Hill, named for the gopher tortoise, a species that lives a protected life in the sand hills of Jasper County.

Savannah

Savannah Film and Video Festival (912-525-5050. www.scad.edu., P.O. Box 3146, Savannah, GA 31406) Several days of screenings and lectures sponsored by the Savannah College of Art and Design.

Savannah Greek Festival (912-236-8256; St. Paul's Greek Orthodox Church, 14 W. Anderson St., Savannah, GA 31401) A day-long celebration of Savannah's Greek heritage with food, music and dancing.

Tom Turpin Ragtime Festival (912-233-9989) A city-wide tribute to one of the innovators of ragtime music. Formal and informal concerts.

NOVEMBER

Charleston

Holiday Festival of Lights (843-762-2172; www.ccprc.com., James Island
County Park) See more than 100,000 holiday lights strung in the park, a dazzling display in a place that rarely knows a white Christmas. Family entertainment and special events scheduled through Christmas.

Plantation Days (843-556-6020; www.middletonplace.org. Middleton Place,
Hwy. 61, Charleston SC 29414) The spirit of harvest days on a Lowcountry
plantation is recreated through activities such as blacksmithing, wool dying
and spinning, candle-making, and pottery. Traditional music and crafts, too,
in the stable yards and green at Middleton Place.

St. Helena Island

*Dancers from Sierra Leone —
a country with linguistic and
cultural similarities to St.
Helena Island — perform at
Penn Center's Heritage Days
Festival.*

Wade Spees

Heritage Days (843-838-2432; Penn Center, P.O. Box 126, St. Helena Island, SC
29920) Held the second weekend in November on the historic Penn Center
campus, Heritage Days celebrates Sea Island culture in its many forms.
Thursday there is a special community sing; Friday there are lectures and
presentations followed by an old-fashioned fish fry with musical entertainment; on Saturday, a parade and performances which include Gullah games
and storytelling, dance, music, and demonstrations of traditional Sea Island
crafts such as basket-making, net-weaving, and boat-building.

Savannah

Crafts and Cane Grinding (912-897-3773; Oatland Island Education Center,
711 Sandtown Rd, Savannah, GA 31410) More than sixty artisans from the

southeast come to sell their work and demonstrate how it's done; farmers grind cane to make syrup; folk musicians play outside.

DECEMBER

Beaufort

Christmas at the Verdier House (843-524-6334; 801 Bay St., Beaufort, SC 29902) The late-18th century planter's home is decorated during Christmas week as it might have been during holidays of long ago.

Night on the Town (843-525-6644; Main Street, Beaufort, USA) Join an informal, local street party as the downtown merchants welcome patrons to partake of holiday snacks and libations. There are decorations everywhere; jazz musicians, carolers, and even Santa make special appearances. An evening of small-town fun.

Bluffton

The decorations at Charleston's Joseph Manigault House recall the festivities of Christmas past.

Wade Spees

Christmas Parade (843-757-3855).

Charleston

African-American Spirituals (843-766-0188; Drayton Hall, 3380 Ashley River Rd., Charleston, SC 29414) "The Senior Lights" singing group of Johns Island present a moving concert of music of the Sea Islands at Drayton Hall.

Christmas in Charleston (800-868-8118; P.O. Box 975, Charleston, SC 29402) The season brings special tours and holiday events such as a parade of boats strung with lights and open-air marketplaces. Many restaurants and hotels offer holiday specials, too.

Hilton Head

Lowcountry's Twelve Days of Christmas (843-681-4000; Westin Resort) A series of daily events (Dec. 15–26) including teas, fireside story telling, and illumination ceremonies. The holiday decorations are the island's best.

Savannah

Christmas in Savannah (912-944-0456 or 800-444-2427; Convention & Visitors Bureau, P.O. Box 1628, Savannah, GA 31402-1628) All month long, Savannah comes alive with special holiday events: tours, performances, 19th-century style holiday presentations in old homes, crafts shows, and celebrations at the beach and on the river.

TOURIST INFORMATION & ON-LINE ADDRESSES

Here is a listing of the organizations in the Lowcountry that cater to visitors' needs. You may benefit from them during your stay; or you may simply want to have their addresses in case you wish to follow-up on a yearly event or request further information. In many cases, booklets, videos, and pamphlets are available at a nominal charge; general information is free.

FISHING AND HUNTING REGULATIONS

Licenses, permits, and wildlife stamps, whichever apply, must be in your possession while in the field or on the water. They may be purchased at tackle shops, sporting goods shops, and from the state.

Georgia Department of Natural Resources, Game and Fish Division Route 2, Box 219-R, Richmond Hill, GA 31324; 912-651-2221.

S.C. Department of Natural Resources P.O. Box 167, Columbia 29202; 843-734-3888.

Wade Spees

*The ideal pace for a
Lowcountry visitor is to be
slower than a scuttling crab.*

VISITOR INFORMATION

Charleston Area Convention & Visitors Bureau P.O. Box 975, Charleston, SC 29402; 843-853-8000 or 800-774-0006; fax 843-853-0444; www. charlestoncvb.com

Edisto Island Chamber of Commerce P.O. Box 206, Edisto Island, SC 29438; 843-869-3867 or 888-333-2781; www.edistochamber.com.

Greater Beaufort Chamber of Commerce P.O. Box 910, 1108 Carteret St., Beaufort, SC 29901-0910; 843-524-3163 or 800-638-3525; fax 843-986-5405; www.beaufortsc.org.

Hilton Head Island Chamber of Commerce P.O. Box 5647, Hilton Head Island, SC 29938; 843-785-3673 or 800-523-3373; fax 843-785-7110; www. hiltonheadisland.org.

Lowcountry Tourism Commission P.O. Box 615, Yemassee, SC 29945; 843-717-3090 or 800-528-6870; www.southcarolinalowcountry.com.

The Savannah Area Convention and Visitor's Bureau P.O. Box 1628, 101 E. Bay St., Savannah GA 31402-1628; 912-944-0456 or 800-444-2427; fax 912-944-0468; www. savcvb.com.

S.C. Division of State Parks PRT, Edgar Brown Building, 1205 Pendleton St., Columbia, SC 29201; 803-734-0156; www.travelsc.com.

IF TIME IS SHORT

The Lowcountry divides easily into three parts: the major cities (Charleston and Savannah), the more rural areas (Beaufort, Edisto, Bluffton, and the Sea Islands), and the beach resorts (on Hilton Head Island, Kiawah, Isle of Palms, etc.). Concentrating on one of these locales is a sure-fire way to have a satisfying, if brief, visit.

Each place has its special qualities, refer to individual chapter openings for a sense of them. In general, the resorts are self-enclosed and limited in terms of history, culture, and sightseeing, yet their on-site recreational resources are exemplary and their use may determine your schedule. Beaufort or Edisto are lower-keyed destinations, where beachcombing and modest shopping might wrap around a day's worth of walking, biking, kayaking, or sightseeing. The cities, of course, are full of opportunity for touring and shopping. (A car is not necessary for a weekend trip to a city, although helpful if you want to explore the countryside or visit both Charleston and Savannah.)

Here are some recommendations:

In Charleston

Two Meeting Street Inn (843-723-7322; 2 Meeting St.) is located in the Historic District, and waking up there makes you feel as if you're a native. *Maison DuPre* (843-723-8691 or 800-844-4667; 317 E. Bay St.) is a lovely oasis, with a courtyard, a bit further uptown. These inns will be booked months in advance during the annual *Spoleto Festival* (843-722-2764), a series of music, dance, and theatre performances, and art exhibits, that occurs in late spring.

My favorite house museums and military sites are the *Heyward-Washington House* (843-722-0354; 87 Church St.) built in 1772 and representing the height of colonial living; the *Nathaniel Russell House* (843-724-8481; 51 Meeting St.) completed in1808; and the *Joseph Manigault House* (843-723-2926; 350 Meeting St.), designed in 1803 by a native son and a marvelous example of adapting European taste for the Lowcountry elite. Slightly father afield on Hwy. 61 are two nationally recognized historic sites: *Middleton Place* (843-556-6020) where the oldest landscaped gardens in America were laid out in 1741; and *Drayton Hall* (843-766-0188), an 18th-century Georgian home which is a magnificent, unfurnished example of the Palladian style. Military history buffs should visit *Fort Sumter National Monument* (843-722-1691; in Charleston Harbor) where the Civil War began; and *Patriot's Point* (843-884-2727; Mt. Pleasant) the berth of battleships and submarines.

Popular shops among locals are along *King St.* (housewares, antiques and clothing), *Queen St.* (boutiques and art galleries), *Meeting St.* (bookstore, informal lunch spots), and *Church St.* (boutiques, art galleries/ antiques stores, children's clothing). *G&M* (843-577-9797; 96 Broad St.), *Hominy Grill* (843-937-0930; 207 Rutledge Ave.), *Peninsula Grill* (843-723-0700; 112 N. Market St.) and *McCrady's* (843-577-0025; 2 Unity Alley) are excellent restaurants.

In *Savannah*

The Gastonian (912-232-2869 or 800-322-6603; 220 E. Gaston St.) and the *Magnolia Place Inn* (912-236-7674 or 800-238-7674; 503 Whitaker St.) are downtown luxury inns with a flair for style and comfort.

Historic sites of architectural and military interest include: the *Green-Meldrim House* (912-233-3845; Madison Square) where General Sherman lived during the occupation of the city; the *Owens-Thomas House* (912-233-9743; 124 Abercorn St.), a Regency-style urban villa designed by William Jay in 1816; and *Fort Pulaski* (912-786-5787; U.S. 80) a masonry fort that was, in 1847, state-of-the-art, and now is a great place for a picnic. Established in 1865, the *Beach Institute* (912-234-8000; 502 E. Harris St.) includes a permanent display of folk art sculpture that celebrates the talent of Ulysses Davis and other African-American artists.

Antiques stores proliferate downtown on *Bull St., Abercorn St.,* and *Whitaker St*; there are galleries and cafes in the *City Market; Factor's Walk* offers a variety of boutiques for clothing and crafts. Locals eat breakfast at *Clary's* (912-233-0402; 404 Abercorn St.) and dinner-at-the-beach at the *Crab Shack* (912-786-9857; Chimney Creek, Tybee). The best fancy restaurants are *Georges'* (912-786-9730; 1105 E. Hwy. 80, Tybee Island) and *Sapphire Grill* (912443-9962; 110 W. Congress St.).

In *Beaufort and the Sea Islands:*

The *Rhett House Inn* (843-524-9030; 1009 Craven St., Beaufort) is the most gracious inn outside the cities. The innkeepers may also arrange kayak and bicycle outings, prepare picnics, and suggest forays to *Edisto Beach State Park* (843-869-2156), *Hunting Island State Park* (843-838-2011) and other, more out-of-the-way places.

For a quick sandwich in downtown Beaufort, head for *Plums* (843-525-1946; 904 1/2 Bay St.) but for a fancy dinner choose the *Beaufort Inn* (843-521-9000; 809 Port Republic St.). On Edisto Island, *The Old Post Office* (843-869-2339; Hwy 174) is the best place for dinner; *Po Pigs Bo-B-Que* (843-869-9003; 2410 Hwy. 174) for lunch.

For a sense of history, visit the *John Mark Verdier House* (843-524-6334;

801 Bay St.) the home of a wealthy 19th-century Beaufort merchant; **Penn Center** (843-838-2432; St. Helena Island) the nation's first school for freed slaves; and the **Edisto Museum** (843-869-1954; Edisto Island), which reveals the history of the island, from the time of Native Americans to the present. The **Marine Corps Recruit Depot** at **Parris Island Museum** (843-525-2951) features the history of the Marines and the Corps' training.

Beaufort's **Bay St.,** and the narrow streets that lead off it, has a classic main street feeling: plate-glass display windows, awnings, and family-run stores. On St. Helena, **Red Piano Too** (843-838-2241; Hwy. 21 at The Corner) an art gallery and store, is the best place in the Lowcountry, perhaps in the southeast, to see native and outsider art on display and understand how that tradition fits in today's island culture.

Wade Spees

One ideal end to a Lowcountry day.

Index

LODGING BY PRICE CODE

DINING BY PRICE CODE

DINING BY CUISINE

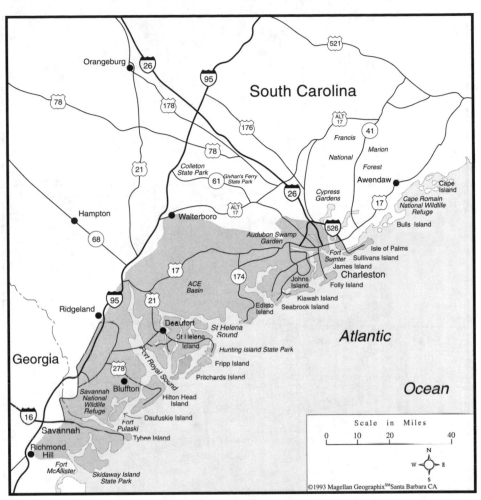

THE LOWCOUNTRY

Courtesy of The Charleston Trident Convention & Visitors Bureau (used by permission)

CHARLESTON

Savannah River

River

Riverfront Plaza

St

Walk

General McIntosh Bl

Factors

TO: 80 West, Hwys 17 & 21 N.

W Bay St

E Bay St

TO: 80 East Forts & Beach

W Bryan St

E Bryan St

Franklin Square

City Market

Ellis Square

W St Julian St

Johnson Square

Reynolds Square

Warren Square

E St Julian St

Washington Square

W Congress St

E Congress St

W Broughton St

E Broughton St

W State St

E State St

Liberty Square

Telfair Square

W President St

Wright Square

Oglethorpe Square

Columbia Square

E President St

Greene Square

W York St

E York St

W Oglethorpe Av

E Oglethorpe Av

Houston St

E Broad St

(W Broad St)

W Hull St

E Hull St

Colonial Park Cemetery

Elbert Square

Orleans Square

W McDonough St

Chippewa Square

E McDonough St

Crawford Square

Civic Center

W Perry St

E Perry St

Barnard St

W Liberty St

E Liberty St

Visitors Center

Montgomery St

Martin Luther King Jr Bl

W Harris St

E Harris St

Pulaski Square

Madison Square

Lafayette Square

Troup Square

E Macon St

W Charlton St

E Charlton St

16 West

Jefferson St

Tattnall St

W Jones St

Whitaker St

Bull St

Drayton St

Abercorn St

Lincoln St

Habersham St

Price St

E Jones St

W Taylor St

E Taylor St

16 East

Chatham Square

W Wayne St

Monterey Square

Calhoun Square

Whitefield Square

E Wayne St

W Gordon St

E Gordon St

W Gaston St

E Gaston St

W Huntingdon St

Forsyth Park

E Huntingdon St

W Hall St

E Hall St

N

Victorian District

E Gwinnet St

Scale in Miles

0
.25
.5

E Bolton St

SAVANNAH

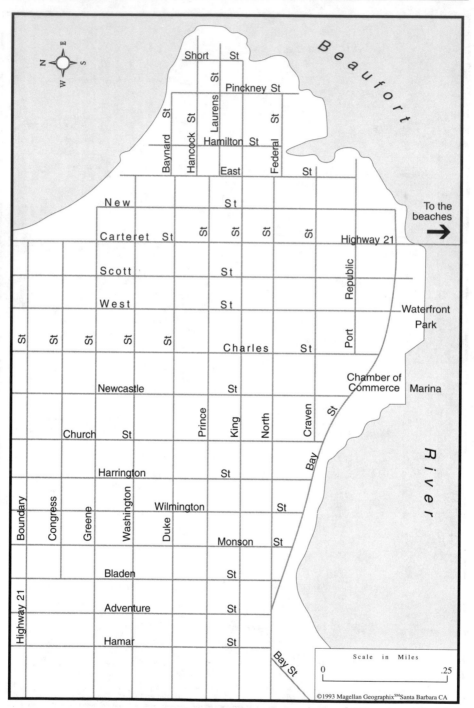

Courtesy of The Greater Beaufort Chamber of Commerce (used by permission)

BEAUFORT

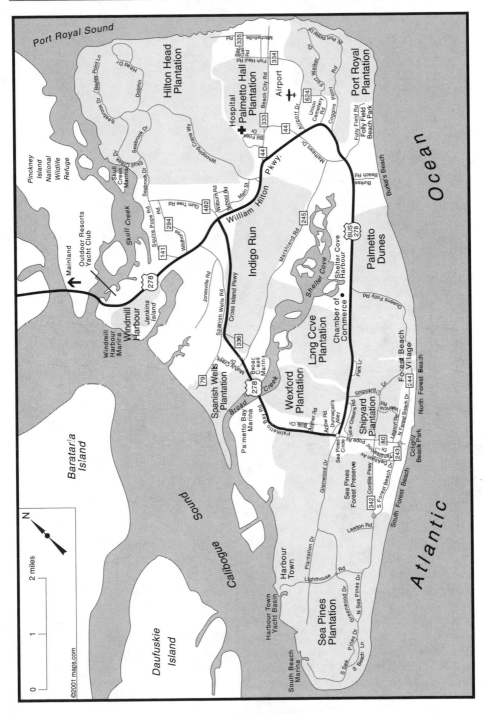

HILTON HEAD

About the Author

Cecily McMillan moved to the Lowcountry of South Carolina in 1980, having graduated from Harvard University and worked as a journalist for *The Real Paper* in Cambridge, Mass., and the *Baltimore News-American*. In addition to freelance writing on southern topics, she handled public relations for the South Carolina Education Television Network station in Beaufort, South Carolina. She came to know the Lowcountry further during her terms on the local planning commission, as a board member of a rural health center, as an officer of the Beaufort County Democratic Party, and as a young mother.

Her writing on the South has frequently appeared in the *New York Times* Travel Section and the Sunday Style Section, and in magazines such as *Southern Changes* and *Southern Exposure*.